A THEOLOGY OF RELIGIOUS CHANGE

A Theology of
Religious Change

What the Social Science
of Conversion Means for the Gospel

DAVID J. ZEHNDER

◥PICKWICK *Publications* • Eugene, Oregon

A THEOLOGY OF RELIGIOUS CHANGE
What the Social Science of Conversion Means for the Gospel

Copyright © 2011 David J. Zehnder. All rights reserved. Except for brief quotations in critical publications or reviews, no part of this book may be reproduced in any manner without prior written permission from the publisher. Write: Permissions, Wipf and Stock Publishers, 199 W. 8th Ave., Suite 3, Eugene, OR 97401.

Pickwick Publications
An Imprint of Wipf and Stock Publishers
199 W. 8th Ave., Suite 3
Eugene, OR 97401

www.wipfandstock.com

Biblical citations are from the *New International Version*. Grand Rapids: Zondervan, 1984.

ISBN 13: 978-1-61097-359-5

Cataloging-in-Publication data:

Zehnder, David J.

    A theology of religious change : what the social science of conversion means for the gospel / David J. Zehnder.

    xxii + 180 p. ; 23 cm. Includes bibliographical references and index.

    ISBN 13: 978-1-61097-359-5

    1. Conversion—Christianity. 2. Conversion. 3. Psychology, Religious. 4. Religion and science. 5. Religion and sociology. 6. Evangelistic work. I. Title.

BL 639 Z34 2011

Manufactured in the U.S.A.

To Mom, Dad, and Grace

Contents

List of Images and Tables · viii

Preface · ix

Acknowledgements · xi

Introduction: Religious Change and the Quest for a More Adequate Understanding of Belief · xiii

1 The Gospel as the Criterion of Religious Change · 1

2 Change in Religious Experience · 11

3 Transformation of the Individual · 38

4 The Individual and Parental Influences · 66

5 The Lure of Ideology · 88

6 The Web of Social Ties · 117

7 Conversion and the Divine Choice · 141

Bibliography · 169

Index · 177

List of Images and Tables

Starbuck's Change Dynamic · 19
Religious Change Motifs · 40
Converts' versus Controls' Perception of Parents · 77

Preface

THIS BOOK IS THE product of research on and off for the last fourteen years. In my early college days at Michigan State I became actively involved in combative theological discussions that sparked this project's beginning. There might be no better field for debate than theology, and within theology there is probably no better topic to debate than predestination, and that topic led to writing about religious change. I saw that there was a lot of confusion about the different positions concerning predestination and a fair level of hostility between the different schools of thought. The debate seemed deadlocked, forcing a choice between God's universal love of the world and the particularity of salvation that is only possible from God's initiative.

Though I always thought that my job would be to write something of a mediating position that honors the best insights of each position, I began to realize that it would not be possible without asking new questions. If we could understand the human side of predestination and answer more thoroughly than ever before how people go from unbelief to faith, then this new angle on the problem might furnish insights that were previously unavailable. In the end, I do think that this approach has helped to form a more adequate concept of God's election, which is outlined in chapter 7. However, in working through this issue, I discovered that the true benefit of inquiring deeply into the human side of conversion has little to do with solving divine puzzles. I did not initially foresee that understanding religious change helps to clarify how people come to faith, which in turn informs theology about what resources it has to care for people as they develop new beliefs. The initial project on predestination turned into a much more practical project that asks how theology can be communicated to people developing faith under diverse influences.

Preface

    In order to account for the human side, an in-depth exploration in the psychological and sociological literature was necessary. Though much data exists on this subject, it has never before been organized and put to use for a specifically theological agenda in this way. Thus, I hope that in reading the vast accounts of religious change from science's and theology's perspective, students of theology will find a sophisticated method for strengthening both their insights into faith development as well as the doctrinal positions that guide the church's ministry.

David J. Zehnder
St. Louis, Missouri

Acknowledgements

FOREMOST I WOULD LIKE to thank Drs. Bruce Hartung and Robert Kolb for never doubting the viability of a study such as this one. Their inspiration was essential. Most especially I thank my adviser Dr. David Maxwell not only for his sympathy for my ideas but his insights that contributed helpfully to the discussion and improved both the clarify and form of the writings themselves.

Ph.D. candidates often hear people ask: "What are you writing your dissertation on?" and sometimes they even hear something like: "That sounds interesting; send me that chapter!" Almost always the material you discussed with the supposedly interested will never again cross their minds, nor will the chapter you sent them find anything but a lonely existence in cyberspace, getting inched away from mind and memory by every new email that enters the inbox. However, there are occasionally people who really do read the chapters you send them. Thus, I thank David Coe, Richard Blythe, Guntars Baikovs, Aaron Franzen, Rick Marrs, Dave W. Zehnder, and Mary Zehnder not only for reading the files I sent them but for giving me constructive feedback as well.

Three parts of this book are taken and modified from previously published essays in *Pastoral Psychology*, *Reformed World*, and *Zygon*.

David Zehnder, "Negative Parental Influences on Religious Conversion: Implications for Pastoral Care." *Pastoral Psychology* (forthcoming, 2011).

———, "Social Theory's Active Conversions as a Challenge to Divine Grace." *Reformed World* 60.3 (December 2010) 159–70.

———, "A Theologian's Typology for Science and Religion." *Zygon* 46 (2011) 84–104.

Acknowledgements

My thanks to the publishers of those journals for permission to use the material here.

The folks at Wipf and Stock, especially Christian Amondson, Robin Parry, and Heather Carraher, deserve thanks for giving this work the chance to see the light of publication and for working efficiently with me through this process. Their model is the frontier of publishing in religious studies and does this field a great service in making a wide variety of books available.

Finally, my wife Grace deserves special thanks not only for her inexorable support of me and my academic pursuits, but she also read the early drafts of this project and hammered them into shape in such a way that never would have been possible otherwise. As anyone who has worked with academic projects knows, that feat takes an equal degree of editing deftness and skill in resisting boredom. Thanks Grace!

Introduction

RELIGIOUS CHANGE AND THE QUEST
FOR A MORE ADEQUATE UNDERSTANDING OF BELIEF

UNTIL NOW THEOLOGY HAS lacked a sufficient method to address the wide variety of conditions under which people develop new faith. Being more concerned with official doctrines of salvation, theologians have invested great energy and clashed in many debates over doctrinal rules, and although church history contains significant *theological* controversies, it features very few disputes on how salvation doctrines *actually apply to life's concrete instances* and speak to *real people* amid their struggles for faith. This study is therefore an effort to correct this imbalance; not only to develop theological doctrines but to ask the more immediate question about how they function within conversion's *human* side, what this book calls "religious change."

The theologian—including anyone propagating religious claims—stands as a mediator and translator between theology's content and its audience. In the current era, it is time for theologians to take their *audience* more seriously than ever before by determining how the gospel *actually communicates to and helps* individuals, especially those struggling to understand and believe the Christian message. Even if academic theology has faced an institutional gap between its systematic and practical departments, this gap need not imply systematic theology's inaccessibility to a wide audience. If doctrines are constructed with one eye on the people they address, they will undoubtedly fill those lives with richer meaning and ethical weight than if constructed with both eyes on textbooks alone; and there is no reason why all theology cannot finally be life-informing and practical.

Introduction

This particular project, which eventually resulted in a serious study of theology's *audience*, was originally a product of my personal fascination with the far more theoretical problem of predestination that asks (but never satisfyingly concludes) why some people believe the gospel and others do not. Years ago I was inadvertently caught up in an effort to try to reconcile the tension between God's lordship over creation and human care of creation; the divine choice in salvation and the human ability to receive and acknowledge grace; the universality of God's love and the particularity of his choosing individuals. Unable to resolve these tensions—tensions that have not been settled in church history (and have, in fact, caused much controversy)—I decided that perhaps the traditional way of looking at these problems was incomplete. Determined to find a new whole within which to conceptualize the universality and particularity of salvation, I decided that theology might benefit from taking religious change (conversion's human phenomenon) seriously and attempt to reconcile doctrinal claims *with the claims of experience*. This initial insight led to this more mature study that uses the psychology and sociology of religious change to help explain the human side of salvation. The social sciences are one way to find a limited viewpoint into what pressures cause people to change, how theology becomes meaningful to them under different changing pressures, and how one's parents and social networks have determinative influences on faith development.

Though I initially set out to solve a doctrinal problem, I discovered that social science accounts of religious change serve a far more immediate function, which is to explain how theology communicates to people undergoing various kinds of changes. The principle is fundamental to all communication: that if we want to explain concepts meaningfully to our audience, we must know something about audiences and how they process concepts—we cannot teach effectively unless we know something about how people learn. Though surely limited in explanatory power, empirical accounts of religious change still give a useful perspective into human reality that helps theology to determine which concepts and axioms it has that might be helpful to its audience and how it might present them effectively.

This study therefore invites its readers on a trek to find a more adequate understanding of conversion's human side by interacting with the social science of religious change. Its question is no more complicated than asking: How does a person come to believe the gospel? Though a richer conception of conversion is the broadest goal, this study's path leads more immediately to the goal of discovering the causes of religious change and their implications for communicating theology to various audiences. In order to reach the broadest goal, we must tackle the immediate goal in its diversity to build a complete picture of the factors that inspire people to change religiously and, eventually, believe the gospel. When we understand the diversity of religious phenomena associated with conversion, then we will be in a better position to understand how this completed picture of conversion might better address the issue of why some people believe the gospel and others do not in a constructive way that still does not let the particularity of God's grace contradict his love's universality. Readers will not always agree with my conclusions about doctrine or the implications of social science for doctrine. In an experimental study of this kind, disagreement is both expected and helpful to strengthening the insights. But ultimately the importance lies not in reconciling everyone's conclusions but in understanding more about what it means to be human and to begin conceiving of theology through a method that honors its personal significance.

To begin any voyage, the proper equipment must be packed, meaning here that we must have a clear *method* for using social scientific accounts of religious change. Such accounts are so diverse in their expressions and levels of abstraction that they will easily confuse the theologian who is not wearing adequate hermeneutical glasses. This introduction's primary constructive task is to outline a method that will inform the entire study. Though many potential methods exist to integrate theology and science, this study favors a "correlational" approach that holds theological and scientific claims in tension as different explanatory means that cannot directly contradict each other. Certainly, other methods of relating science and theology are also insightful, but only the correlational is ideal for this particular task because it allows an earnest dialogue between science and theology that honors the integrity and independent authority of each discipline. At bottom, if we recognize conversion as a divine gift that cannot be harnessed by any human efforts, then we need a correlational distinction between the natural things observable by science and the supernatural work of the

Holy Spirit that is only visible in faith. The following discussion is designed to clarify this method in *general* terms. We will be able to give a more definite shape to the method once we begin to explore the science of religious change in more detail.

The Correlational Method

In his typology for defining theology's relationship to science, psychologist John Carter categorizes correlational methods under the heading: "Scripture *Parallel to* Psychology," capturing the idea of science and theology as dialectically parallel but never effacing each other.[1] They function as dialogue partners, offering different perspectives on a topic. The fundamental stake of this approach is to depict scientific and religious truth claims as valid within their respective levels of explanation, recognizing that each discipline operates according to its own peculiar logic. While they can be juxtaposed, they ultimately explain different things, and even if they describe the same phenomenon they do so from different concerns and presuppositions, precluding any single interpretation that brings both accounts into harmony. For example, if biological science finds that humans are, in their very genes, greedy, self-interested, and lacking sympathy for the preservation of the whole human community as opposed to individual legacies,[2] then it seems plausible *on the surface* to say that science has really discovered Original Sin—a biological root of rebellion in us all. This surface view is really closer to methods that try to unify both disciplines. The correlational approach, by contrast, will recognize that while biologically-based greed *can* be legitimately interpreted as an expression of depravity, this conclusion is reached by applying our own theology to a particular phenomenon without hanging theology's credibility on science's results. It recognizes that the doctrinal authority can never depend directly on a scientific foundation. If biology eventually overturned that conclusion and argued that humans, when researched even more extensively, are actually good-willed and magnanimous at heart, the change in result would not shake the depravity doctrine's scriptural basis. Even *if* theology and

---

1. Carter, "Secular and Sacred Models," 433–56.
2. Dawkins, *The Selfish Gene*.

science recognize inherent avarice in the human race, the difference is that they do so for vastly different reasons and with different expectations: the one, to attempt to understand human nature and improve society, the other to bring people closer to God.

Because the correlational method gives a forum for multiple voices, it is notably loose and versatile, according to psychologist Gary Collins.³ Rather than a formal method taking precedence over a certain theological problem, the problem defines which sources of input are best-placed to handle it. In this respect it is similar to existentialist thinking by putting existence before essence,⁴ acknowledging that theological reflection takes place within the context of concrete human problems (in this study the problem of how faith develops) and that handling them is the process by which the church's ultimate values are both determined and revealed. These values are revealed when problems force theological thinkers to *act*, and they are determined by the problem-solving process that translates values into action.

To illustrate, let us suppose that a church decides to evangelize to a nearby city by handing out tracts at an annual street festival. The church's action in evangelizing, as opposed to merely discussing a theology of missions, reveals the sincerity of its missional convictions, but it might find that its methods do not have a lasting impact on the people they have reached. Though the values motivating the action were solid, their results were disappointing. This lack of effectiveness might cause the church to rethink its beliefs about how best to do evangelism and might motivate them to take up a new approach, perhaps to start a social outreach for people who are hurting most. The theology and convictions stay the same, but experience shapes how they function in real time.

This example is intended to demonstrate that the correlational method's practical focus entails that its general framework has few rules, allowing individuals to decide their own goals and use whatever resources are available to accomplish them. Perhaps this method accounts for people's tendency to choose their own way regardless, but in either case, it is intended not to produce a certain theology but to provide a discussion forum for theology to find its life-significance. The

---

3. See "An Integration View," 112. Collins actually calls it "indefinable."
4. Sartre, *L'Existentialisme est un humanisme*, 21.

reward of this method is its versatility; the risk is its vagueness in lacking inherent criteria of value.

The lack of value criteria appears in the correlational method's openness to secular research. It does not require research to be *Christian*, only that it be put to Christian use, and it thereby presupposes that secular anthropologies are valid conversation partners in Christian anthropology. In fact, its vagueness allows that any sources of information might be useful if held far enough apart that the presuppositions of one do not obscure the claims of the other. This general tone expresses optimism in science but a *qualified* optimism because it is designed to keep secular sources of knowledge from swamping the conversation by a basic recognition of their limitations. The heart of correlational thinking is what H. Richard Niebuhr calls "Christ and Culture in Paradox,"[5] acknowledging that there will always be tension between secular and theological accounts of religion. We should not try to use one to vanquish the other, and we should not expect to find an ultimate resolution between them because no meta-theory will ever handle all of life's unpredictability.

A provocative case of this tension is evident in studies such as a particular "sanctification test,"[6] where psychologists replicated the Good Samaritan parable, testing forty Princeton Theological Seminary students to determine if they would stop to help a young man "shabbily dressed, slumped, coughing and groaning, in a doorway in an alley." Results showed that only sixteen people stopped, leaving a solid 60 percent of "bad Samaritans." The only predictor the researchers could find to determine why some stopped and others did not was the degree to which these seminarians were in a hurry. Studies of this kind are humbling to theology because they point out the lack of discernable difference between Christians and everyone else, but at the same time, a correlational approach will detect that these studies do have an entrapment quality and that sanctification is a deeper concept than what the behavioral sciences are able to measure through empirical means. The method, however, is unable to eliminate this basic tension that steadfast Christianity *should* be evident through action and that those

---

5. See Niebuhr, *Christ and Culture*, 149–89.
6. Batson et al., *Religion and the Individual*, 346–47.

seminarians really *should* have had their priorities in line so as to stop and assist the ailing young man.

Because it handles problems in their concreteness and deals with the intrinsic tensions between doctrine and culture, this method has some precedence in Lutheranism. Correlational thinking has a specific expression in the so-called "Wittenberg Theological Method" that guided the Protestant Reformers in their efforts to establish doctrinal norms from Martin Luther's time to their last official confession in the Formula of Concord (1577).[7] This theological style placed life over theory, directing doctrinal statements toward the comfort of the sinner before God and the dual, irreconcilable responsibilities of God and humankind. Nowhere is this style clearer than in the debates over predestination and the final resolution of the Formula of Concord Article XI that urges the church to seek its election in Christ and not to explain salvation and damnation entirely from God's decree or from free human choice.[8] Abstract resolutions of God's will would transcend the gospel's limits and rely on a philosophy to resolve the tension between the particularity and universality of God's saving action. In effect, it would put essence over existence and possibly relativize the incarnation under an abstract providence doctrine that, based on their own version of research, the Reformers felt was deficient in comfort.[9] Instead, Article XI lets pastoral concern color the doctrine's application in practice, one intended to comfort the troubled conscience by resting speculative concerns in the experience of Christ. The Wittenberg method stands as an early example of correlational thinking in that it used the experience of comfort and the gospel as parallel dialogue partners. If its proponents had disregarded comfort, then they would have too readily dismissed the psychological side of religion; but if they had made comfort, rather than belief in the gospel, theology's primary goal then they would have eclipsed theology's independent authority. Indeed, if comfort were the central goal, they might have attempted medieval psychiatry by hedging the gospel with ale! But they continued to take the gospel on its own authority and used it to comfort troubled consciences, and even if

---

7. Kolb, *Bound Choice*, 1–6.
8. See the Formula of Concord XI in Kolb and Wengert, *Book of Concord*, 642.9.
9. See Frank, *Theologie der Concordienformel*, 4:140–41.

Introduction

consciences were not automatically unburdened, they did not give up faith in the gospel's effectiveness.

This point illustrates one of the correlational method's greatest strengths in allowing the various disciplines freedom to operate on their own terms yet in dialectical fashion, so that the theology's practice can benefit from both. Correlational methods do not naturally force scientific and theological conclusions about faith to compete directly because they generally describe different objects and, even if they do describe the same object, they work on such different levels of explanation that one description does not cancel the other as in a zero sum game.

In modern theology, this stratification of levels, in part, explains Rudolf Bultmann's theological method in that he refused to let the validity of the kerygma (gospel proclamation) be contingent on a particular culture's success—as in nineteenth-century liberal theologies (e.g., Schleiermacher; Ritschl)—or on Christianity's ability to fabricate a complementary theological account of natural science's predominance. Instead he emphasized the uniqueness of Christianity's concept of justification in contrast to anything that natural reason is able to understand on its own terms of inquiry.[10] Following the Neo-Orthodox spirit, he resisted the attempt to do natural theology and emphasized revelation as the only means of knowing God. Like Karl Barth, he resisted building any philosophical foundation for the gospel and instead emphasized faith's suspension above any rational ground.[11]

The description so far has hopefully clarified a few important points. (1) Scientific and theological assertions are different in kind

---

10. Bultmann, *Kerygma and Myth*, 211, states: "The whole world is profane, though this does not make any difference to the fact that '*Terra ubique Domini*,' which is something which can only be believed in contrary to all appearance. It is not priestly consecration which makes the house of God holy, but only the word of proclamation. Similarly, the framework of nature and history is profane, and it is only in the light of the word of proclamation that nature and history become for the believer, contrary to all appearance, the field of the divine activity." Note how the only revelation is that received in proclamation.

11. "The man who wishes to believe in God as his God must realize that he has nothing in his hand on which to base his faith. He is suspended in mid-air, and cannot demand a proof of the Word which addresses him. For the ground and object of faith are identical. Security can be found only by abandoning all security, by being ready, as Luther put it, to plunge into the inner darkness" (ibid.).

and grounded in different authoritative bases. Even if both assert factual statements, it is for different purposes and with different goals. (2) Though these assertions are different, tension still exists between them. Scientific knowledge inevitably influences theological claims, and theological concerns will influence and give meaning to scientific practice. (3) Concrete problems are the focus, and correlational thinking invites diverse sources into the discussion of how to address them. This diversity in correlational thinking is simultaneously a great strength and a potential liability that can easily cause a lack of clarity. Because it lets individuals determine their own goals and balance information sources, it creates a kind of relativism, even within its own parameters, meaning that the problem's best solution might become unclear both in terms of defining what is best and determining how to get there.

Though this book generally follows a correlational method, its challenge is to ensure that in listening to diverse sources from psychology and sociology it does not lose its central purpose to communicate theology's central claims to people developing faith in various stages. If communicating the gospel is the central goal, then correlational use of social science will help to describe the gospel's *audience* so that theologians will be able to find the most meaningful ways to explain the gospel to that audience. Though this study cannot explain every audience and means of communicating to it, the study can offer social science's best insights into religious change at levels of generalness that will apply to most theological contexts. Even if the reader disagrees with my theological correlations to the data, it is still helpful simply to have the data and know that theology's task is to find resources within its independent tradition and authority that can speak meaningfully to people undergoing the developments featured.

A Map into the Territory of Religious Change

This trek into the science of religious change cannot begin immediately but must pick up its essential orientation in chapter 1. The correlational method is only a frame that needs a specific picture of what is most important. Or, to repeat a metaphor used above, the method is only like the frame of eyeglasses that need lenses for clear vision. Chapter 1 gives this clear vision by offering a theological definition of conversion that will serve as the primary theological matter that correlates to the varied religious changes explored by the social sciences. The next five chapters follow conversion experience's three constituent parts: a convert, a creed, and a social group. Chapters 2–4 discuss the convert, chapter 5 the creed's role, and chapter 6 the role of social influence. Chapter 2 begins the trip in earnest with a robust description of religious change's dynamics, or what happens as people's minds are converted and they begin to live out a new faith. It continues in the next chapter by asking why change occurs both through cognitive and emotional influences, and chapter 4 explains how parents significantly influence children's faith development. Chapter 5 uncovers an elusive area of sociology to explain how theological doctrines themselves play a role in the care of people's needs and in leading them into a faith, and chapter 6 explains how social networks tie together everything the preceding chapters explain in a social context. The reader who has hung on with these diverse accounts into religious change will be rewarded in chapter 7, which seeks to show how a more adequate understanding of conversion is now possible, how the immediate goal of this research has served the ultimate goal in giving the church a fresh way to understand why people believe the gospel, and what implications this new perspective has for the church's life.

1

The Gospel as the Criterion of Religious Change

As stated in the introduction, the correlational method for relating science and theology has no built in direction unless someone defines it independently. The psychosocial accounts of religious change that follow this chapter will be confusing to filter and use unless we have a definite theological concept of conversion intended to address these cases. This chapter provides this definition by arguing that the gospel's presence in people's faith is the one thing that makes religious changes theologically significant. The gospel is thus the criterion of salvation, or that which identifies Christ's presence amid any variety of religious experiences.

Conversion's Spiritual Dimension

That salvation comes through the Holy Spirit there can be no doubt. There is also no doubt that human beings are unable, by their thoughts and actions, to tame, control, or direct this transcendent source of faith that takes a budding development in religious preference and illuminates it with Christ. The vitality of church ministry hangs on this one point: that, contrary to reason, Christian life begins with recognition of human helplessness before God.[1] Though an uncomplicated truth, what the church teaches children about their spiritual dependency on their heavenly Father and the necessity of his forgiveness is perhaps the

---

1. Wenz, *Theologie der Bekenntnisschriften*, 563.

most difficult theological truth to believe, being difficult on a qualitatively different level from daily operations of human thought because, as St. Paul testifies, it is only understood as a consequence of the Spirit's miraculous intervention.[2] It should not be surprising, then, that scientific research into religious change is wholly unable to understand the transcendence that it continually dances around but never finds. Rationality neither finds nor espouses this human dependence on grace because of its very orientation as an active pursuit of knowledge and conquering of nature. Like a jungle explorer caught in quicksand, its struggles only embed it deeper, and by its own presuppositions it cannot see that to find a solution it must first be still. Grace, that is, cannot be caught through active strivings or scientific method. Ironically, it must catch.

The church confesses its dependence on grace not to efface the human being and thereby deny conversion's observable side; it confesses grace to acknowledge the ultimate meaning of a process that science can conceptualize on its own level but cannot value. The wealth of insight that social science provides into how individuals change religiously, affiliate with faith networks, suffer worldview breakdowns, and search for new meaning systems still never harnesses the significance of these processes or finds what theology calls "salvation." That task—which begins in acknowledging human dependence on grace—belongs to theology alone and is invisible to rational structures.[3] Though a conversion theology may use science to explain how the gospel speaks to people amid life's changes, the starting point must be a theological account of conversion that preserves its independent authority.

Conflict in Human Nature

Salvation is meaningful only amid an absolute quandary, something irresolvable by human methods. As Paul says: "All have sinned and fall short of the glory of God."[4] This biblical maxim does not imply that humans tend to fall short such that they can, through trial and error,

---

2. See 1 Cor 2: 8–10.

3. Cf. 1 Cor 2:14, "The person without the Spirit does not accept the things that come from the Spirit."

4. Rom 3:23.

correct their aim and fall perfectly on God's glory. In its own way, that presupposition characterizes contemporary science. It means rather that humans have a fundamental conflict with God in their nature, what theology calls "Original Sin" or "depravity." Though human nature is good in its created essence, its fallenness blinds it to spiritual things. Though humans are created as responsible moral agents,[5] their capacity to choose moral good is limited to mundane things, or "matters below us."[6] These matters include civil affairs such as social ethics and things (including science) that reason is intended to govern, but it excludes the ability to change one's heart. Spiritually speaking, the human will is not the neutral choosing apparatus that it might seem to be. Its inherent choosing capacity cannot apply to impossibilities (i.e., choosing to love God). In spiritual matters the will is an inner orientation, a state of heart that, left to its own ability, will always orient away from God as though sin were north and God were south on a spiritual compass.

The depravity doctrine does not explain every problem of humanity directly, nor does it encourage the church to delight when scientific arrogance is leveled, where illnesses go uncured or space shuttles explode mid-flight. It rather expresses the fallenness of all affairs because of their distance from God, not that humans are incapable of great things, but they are incapable of achieving God's righteousness in their accomplishments. Humanity's fall means that we narrow our vision to the horizon of human potential (*incurvatus in se*) but fail to understand the futility of the greatest human goods if their grandeur lacks divine blessing.[7] It might seem that human claims to self-sufficiency would arise exponentially in a modern age where feats in technology (even the computers we take for granted) would appear miraculous only a few generations ago, but the human claim to self-sufficiency, as it forms an ultimate horizon of expectation and meaning, has persisted from the earliest times. Humankind continues to reach at God from towers of

---

5. Brunstad, *Theologie der Lutherischen Bekenntnisschriften*, 69, says (translated): "Man is not responsible because he is free but he is free insofar as he is responsible."

6. Luther, *Bondage of the Will*, 107, says: "man should realize that in regard to his money and possessions he has a right to use them, to do or to leave undone, according to his own 'free-will'—though that very 'free-will' is overruled by the free-will of God alone, according to His own pleasure."

7. See Forde, *Theology is for Proclamation*, 48. Forde calls the fall an "upward fall" because it lands in pride.

Babel,[8] and when people discover that God cannot be reached through rational abilities, they do not, on their own understanding, retreat from their pursuits but will manufacture idols, redefining God in domesticated forms unlike the transcendent creator and redeemer. Science will even tempt us to conclude that to discover God and to discover mental health and peace in oneself are not particularly different things.[9]

The Bible's prophecy to all generations is that human strivings to self-salvation are impossible because they operate on a basis that is doomed to fail. "The wages of sin," Paul says, "is death, but the gift of God is eternal life in Jesus Christ our Lord."[10] Without beginning and ending in this fundamental place between death and life, sin and redemption, the Scriptures declare that any human efforts to build cultures and businesses, to seek moral rectitude, or even to convert to true religious faith cannot bring about salvation because humans cannot escape their natural fallenness. The problem that plagues conversion theology lies here: that the heart of humankind is corrupt and standing in need of faith.[11]

On Acquiring Faith

But how is faith obtained? Church doctrine will typically state that the Spirit inspires faith through the word and sacraments.[12] This rule confirms faith's normative source, that it cannot come without the word; but it does not attempt to detail God's action or how people develop religiously. Its best function is to say how faith is recognized through the word. In addition, the Scriptures communicate that however mysteriously God works on people through his word, *Christ* is the way to God, unlike humanly conceived solutions.[13] Protestant theologies have emphasized justification, that God's saving gift of Christ is complete in the instant that God gives it. Christ cannot be accumulated through moral efforts because, like Babel towers, these strivings are human measures

---

8. Gen 11.
9. Meyers and Jeeves, *Psychology through the Eyes of Faith*, 159–74.
10. Rom 6:23.
11. Cf. Heb 11:6.
12. Augsburg Confession V in Kolb and Wengert, *Book of Concord*, 41.1–3.
13. Eph 2:4–5; John 14:6.

to tame an untamable Spirit. Justification couples with "divine monergism" to communicate the human state of inability before God's mercy and to curb the inherent impulse to seek God's approval in good deeds. "Monergism" is simply the acknowledgment that humanity, due to its fallen condition, is unable to cause the Spirit to illuminate itself with Christ, that there is no leverage humans have over God's grace.[14] It contrasts historically with synergism, which posits salvation as a result of God's grace and human decision for that grace, however little. History exposed a problem with synergism; that if salvation were made contingent on a choice, then no matter the degree to which the church emphasized grace, salvation would not be certain. Salvation's comfort for synergism would have to anchor in a personal sense of achieving right belief regardless of the church's assurance. It dramatically changes the paradigm of salvation's certainty, however subtly, by placing final emphasis on the individual rather than on God. As much as the pastor should say with Jesus: "Your sins are forgiven,"[15] the church could believe this message not because of its reality but because of its confidence that it has believed the pronouncement rightly. And to leave justification contingent on human subjectivity is to leave room for doubt that maybe my faith is not solid enough or maybe I do not understand doctrine sufficiently to be saved.

The tension between monergism and synergism arises because there are divine and human sides to salvation, and no broad consensus has appeared across denominational lines to demonstrate how they work together. Certainly right human belief is necessary for salvation. Individuals cannot spurn God's grace and obtain grace simultaneously, but can belief (or any religious experience) be a kind of meritorious ground for salvation? Thus the problem turns, and the theologian is forced to decide which emphasis best represents the picture of salvation that God has revealed. Though it can prove neither its choice of

---

14. Monergism literally means "one worker," referring to God's sole causal action in saving a person. Synergism means "work together," implying, in this case, two workers. Cf. Miller and C'de Baca, *Quantum Change*, 14, "Quantum changes are rarely remembered as willful or volitional events, like changing your mind or making a resolution. They are more like waking up one morning to suddenly discover that your skin is a different color."

15. Luke 7:48–49 continues, emphasizing Jesus' authority: "The other guests began to say among themselves, 'who is this who even forgives sins?'"

authoritative sources nor its interpretations to satisfy all objections, this book favors a Christ-centered approach to this problem—one that emphasizes the gospel's character as a pure gift—meaning that faith must originate from Christ, outside of the human capacity to believe. If we are not required to believe to a certain degree but only to believe in Christ, then we have the assurance that Christ is responsible for our salvation rather than our powers of credulity.

Scripture clarifies that Christ is the answer to sin's dilemma for those who believe in him because faith binds them to his death and resurrection.[16] This belief in a dying and rising Christ is truly a human phenomenon known in experience, yet it is not possible without the Spirit. By itself human belief can conceive of Christ as, at best, a fact, but the Spirit gives the belief *life* and personal significance, turning belief into faith. Though the Spirit does not usurp people's cognitive powers and alienate them from their wills and intellects, he opens Christ to them.[17] Though he does not quicken individuals by compulsion or turn them into automatons, he heals their wills, allowing them to turn to Christ.[18] Though many definitions of conversion are available, this study follows the Formula of Concord as a helpful summary of the scriptural witness to portray conversion as a spiritually enabled "spark of faith" in Christ that grounds a person's change in "mind, will, and heart."[19]

---

16. Rom 6:5.

17. The story of Lydia's conversion at Philippi (Acts 16:14) is perhaps the nearest biblical testimony of this point. Paul was speaking to some women and, "One of those listening was a woman named Lydia, a dealer in purple cloth from the city of Thyatira, who was a worshiper of God. The Lord opened her heart to respond to Paul's message," after which she and her household were baptized.

18. See Brunstad, *Theologie der Lutherischen Bekenntnisschriften*, 65, and Wenz, *Theologie der Bekenntnisschriften*, 565–67. These sources argue that God works through means such that he does not abolish selfhood or alienate people from their own choices as the term "brainwashing" connotes.

19. FC II in Kolb and Wengert, *Book of Concord*, 554.54 and 560.83 respectively. In general, "faith" is a divine and human property. Though faith is a divine gift, it is also realized in human consciousness. The gift is not earned but known through experiencing Christ in time.

The Sacramental Encounter

Though it is fascinating to speculate about the variety of ways the Spirit ministers to the world, the reliable path to finding the Spirit's work must follow the revealed word. If the Spirit is the living force of God's work in creation, then the word is the DNA directing that life. Without discerning ostensible manifestations of the Spirit by the word, the church opens itself to drastic abuses. Like Deut 18's false prophets who practiced divination and sorcery, today's church will be tempted to use the Spirit's supposed presence for its self-directed ends if it does not seek the word as its true guidance. This point is crucial for interpreting religious change in that when typical religious changes find salvation, they only do so in an encounter with Christ, that is, a sacramental encounter.

The sacramental encounter, though perhaps lofty sounding, means only that when individuals enter a community of believers and encounter Christ, that encounter itself is saving to them in that it is received by the very center of their Christian identify: their faith. Christ is encountered as the divine word, who reaches the church through oral and written forms as well as the sacraments of baptism and the Lord's Supper; but the important part of this encounter is the word itself, however conveyed. The "church" referred to as the context of this sacramental encounter need not find precise definition here but simply recognition that a church bears the means of grace in order to make faith possible for its congregants and thereby give them a new identity as God's children. However liturgical or informal, the church is a medium where salvation is possible because it preaches Christ as the answer to humanity's spiritual dilemma and offers his presence. While attempts to understand God's will and the Spirit's workings in other religions and secular affairs cannot help but to be ambiguous, the church and its gospel remain an unswerving norm for discovering God's saving action and the futility of trying to find salvation elsewhere, through means scientific, experiential, or affective.[20]

---

20. Luther argued in the Heidelberg Disputation (1518), *Luther's Works*, vol. 31, 39, "That person does not deserve to be called a theologian who looks upon the invisible things of God as though they were clearly perceptible in those things which have actually happened [Rom 1:20]. He deserves to be called a theologian, however, who comprehends the visible and manifest things of God seen through suffering and the cross."

What Conversion Is

With these presuppositions in place, a specific model of salvation's experience is helpful for this study's correlation with scientific accounts of religious change because it describes conversion's content theologically and thereby provides a definite criterion for judging religious change and determining how the gospel speaks meaningfully to people undergoing these changes. Despite vast differences in religious experience, the gospel, as defined by its Spirit and word—its motion and information—must have a consistent theological expression to brand its followers and delineate the church.

This description can be summarized under the concepts of *despair* and *trust*. If God's saves through the law's destruction and gospel's vitalizing (that is, through condemning human fallenness and then bringing new life in Christ) then human recipients will sense these divine actions through despair and trust.[21] The symbol of despair is intended to portray an existential judgment. *Despair* is not theology's prescription of an emotion (though it accompanies a range of them) but of a certain conviction that any hope of salvation rests outside of human pursuits. When people are faced with their fallenness there can be no response but despair of self and a fall into God's mercy. Here is the striking difference between the Kierkegaardian leap of faith, involving personal resolution, and the faith beginning in despair, a kind of existential collapse.

Theologically understood, conversion can only begin in a state of helplessness before God in recognition that all of the temporal structures humans obsessively heed—be they scientific, cultural, or moral—cannot exact the slightest leverage in obtaining salvation.[22] Attempts to find salvation in social structures and personal desires, indeed, in any created things are ultimately in vain. At its extreme, despair stands in contrast even to theology. While theology can define conversion and clear away false notions of self-sufficiency to direct minds and actions, only the Spirit can finally imbue a person with faith, and only Christ

---

21. The argument for despair and trust as faith's two modes is that these symbols accurately summarize the human reception of God's condemnation and forgiveness (law and gospel). They are defined theologically, not psychologically, meaning that they do not prescribe any precise emotional pattern to conversion experience.

22. Cf. Isa 64:5–8.

himself can save, never the *doctrine* of Christ. In its human capacity, faith too is unable to ground salvation; it rather opens people to what God has already accomplished in them.[23] To those that truly understand their helplessness before God, there remains the single option of falling into Christ's arms.

Consequently, *trust* is the conviction that despite this fallenness, acknowledged in despair, Christ has atoned for me. This sacramentally given realization grounds the church's knowledge of salvation. It reveals, however cloudily, the eschatological hope for all of creation that creation can neither direct nor achieve. The church trusts Christ as a transcendent source of salvation's promise. Trust is not an affection theologically prescribed but the conviction or disposition that most clearly senses salvation's reality, both the efficacy of Christ's atonement and its pertinence to individuals in time. The Spirit's gift of faith mediated through the word will comprise these two convicting moments (despair and trust) that most clearly reveal salvation. If other theologies cannot appreciate this account of faith, they may still have Christ's presence but, by this account's standards, await its clearer revelation. The ontology of salvation, that is, is not completely dependent on the epistemology of doctrine. But theology centering on Christ's free gift must confess that despair and trust most clearly align the church with God's condemnation of sin and promise of salvation and thus his primary disposition toward humankind.

This definition places conversion on a different level than anything controlled by human aspirations. If even church dogmatics can only blaze a path for the Spirit, then conversion cannot be forced or calculated by human methods. Salvation cannot be discerned through rational powers but through trust that the word reliably mediates the Spirit. If anything, knowledge of salvation only begins to glow in the abdication of rational structures along with every other worldly measure of value. These structures not only include means to use religion for personal ends but also any patterns of experience or emotion that people might prescribe as a basis for salvation's certainty. As much comfort as rituals provide, as much trust in Jesus that they cultivate, they only point the

---

23. "Faith saves" in terms of its being a divine gift. In terms of its human capacity it does not ground salvation; it grounds the knowledge of salvation and entails responsibility to continue placing oneself under the sacramental encounter and to pursue human righteousness.

church to its transcendent source and hope that it will be saved despite its attempts to systematize the Spirit's work in time.[24]

To this point it might seem that the material world is represented as inferior to the spiritual because salvation is tied so fundamentally to the Spirit's transcendent work. But the Christian church has always believed that created reality is good because God has fashioned it and called it good. Its fallenness means only that creation cannot find spiritual orientation through its own resources. Nevertheless, its resources are redeemable by God's intervention into time. John says: "The Word became flesh and made his dwelling among us," indicating that the material world is inherent in God's redemptive action. It is, for its corruption, the context in which God's glory, grace, and truth appear.[25]

Theology is thus in tension with science as a quantifier of matter. Though empirical research into religious change cannot harness God's grace, it still enlightens the phenomena under which grace appears. If theology's sacramental encounter with Christ forms the basis of salvation's certainty, science cannot influence the verity of this confession. But the precursory conditions and emotions, explanations of how people find themselves bonding to a faith community; these things fall within science's domain. Because God has chosen to work through means of grace, people, church ministry, and the incarnation itself, a comprehensive conversion theology must consider the question's human side, a task in which theology has thus far proven highly negligent. It must hold the tension that material conversion dynamics instigated by impure motives are the matter into which God breathes life. However tainted religious changes are, they still place individuals under a sacramental encounter, where despair of humanity and trust in Christ become as daily bread and the hope of salvation transcends worldly values.

---

24. Tillich is helpful in defining a symbol as a communicator of transcendence but never an end itself. See Reetz, *Das Sakramentale in der Theologie Paul Tillichs*.

25. John 1:14.

2

Change in Religious Experience

THE FIRST STEP IN exploring religious change (conversion's human side) is to provide a robust description of the process through which a person becomes newly focused. To understand this definition's context it will be helpful, first, to discuss the scientific study of religion as theology's conversation partner. Both disciplines have demonstrated religion's importance in human nature, a principle that sets up discussion of religious change's dynamic, the process in which this natural capacity for faith becomes focused on a certain theology. Because the dynamic depicts change's internal process and not its effects, the last section uses sociological research to describe religious change's lasting effects on people's thought and language.

Religious Human Nature in Theology and Science

The Bible narrates that humans are created spiritual beings. From the Genesis creation story to the New Testament's anthropology, humans are portrayed in their religious orientation. Because Christ is the image of the invisible God, the firstborn over all creation, "all things were created by him and for him,"[1] most especially the pinnacle of his creation.[2] But the stories of the fall and flood qualify that this religious orientation does not always finds its true destination. Without the Holy

---

1. Col 1:15–17.
2. Gen 1:26.

Spirit's inbreaking into human consciousness, people continually worship idols;³ and unless religion realizes conversion's spark of faith—a point of helplessness before God and dependence on Christ⁴—it will remain self-serving. Without Christ it will remain in idolatry's self-centeredness rather than finding redemption beyond worldly securities. Yet, as corrupt as human nature is, it is the means through which God has determined to build his church, through fallen agents and on them.

This flawed, self-serving religiousness is where social science meets theology, although, from a correlational perspective, the meeting resembles a Dostoevskian "Inappropriate Gathering."⁵ Theology does not need science's confirmation that humans are inherently religious because it bases its proposition on Scripture. But in serving the church and world, theology benefits from using science not only to understand the world, but to help reveal falsely directed religious motives present in us all. If humans are spiritual and material composites, then science may help to describe this composition from the material perspective.

Religion's universality is one topic on which science and religion correlate closely. Through different methods, both disciplines contend that whether or not faith systems can be proven, humans are unquestionably created to have faith.⁶ For example, research at the turn of the century turn showed that 97 percent of United States residents believe in God and that 90 percent pray.⁷ Even from the broadest polling a remarkable coincidence exists between the Bible's claim that all things were created "by him and for him," fallen though they are, and the survey demonstrating religious faith's pervasiveness in America. This pervasiveness shows that religion is a significant factor in many lives and

---

3. In Rom 1:22–23 Paul discusses this problem: "Although they claimed to be wise they became fools and exchanged the glory of the immortal God for images made to look like mortal man and birds and animals and reptiles."

4. See chapter 1 for this definition of conversion.

5. From *The Brother's Karamazov*, it is a meeting of agents with radically different agendas.

6. The term "faith" in this chapter indicates the human capacity to believe religious things. Theology sometimes defines it as a divine gift, but this meaning is not the assumed sense unless otherwise noted.

7. See Spilka et al., *Psychology of Religion*, 1. Other cultures might demonstrate that belief in a personal god is much less pervasive; however, the need for ultimate meaning and values will generally not diminish across cultural borders.

tentatively suggests that theology's challenge is less to argue for a spiritual reality but to give preexisting religious beliefs a better content.

Other sources argue similarly through different means. Medical doctors Andrew Newberg, Eugene D'Aquili, and Vince Rause, hooked up a meditator to a SPECT (single photon emission computed tomography) camera to track blood changes in the brain during meditation.[8] They found that the orientation section of the brain's rear, left hemisphere showed blood deprivation during meditation. No longer did the meditator sense sharp dimensions or angles in spatial reality but space itself began to appear as a unity once activity in the brain's orientation area quieted. Newberg and his colleagues argue that humans have a religious sense unlike other neurological properties, one un-inducible through chemicals. They conclude that humans are hardwired to believe in faith-based tenets and that this capacity is connected, however murkily, to a greater spiritual reality. What John Calvin called the "sense of divinity"[9] is strangely correlated by recent advances in neurological imaging. The reasons for acknowledging the religious sense are obviously quite different between Newberg and Calvin, and theologians would be wise not to use Newberg to prove their doctrine.[10] But this scientific contention for a religious sense clarifies theology's task to direct inherent religiousness to Christ and to expose misdirected faith's idols.

Newberg and his colleagues are important commentators on the link between biology and religion but not exhaustive. Many theorists attempt to answer the question of humanity's hardwired religiousness through biology, evolutionary theory, or other neuroscientific approaches.[11] Though the results are fascinating, they are far from conclusive in a young science. The theologian cannot help but see these studies pointing to transcendence. Thus far they have only managed to

---

8. Newberg et al., *Why God Will Not Go Away*, 1–5. The meditator was Buddhist, however his religion is not the point for these authors who argue for the brain's inherent ability to have religious experiences.

9. "*Divinitatis sensum.*" Calvin, *Institutes*, I.iii.1, says: "There is within the human mind, and indeed by natural instinct, an awareness of divinity. This we take to be beyond controversy. To prevent anyone from taking refuge in the pretense of ignorance, God himself has implanted in all men a certain understanding of divine majesty."

10. Matthew Alper interprets Newberg's data in an atheistic fashion, citing the religious sense essentially as an illusion. See Alper, *The "God" Part of the Brain*.

11. Spilka et al., *Psychology of Religion*, 59–65.

prove that religion's importance to people is not purely due to sociocultural influences but has a rooting in their biological nature, stressing an important point easily missed in sociology. To check a survey's "atheist" box does not rule out a religious kind of belief.

The insights from neural imaging corroborate clinical psychology's century-old claims. Though Sigmund Freud viewed religion as a neurosis causing individuals to project an exalted father figure, his sense of religion's pervasiveness and importance inspired his devotion to the topic.[12] His disciple Carl Gustav Jung also devoted much attention to religion, though in a contrastingly positive light. His work on mythology concludes that humankind has a collective subconscious that governs all of human thought with nonrational, essentially religious values.[13] As coldly objective as some science appears, it is loaded with dogmas that stem from its historical particularity and its culture's means of determining fundamental values of life and survival. Jung's notion of translation is significant for arguing that cultures reinterpret religion as they become secular, but they cannot abolish it. Myths of starry deities moving planets become myths of cosmic physical powers. To wage war on deity is to attack one's very human identity.

Though religion receives less attention from Freud's other successors, it does appear in developmental accounts, most notably Erik Erikson and James Fowler. In developing his "eight ages of man," or stages of human development, Erikson's first patients were babies. His first stage covers the most formative time in a person's development: "basic trust vs. mistrust" in which basic trust is essential to an infant's rudimentary sense of ego identity. Basic trust is the infant's "willingness to let the mother out of sight without undue anxiety or rage, because she has become an inner certainty as well as an outer predictability."[14] The affective bond between the mother and child is essential to healthy development, meaning that trust is expressly related to the person and not necessarily to behavioral demonstrations of love or to the amount of food the child receives. In a life that will inevitably suffer many disappointments, people's capacity to rebound mentally from sufferings is influenced largely by their sense of certainty in their mother's (and

---

12. E.g., *The Future of an Illusion*.
13. Jung and Kerényi, *Essays on a Science of Mythology*, 74–79.
14. Erikson, *Childhood and Society*, 247.

later the father's) commitment to them from life's earliest stages.[15] Trust takes different forms throughout human development, and though not all people grow to trust in a formal religion's deity, basic trust itself "becomes the capacity for faith—a vital need for which man must find some institutional confirmation."[16] Erikson does not claim directly that all people are created to be religious in the same sense that Scripture does. His approach is nuanced to show that in maturing, humans never lose their need for an object of trust that provides for their needs and, more importantly, orients their identity and purpose, which is partly the outcome of infants coming to terms with the meaning of the parents' care and consequent sense of their place in society.[17] Though not everyone develops specific religious faith, all people are born with a capacity for faith that takes different forms wherever their lives' meanings take root.[18]

Erikson's insights continue in the work of James Fowler, who uses his developmental psychology to define six stages of faith. Fowler's conclusions on basic trust are like Erikson's, though in Fowler's scheme, the place of an infant's "undifferentiated faith" in its mother for basic care and affection serves as a pre-stage, presupposed in the six actual stages.[19] *Undifferentiated* means that though the infant is too young to have a specific concept of faith's object, it still senses comfort and abandonment according to the mother's treatment. This placement before the six proper stages demonstrates that this link between parental care and healthy faith development is universal, whereas later stages of faith are unattainable by many people. Fowler links his concept of basic trust with Jean Piaget's "scheme of object permanence," demonstrating

15. Erikson, *Identity, Youth, and Crisis*, 106, holds that hope is "the enduring predisposition to believe in the attainability of primal wishes in spite of the anarchic urges and rages of dependency."

16. Ibid., 106.

17. Erikson, *Childhood and Society*, 249, says: "Parents must not only have certain ways of guiding by prohibition and permission; they must also be able to represent to the child a deep, an almost somatic conviction that there is a meaning to what they are doing."

18. A more recent account of trust from sociology's side portrays foundational trust as manifest in ten levels of analysis such as roles, beliefs, social models, religious organizations, symbols, and governments. See Blasi, "The Meaning of Conversion," 11–32.

19. Fowler, *Stages of Faith*, 119–21.

that somewhere between seven and eight months of age infants begin to sense that their perceptions have permanent referents, remembered even when the perceived object is absent. Here, Fowler believes, is the beginning of basic trust. Though a caregiver is not phenomenally present, the child begins to trust the mental impression that the caregiver is real and will return. This part of development evinces humanity's inextricable impulse to believe in unseen things.[20]

Though not all scientists agree that humankind is created for faith much less to love God, a significant variety of reports show religion's pervasive importance. Where atheists are discovered, it need not trouble biblical anthropology. As Jung contended, atheists exist under the collective subconscious just as all people; and as theology holds: "man's nature, so to speak, is a factory of idols"[21] of which no one is free. The universal divine sensibility as attested in Scripture and empirical research warrants further study into human nature and its implications for ancient doctrine. Science catalogs the dynamics of religiousness but inevitably discovers idols. It finds idols because idols are always self-serving gods offering the believer a rational reciprocity for faith. Because science is always concerned with rational explanations for phenomena, its theories consistently point to the benefits, the this-worldly payoffs of having religious faith. Even when considering otherworldly payoffs such as heaven and hell, it only addresses these beliefs' impact on this world. But this point only emphasizes the frustration and yet the wonder of this research. Though science seems to explain so much to the detriment of theology's claims, it never leaves the level of material causality; it itches for a transcendence on which it borders but never reaches: the place where all idols and impure motivations to believe find redemption in Christ's dying and rising.[22] Though the rational motives for believing religious things (discovered by science) must finally be given up insofar as they replace God, this incarnate plane of religion, though distorted, is still where grace appears. As long as science and theology are used correlationally, religious pervasiveness and

---

20. Note the correlation with Heb 11:1–2, "Now faith is being sure of what we hope for and certain of what we do not see."

21. Calvin comments on Gen 31:19 in *Institutes*, I.xi.8.

22. Rom 6:1–14. In chapter 1 this theology is called "despair of self and trust in Christ."

the universal sense of divinity legitimate further inquiry into these perspectives' relationship.

The next section explains how faith's object changes when the sense of divinity becomes focused on a particular theology. Studying religious change does not impinge on conversion's theological definition as a Spirit-enabled change in "mind, will, and heart,"[23] but it enriches our knowledge of change's process, precursory factors, and dynamic: the material basis through and on which God works.

Dynamics of Religious Change

Because the church maintains its doctrinal norms independently of external authorities, only its theological convictions can define conversion. The definition cannot be universal because its very basis is the authority structure of a *particular* theology. However, the church's judgment of a true conversion according to the gospel criterion accompanies a general dynamic of religious change that might appear in Buddhism, Islam, or even secular social movements. Though the ideology in these instances of religious change is drastically different, psychology has emphasized that the process of reorienting one's mental structures toward a new faith system is common to humanity. A possible objection is that this claim denies the particular truth claims of all faith systems. Christians, believing that Christ is the only way to the Father,[24] might expect that their experiences are special or different than other faiths. The church must rather remember that its uniqueness comes from the word itself (faith's object) and not any speculation into how the Spirit might create Christians in an empirically testable manner.[25] The general applicability of religious change's dynamic correlates with theology's claim that God does not coerce people.[26] The Spirit works inscrutably

---

23. See Formula of Concord (FC) II in Kolb and Wengert, *Book of Concord*, 560.83.

24. John 14:6; Acts 4:12.

25. Recall FC II in Kolb and Wengert, *Book of Concord*, 554.56, that "the presence, effectiveness, and gift of the Holy Spirit should not and cannot always be assessed *ex sensu* [from sensation]."

26. "[Conversion] happens not like a picture being etched in stone or a seal being pressed in wax; these things do not know or feel anything" (ibid.).

through normal human processes and is known only as those processes begin to orient toward Christ.

Early Groundwork

Few psychologists have attempted to define religious change's dynamic, or what actually happens to the person. Though change is common, it occurs over different time periods and under different influences discoverable in the scientific study of religion. These difficulties have led researchers to conclude that the mental process of religious change is still unknown and can be grasped only by analogy. About one hundred years old, E. D. Starbuck's *Psychology of Religion* is arguably the best introduction to the phenomenon that modern psychology has produced. Devoting about two hundred pages to religious awakenings, he offers a basic model that later psychology has expanded but not overturned.[27] He influenced his teacher William James to follow his model. In an oft-quoted passage James summarizes it: "To say that a man is 'converted' means, in these terms, that religious ideas, previously peripheral in his consciousness, now take a central place, and that religious aims form the habitual centre of his energy."[28]

Both James and Starbuck believed that extreme awakenings held the key to the more prolonged and moderate, where the mental processes involved were similar but less salient. Their central framework shows that consciousness's focus on immediate sensations and thoughts is easily influenced by subconscious or peripheral thoughts present in the mind but awaiting attention. Weighty mental input such as gospel proclamation can influence a person effectively at the conscious and subconscious levels. Even if consciousness is not focused directly on the message preached, in converts it creates tension between the new life proclaimed from the pulpit and their current life estranged from that higher spiritual place. The tension incubates in a person's peripheral mental life and prepares him or her for a transforming moment where a trigger (perhaps the reiteration of the proclamation) causes an upsurge into the consciousness resulting in a moment of clarity and awakening

---

27. Starbuck, *Psychology of Religion*, 211–12.
28. James, *Varieties of Religious Experience*, 165.

to new life. The figure below outlines this change from Starbuck's own pen. If r hypothetically stands for the "spark of faith" in Christ, we see in the first diagram that it stews in the peripheral mind but is not yet realized. The concerns of a, b, c, and d are still primary in consciousness, and though r is subliminally present creating tension, the four lower values are still the person's primary values. But once the awakening is triggered, we see that R solidifies with an upsurge into consciousness and though a, b, c, and d are not eliminated, their preferential place in determining the convert's values is subverted by R's higher plane. Now they are interpreted in light of R. In a Christian interpretation, for example, thoughts of Christ and the Scriptures' prescription for living reinspire and reorient secular values such as justice, love of family, and charity.

Figure: Starbuck's Change Dynamic.[29]

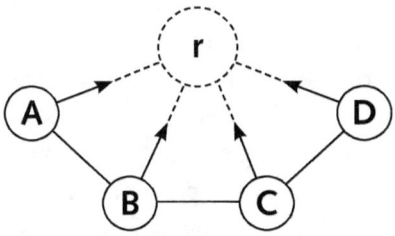

Before Conversion

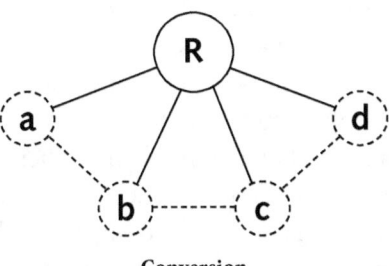

Conversion

Contrasting modern paradigms that portray converts as active in accomplishing their new life,[30] Starbuck believed that realizing new

29. Starbuck, *Psychology of Religion*, 110.
30. E.g., Zock, "Paradigms in Psychological Conversion Research," 55.

spiritual life through willpower was impossible in this dynamic because of the uncontrollable elements in peripheral consciousness and because accounts of religious awakenings portrayed converts' passiveness. A male at nineteen reports:

> Knowledge of sin had ripened into the sense of sin; at church one sentence in the sermon caught my attention, though I was usually inattentive. The impression faded away immediately. Two days later, while in business, there was a sudden arrest of my thought without a consciously associated natural cause. My whole inner nature seemed summoned to a decision for or against God; and in five minutes I had a distinctly formed purpose to seek him. It was followed immediately by a change, the principal manifestation of which was a willingness to make known my decision and hope of divine forgiveness.[31]

Though the quote speaks of decision, Starbuck saw that the decision took place in a greater context of inevitability. Once the "knowledge of sin" first mentioned began to incubate in the person's consciousness it would eventually release into a full-blown realization of religious insight, here of the need for forgiveness. Starbuck postulated that these experiences must happen along ordinary lines of cognition rather than coercion by one's effort or another person's pressure (though these elements do have a role). If the change is forced, his model dictates, the aim will be too low by trying to force belief in a false version of R rather than R itself. In their respective contexts Starbuck and conversion theology both admonish: "Be still, and know that I am God."[32] Religious change requires patience on all sides.

Lest their audiences find radical converts to be a nearly different class of people, both James and Starbuck emphasized that this dynamic, though represented in extreme form in their research, functions through ordinary mental operations. They likened it to lapses in memory where a certain word is "on the tip of my tongue" and cannot be retrieved by hard concentration.[33] The only way to remember is to relax, and many times the word suddenly appears to mind. A more important analogy that current psychologists have also seized is problem solving

---

31. Quoted in Starbuck, *Psychology of Religion*, 107.
32. Ibid., 117. Starbuck quotes Ps 46:10.
33. Shaw, "Paradoxical Intention," 5–16.

genius. Starbuck mentions a Sir William Rowan Hamilton whose discovery of quaternions (a mathematical operation) troubled him for fifteen years until a solution simply occurred to him on a walk in Dublin.[34] Psychologists cite inspired moments, not just in mathematics but also in art, poetry, and literature as analogues for the clarity of religious awakening.

This explanatory approximation of religious change remains dominant today, but social psychology has expanded and nuanced the model by breaking it into distinct points. The model's new version offers perhaps the best approximation of mental processes underlying the convert's change in mind, will, and heart.

Later Developments: The Problem Solving Motif

The mystery of religious change has impeded many researchers from attempting to explain the dynamic after Starbuck's spirit. Notable exceptions are social psychologists C. Daniel Batson, Patricia Schoenrade, and W. Larry Ventis (hereafter, BSV).[35] While researchers are generally apt only to look for statistical commonalities in converts, these social-psychologists have attempted to explain the mental process itself, albeit by analogy. They follows James's belief that dramatic religious experiences contain the key for understanding less dramatic religious experiences; in this case, that sudden changes follow the same course as gradual changes, only at greater speed. Their nine component model helps to explain the mental operations associated a spiritual change in mind, will, and heart.

1) To follow BSV, the reader must grant that all human perception is constructed. This claim is a philosophical presupposition that these researchers use to apply Gestalt psychology to religious awakenings. Gestalt was conceived by Max Wertheimer (1912), whose inspiration came from the motion picture's inception. He reasoned that the ability to perceive a movie from quick succession of still camera shots on a reel demonstrated that the motion picture's reality depends entirely on the mind's ability to construct its reality. Though this thesis links back

---

34. Starbuck, *Psychology of Religion*, 110–11.
35. Batson et al., *Religion and the Individual*, 88–108.

to the thought of George Berkeley (1685–1753) at least, Wertheimer used it to build the Gestalt psychological school where he focused his labor less on metaphysics and more on how people's perceptions of particular objects and relations evince innate laws of thought. Though Wertheimer did not venture far into deconstructing people's value hierarchies, he did establish how our attributions of meaning arise out of contexts. For example, perception of a spider might be fascinating or unnerving. It depends on context (the woods vs. one's house) and personal constitution. The meaning of "spider" is not a stable universal but a constructed reality.

2) Constructed reality's building blocks are certain mental structures that serve as perceptual tools. Unlike structuralist literary criticism that attempts to uncover deep, universal patterns of mental life in literature, these mental structures are changeable. They are the presuppositions and categories of thought, not only for determining spatial relations and quantities but also values and standards. These preconceived notions help us to make sense of the world and survive. Many of us have a notion of "slick" that applies to politicians and salespeople. The slick structure provides an adjective, a category for certain smooth talkers not only to identify them but to link them to our brains' caution impulse. According to Jean Piaget, human development influences these structures, explaining why children are unable to identify the slick politician (or even understand the constancy of liquid's volume when poured into variously shaped containers). Because religious change occurs often in ages twelve through sixteen,[36] the developmental shifting of structures likely plays a significant role.

3) The BSV model's relevance to religious change becomes evident in applying cognitive structures to the problem solving process—their analogue for the experience of change. The different structures are not equally valuable for problem solving. Low level structures such as recognizing roundness to identify a racquetball or basic logic to understand a cash transaction are fundamental to human thought but their explanatory power is limited. If asked: "Is this cash transaction consonant with familial responsibility and societal duty?" or "Should I play racquetball with a $5,000 health insurance deductible?" then their software will find an error, so to speak, and the questions will seem

---

36. Johnson, *Psychology of Religion*, 127.

unsolvable. But these more abstract questions are solvable on a higher level structure that is less indispensable but more sophisticated. Humans tend to develop these more abstract levels of organization with age and education. I recall seeing a sign that advertised a meeting for "All Democrats and Liberals." The students behind this meeting seemed to apply a low level power of association by their simple categorization of democrats with liberals. A higher level sign would probably call out to "Liberal Democrats," acknowledging that Democrats can be both liberal or conservative on a given issue and that so-called liberals are not necessarily Democrats. The point is that problem solving many times requires the mind itself to adapt and conceive of the problem in new terms if the old terms ended in obscurity.

4) A new problem-solving Gestalt is not likely to appear *ex nihilo* but rather from a reorganization of cognitive structures. Like reading a glossy page on a bright day, the proper angle is necessary to see. BSV clarify that the new Gestalt, "through greater differentiation and integration, makes it possible to think what was previously unthinkable."[37] For example, architects synthesize different values in designing buildings. If they design a building completely for energy efficiency its dark rooms and low ceilings will give it a claustrophobic feel, but if designed completely for aesthetics, it will probably lack efficiency. Through a creative process, the architect has to synthesize all of the values that constitute a comfortable and efficient building; so doing takes a high level of mental organization, to see a design's parts and whole simultaneously. BSV use examples such as Archimedes, whose discovery of specific gravity (viz. how to determine if a crown were made of gold) came in a flash of insight when he applied his own body's displacement of bath water to the problem of measuring the crown's volume.

5) The problem solving motif proves a fitting parallel to religious change in that both can happen over long or short periods and both can work either gradually or in flashes of insight. For those insightful flashes, BSV suggest that there are stages of preparation, incubation, illumination, and verification contributing to Gestalt reorganization. This account expands Starbuck's early work, which focused only on incubation and illumination. Preparation is the frustrating phase, as when Archimedes feared for his life if he could not determine the crown's

---

37. Batson et al., *Religion and the Individual*, 94.

authenticity. It is the struggle, where the mental structures are unequal to the problem solving task. Incubation is the stage where, unable to force the solution, the thinker stops thinking about it directly and it stews in subconscious memory. Illumination is the breakthrough itself, where the old ways of conceiving the problem are deemed inadequate in the new insight's light. And verification is the testing and nuance of the new insight.

6) Exactly how illumination occurs is inexplicable. Perhaps humans do not posses even potential mental structures to unravel this mystery. There might be, however, a physiological basis for this operation. Because the brain's right cerebral hemisphere handles perception it is most responsible for apprehending the Gestalt, but the left hemisphere, concerned with logic and language influences, perhaps "edits" the Gestalt's form. When thinking hard about a problem, BSV speculate, the left brain is more active. Though its operations are more precise than the right brain, its horizon of possibilities is more restricted. When left to incubate, the left brain eases up and lets the right brain apply its spontaneous work to the problem. In some cases, the perceptually oriented right hemisphere "sees" something that the left could not and the result is a flash of clarity. Of course, this theory is speculative, and due modesty will recognize that some problems are unsolvable and that flashes of insight, even when they do occur, do not ground their product's truth.

7) The last three stages cover psychological motivations for change that need not be described in detail because of their place in this study's later chapters. However, BSV's discussion of stage 7 makes the important point that the problem solving process is dynamically similar in matters of philosophy, science, or existential problems. BSV suggest that Erikson's eight stages, starting with trust vs. mistrust, are examples of personal conflict between a realized and ideal self in which people continually seek to transcend their level of existence by attaining more willing and mental powers. The problem of reaching that ideal begins the process that, for many, leads to illumination.

8) The stages of preparation, incubation, illumination, and verification can be formally translated into terms of religious awakening. BSV correspondingly call them existential crisis, self-surrender, new vision, and new life. This schema expands Starbuck's problem/solution

diagram and captures the temporal process of religious change. Theological and early science paradigms portray religious change as instantaneous,[38] following Paul's encounter with Christ on the Damascus road.[39] And though the illumination stage might happen suddenly, these other stages demonstrate that it does not occur without a greater context and need. These flashes of insight do not occur arbitrarily or neurotically; they are solutions to particular problems. Though theology cannot portray conversion as an incrementally developed status,[40] it also cannot deny that there are complex factors leading to and proceeding from salvation's temporal appearance.

9) Though the problem solving model offers a plausible correlation to theology's notion of conversion, BSV offer a disclaimer that not all instances of religious awakening are beneficial. Their method is clear in judging the truth of an awakening by its implications for mental health. Illumination can fail, they say, if it encourages people to flee into fantasy and ignore concrete life, if it facilitates emotional dependence on a religious leader or group, or narrows one's viewpoint toward rigid dogmas.[41] Theology can generally support these first two points. God's rule of creation accounts for responsible individuals who are required to act reasonably and justly in civil and social matters. Clearly, flight to fantasy and emotional dependence could impede these responsibilities. But what of rigid dogmas? BSV does not try to hide its bias against anything it considers "fundamentalism," but to confess any theological doctrine (such as "God is three persons, yet one substance") is to work in a realm of absolutes discouraged by BSV. This challenge should inspire theologians to remember that conversion's validity is discernable because of the gospel alone. Neither mental illnesses nor extreme dogmatism disqualify the Spirit's effectiveness. But theology can learn from BSV that the most beneficial changes (from theology's standpoint) are those that teach people to internalize doctrine. Changes like St. Paul's inspire action by making doctrine the orienting center of one's being and a

---

38. See Meehl et al., *What, Then, Is Man?*, 251.

39. See Acts 22:10, "About noon as I came near Damascus, suddenly a bright light from heaven flashed around me. I fell to the ground and heard a voice say to me, 'Saul! Saul! Why do you persecute me?'"

40. An incremental conversion would cross the immediate fullness of God's gift of salvation.

41. See Batson et al., *Religion and the Individual*, 107.

beginning to action.[42] Doctrine is like a rule: "Do not place your hand in front of the table saw blade," that must be followed absolutely, but if followed, it opens the possibility to numerous creative enterprises.

Evaluation

From Starbuck to present day, analogies are psychology's best attempt to conceptualize dramatic changes. Though the problem solving model is an effective tool, it has one major flaw in that its own Gestalt is insufficiently integrative. In centering on dramatic changes and their corresponding problem/solution dynamic, BSV has neglected more subtle forms of change. Psychologist Chana Ullman provides a needed qualification that change is less often a cognitive struggle and more often a result of positive emotion in finding an object of trust, be it God himself, a group, or a charismatic leader. This qualification concurs with Erikson's insights on trust. Though Ullman began her research thinking that religious change is a product of cognitive struggle, she becme convinced that the problem/solution scheme is subordinate to a greater context of falling in love with the object of one's religious trust.[43] This focus portrays converts less as autonomous, scientific inventors and more as social beings craving love and affirmation.

Regardless of the dynamic's detail and these models' fallibility, it confirms James's comment that "religious ideas, previously peripheral in his consciousness, now take a central place."[44] The change dynamics exhibit theology's contention that doctrines are revealed truths that do not operate on a simple, factual level such as dry news articles. Scripture passages such as: "You believe there is one God? Good. Even the demons believe that and shudder!"[45] distinguish between merely acknowledging a true proposition and *taking it to heart*. In discussing the reorganization of cognitive structures BSV's dynamic correlates closely

---

42. The contrast would be to treat doctrine as an end, as though holding certain views were the Christian's primary duty.

43. Ullman, *The Transformed Self*, xvi. The Ullman model need not have a completely different explanatory scheme than the problem solving model, but it recognizes that the problem solving dynamic operates socially and emotionally too.

44. James, *Varieties of Religious Experience*, 165.

45. Jas 2:19.

with theology. Many people know of Christ peripherally (factual or cultural ideas about Jesus' identity), but converts begin to know Christ as centrally important. Their cognitive structures form a hierarchy organized around Christ as their existence's meaning and many times this change increases their creative powers to relate to diverse peoples and circumstances. Because of humankind's sinful orientation, only the Spirit can supplant idols and focus a person on Christ. The dynamic above gives psychology's closest approximation of the material basis through which the Spirit works. To say that the Spirit causes conversion (theologically understood) neither implies that the Spirit causes the dynamic physically nor that its experience guarantees the Spirit's presence. But the Spirit subtly takes typical human religiousness and directs it to Christ through the word.[46] Though anyone can experience the dynamic without the Spirit, no one can have Christ as its end unless the Spirit first operates on the heart.[47]

Even if the dynamic cannot easily pin the Spirit down it can inform theology's task. If religious change refocuses one's attention then theology can facilitate the focus by fully proclaiming Christ's divine and human natures to emphasize his absoluteness as faith's orientating center and his relevance to humanity as the incarnate Son. Any dilutions of Christ's ultimate status though excessive analogies or philosophies of redemption will attenuate this focus's force. However, the dynamics also indicate that religious change cannot be compelled but must happen naturally; neither falling in love nor problem solving can occur by brute force. Though the Spirit heals the will supernaturally, it

46. The Spirit's causal power heals the convert's heart, allowing a turn to Christ, but the Spirit does not force a cognitive reorganization any more than he forces people to carry out good deeds. The Spirit's psychological operations are unknowable on the surface except that in conversion's light (known by the gospel criterion) we can discern the Spirit's operation in a person's entire process of religious change including the factors leading to conversion.

47. Christianity's uniqueness is evident in its concept of self-transcendence. This term typically refers to expanding one's potential and personal strength, perhaps through religious transformation; but in Christian theology self-transcendence begins where a person no longer looks within but relies completely on Christ. I transcend to new life because Christ does so for me. Theology cannot concern itself with finding the Spirit's specific presence in experience because ultimately the Spirit's work transcends (contrasts and works despite of) religion's human expression. Christianity stands alone in recognizing that salvation is possible only in the destruction and resurrection of religiousness by grace.

is without the compulsion that alienates people from their conscious selves. Evangelists can take heed that their task is to proclaim Christianity's truths and embody them in life, but unduly pressuring the unchurched (or parents pressuring children) to believe will compromise change's spontaneous nature. As Starbuck believed, to *force* change is usually to aim for a lesser object than the mind would find through its typical workings.

The dynamics of change are useful to explain how people begin to believe religious doctrines in their hearts, but in concentrating on the change process they say very little about its long-term effects. To complete our description, the last section asks what lasting effects a religious shift might have in someone's thought and language.

Religious Change's Effects: The Markers of Transcendence

To explain (or predict) spontaneous awakening is perhaps psychology's hardest task. The difficulty parallels theologians' curiosity to determine how the Spirit turns people to Christ. Theology handles the problem by setting doctrinal rules around the problem, never pretending to solve the spiritual mystery, and psychology mirrors the problem through analogy with its problem solving and falling in love models. The dynamic's inscrutability, however, does not entail that its effects are equally obscure. Social research has catalogued religious change's identifying marks, or what converts might say and do differently. Though these external signs cannot guarantee a true change, they are normative signs (sociologically speaking) that a person's values have been refocused on a particular theology. These social markers of transcendence offer a useful correlation to the Christian's status as a new creation in Christ and an idea of how theology functions in this birth's newness.[48] This discussion first highlights religious change's uniqueness and then describes its four social marks, thus completing the description of this phenomenon.

---

48. 1 Cor 5:17, "Therefore, if anyone is in Christ, he is a new creation; the old has gone, the new has come!"

The Break's Extremity

Social psychologist Richard Travisano has produced an account of religious change highly regarded throughout his field. It carves out change's special status by distinguishing it from *alternation*, a less radical change more akin to changing opinions rather than hearts.[49] The notion of *alternation* comes from sociologist Peter Berger's work in evaluating the modern world's "social mobility."[50] Berger argues that people, due to constant inundation with information and contradictory meaning systems, tend to construct several versions of themselves through which they alternate back and forth. The plurality of competing narratives makes switching religions, denominations, and political associations typical. Without ultimate loyalty to any one narrative, Berger contends, people may jump narratives like a frog jumps lily pads. This evaluation inspired Travisano to seek a more sophisticated account. Though Travisano does not dispute alternation's reality, he denies alternation as a synonym for true religious change, and in those sentiments he agrees with the dynamics discussed above that demand definite reorientations in focus.

Travisano's splitting maul for separating alternation and religious change is the double-headed sociology of identity and role. Where role has a formal or behavioral feel, identity strikes a more permanent and abstract trait. Modern society contains many people who switch roles, such as a mailman becoming a restaurant manager, a husband becoming a father, a Republican becoming an arms rights lobbyist, or a Catholic becoming Orthodox. These kinds of alternations are common today,[51] perhaps because they are easy. If our primary loyalties remain unchallenged, taking up a new role or task produces little anxiety. If the new role entails an advantage (e.g., the Orthodox church is much

---

49. Travisano, "Alternation and Conversion," 594–606. "Conversion" in Travisano is here represented as "religious change."

50. Berger, *Invitation to Sociology*, 49–50.

51. Matthew Loveland reports that around one-third of U.S. adults "switch" (a synonym for "alternate") denominations. Loveland explains this phenomenon within a religious marketplace framework where consumers join denominations according to a conscious rationale. In "Religious Switching," 154, he concludes: "Childhood socialization does not appear to produce lasting religious preferences . . . When social behaviors that would influence preferences later in life are allowed to predict switching, childhood socialization is not an influential determinant of religious choice."

closer to home, or a new job pays better), it demonstrates alternation's tactical prudence but also its indistinctiveness. Identity, conversely, "is a placed or validated announcement."[52] When Christians confess: "I believe in God, the Father Almighty," this announcement is absolute. It does not announce a role that can be taken up or left until tomorrow; it expresses a *fundamental loyalty*. Symbolic interactionists such as Travisano observe how role and identity influence each other. So simply taking up a role (e.g., casually attending church) might result in an identity change,[53] or a certain identity (e.g., an historian) tends to correlate with certain roles (i.e., teaching history). Nevertheless, the concepts of identity and role are distinct.

Religious change is a break and reformulation in identity itself. In symbolic interactionist terms: "[religious change] involves the adoption of a pervasive identity which rests on a change (at least in emphasis) from one universe of discourse to another."[54] Travisano uncovers a sense of passiveness and selflessness. Self-reliant people such as Ralph Waldo Emerson are poor candidates for this type of change. If their values consistently circle around self-preservation, they will not be overtaken by a new "universe of discourse." True converts of any kind are repentant, even on a secular level. "A whole new world is entered, and the old world is transformed through reinterpretation. The father sees his bachelorhood as youthful fun; the convert sees his as debauchery."[55] "I once was lost but now am found, was blind but now I see," declares the famous hymn. This decisive break with the past and reinterpretation of the old self in terms of the new self's value system marks religious change's identity shift as distinct from alternation.[56] Converts are suspicious characters, according to Travisano, because they obtain clarity unknown to most people.[57] While most people's attention and values are split into several roles and expectation sets (e.g., church,

52. Travisano, "Alternation and Conversion," 597.
53. See Bromley and Shupe, "A Role Theory Approach," 159–86.
54. Travisano, "Alternation and Conversion," 600.
55. Ibid., 601.
56. Note that this change affects a person's value orientation and behavior, not necessarily the broad personality traits such as introvert vs. extrovert or intuitive vs. sensing perception. See Paloutzian et al., "Religious Conversion and Personality Change," 1047–79.
57. Travisano, "Alternation and Conversion," 606.

family, work, local government) that liquefy their identities, the convert's "identity ubiquity" remains more stable in all roles.

Though Travisano's analysis might not apply in every case, his essay honors the church's particularity. A new life in Christ should be something more than an alternation, role assumption, or what one researcher called "a fashion."[58] Because the Spirit many times appears under the cover of great weakness,[59] converts will not evince this sharp kind of break and new identity always. The church should patiently help to inspire the convert's new world of discourse through teaching and explaining the means of grace that the convert, in a newfound sense of clarity, is especially ready to absorb.

The Convert's Social Type

Sociologists have attempted to define the convert's suspicious sense of clarity and differentiate it from the unconverted. Is there something distinct about converts, and if so, what is it? If a sense of transcendence has certain markers, what are they? Dissatisfied with research up to their time, sociologists David Snow and Richard Machalek determined to identify a convert's sociological signs.[60] Many prior studies tended to equate membership or affiliation with religious change. As with alternation, affiliation and membership hover above the true change in identity that distinguishes converts from loose affiliates.[61] Snow's research produced four distinct themes that not only identify religious change but point to the extremity defined by Travisano and later Max Heirich's appropriately-titled essay "Change of Heart."[62]

The first is *biographical reconstruction*. If we follow BSV's presupposition that reality is constructed (in terms of the meanings and

   58. Dericquebourg, "Becoming a New Ager," 131–62.
   59. FC II in Kolb and Wengert, *Book of Concord*, 554.56.
   60. Snow and Machalek, "The Convert as Social Type," 261–66. Snow and Machalek are hereafter abbreviated as "Snow."
   61. Machalek and Snow, "Conversion to New Religious Movements," 56, state: "At present, it can be argued that all conceptualizations of conversion share at least one common theme: the notion that conversion constitutes a radical personal change. More specifically, this change is commonly construed as a transformation of consciousness, especially of self and identity."
   62. Heirich, "Change of Heart," 673–75.

values humans attribute to their perceptions), the convert's biographical reconstruction shows that life's meaning is subjectively rooted. Undoubtedly certain viewpoints are superior to others, yet all are laden by dogma. Converts cannot doubt that their new faith has rescued them from their old ways. "And even now it is difficult for me to strip off and cast aside the doctrine of the pope," writes Martin Luther, "And certainly we have barely begun to hope and to call upon Christ as our savior that He may come through death, famine, and war and set us free."[63] To discover a new religious truth, as the dynamics above demonstrate, is not to stack up new cards but to shuffle the whole deck. The process has retroactive implications. In Luther's case, the pope as former stanchion of the faith becomes a devil. The old self without Christ was blind, but the new self trusting Christ can see.

Snow warns that "biographical reconstruction may even involve the fabrication and insertion of events"[64] to contrast the depths of despair with the heights of redemption. Converts might simply remember their lives differently due to their new theological emphasis. Without intentional deception, they provide a particularly salient example of reality construction's partisan nature. From an outsider's perspective, the convert's old and new selves are probably far less stark in contrast, demonstrating how language and perception many times precede piety. When the church ministers to converts it invests for the long term and cannot expect their lives to match their newfound biography's language exactly. It needs patience for its preaching, teaching, and counseling efforts to ripen, that is, for piety to begin conforming consistently to the convert's new way of thinking and speaking.

Theology's role appears more forcibly in the convert's second mark: the *adoption of a master attribution scheme*. A master attribution scheme is a doctrinal apparatus for making sense of the world.[65] Attribution is the social scientist's term to denote how people explain causal relations. To say: "I feel a storm coming in my knee," is to attribute a physical sensation to a drop in atmospheric pressure that could indicate stormy weather. A master attribution is an abstracted and grand vision of causality found in doctrine. The theological vision centralizing in

---

63. Luther, "Lecture on Genesis 49:11, 12," in *Luther's Works*, 8:256.
64. Snow, "The Convert as Social Type," 268.
65. Snow, "The Sociology of Conversion," 173.

converts' minds separates them from alternators and, as Travisano and Berger noted, raises suspicion from those with a lesser sense of purpose. Though converts acknowledge mundane causal operations such as the sun causing warmth or arthritis causing pain, their sense of physical causality's significance broadens along with their attention toward ultimate problems and solutions.

Snow's particular research indicated a shift toward individual responsibility. The Nichiren Shoshu Buddhists he interviewed showed a change in master attribution from vague social factors to the self: "Before joining Nichiren Shoshu I blamed any problems I had on other people or on the environment. It was always my parents, or the school, or society. But through chanting I discovered the real source of my difficulties: myself."[66] As much as conversion dynamics are similar between religions, the master scheme demonstrates doctrine's impact. Even among Christian denominations the attributions could be very diverse. A Pentecostal might see causality in terms of God's battle with Satan and angelic forces; a Presbyterian might see all things traceable to God's sovereign hand; a Lutheran might combine the Reformed and the Buddhists and decide that there is an irresolvable tension between divine and human responsibilities![67] In all cases, the master scheme does not explain historical events merely from scientific curiosity. In causal attributions it rather employs the convert's new theology, that which identifies life's deepest problem (e.g., sin, alienation from true self, societal oppression of a class) and its solution (Christ, Buddhist chanting, hope for liberation).

Though many people are drawn to churches through affective ties,[68] Snow affirms that the mind's assumption of a master attribution scheme separates the true convert from the casual affiliate. The change highlights doctrine's role and provides a close correlation to conversion. Though many factors influence conversion's process, doctrine's role is vital: "Do not conform any longer to the pattern of this world, but be transformed by the renewing of your mind."[69]

---

66. Snow, "The Convert as Social Type," 271.
67. Kolb, *Bound Choice*, 6.
68. See Stark and Bainbridge, "Networks of Faith," 1376–94.
69. Rom 12:2.

In renewed minds, Snow noticed a *suspension of analogical reasoning* that preserves the new theology's particularity among competing worldviews.[70] At least two varieties of metaphors exist: the analogical and the iconic. While theology cannot help but to employ scriptural metaphors (e.g., God as Father, love, hen gathering chicks),[71] these iconic metaphors point beyond themselves to a transcendent purity. God is the ultimate Father, the purest source of love, the most compassionate protector of his children. Conversely, analogical metaphors (Snow contends) are problematic for the convert's particularism. Unlike the iconic's vertical direction, analogy tends to work horizontally by demonstrating the rough comparability between two things.[72] To say that Jesus is like Mohammed or Confucius, that God is like Allah, or that evangelism is like door-to-door solicitation is to threaten the convert's theological vision.[73] The sacredness of the new way is profaned by analogical disregard for its uniqueness.

Of the convert's four marks, suspension of analogical reasoning is perhaps the weakest represented because it applies centrally to exclusive theologies. Possibly converts from unbelief to liberal denominations that see great continuity between the claims of theology and culture would not be as ready to deny analogical metaphors for God. Snow could deny their true change and call them alternators, but that move would beg the question of this mark. Ideally, the suspension of analogical reasoning accords with Scripture. The Old Testament is pervaded by the theme of Yahweh's incomparability: "You shall have no other gods before me. You shall not make for yourself and idol in the form of anything in heaven or on the earth."[74] Because language influences thought, converts should be discouraged from drawing parallels between profane and sacred matters unless they are able to discern precisely the difference between iconic and analogical metaphors. In many cases, Snow predicts, the convert is automatically sensitive to the difference.

---

70. Snow, "The Sociology of Conversion," 174.
71. Respectively, Matt 6:9, 1 John 4:8–16, Matt 23:27/Luke 13:34.
72. Snow, "The Convert as Social Type," 274.
73. Snow, "The Sociology of Conversion," 174.
74. Exod 20:3–4.

Change in Religious Experience

The theme that doctrinal language influences thought weighs heavily in the first three marks: biography reinterpretation, master attribution, and suspended analogical reasoning. Snow's strength lies in considering theology's often overlooked role. But if religious change really entails a change in will and heart as well as mind, a change in action should accompany that of doctrine. The fourth mark, *embracement of the convert role* covers this theme. In studying many adolescent religious awakenings, Starbuck concluded that awakening's central expression is "unselfing." As youths mature and begin to recognize the world's broadness they turn outside of themselves and often to God.[75] Snow has discovered a similar unselfing phenomenon: "The convert is thus acting not merely in terms of his or her own self-interest but to further the group's cause or mission."[76]

People with definite faith, religious or political, have difficulty compartmentalizing their lives. Their values permeate all aspects of their lives, leading to certain hermeneutical and behavioral tendencies. Converts, Snow contends, typically exaggerate their religious role. Not only do they tend to change their behaviors such as restricting their alcohol use or supporting different political causes, but even in everyday work and leisure they tend to interpret these activities from their new identity's standpoint. A picnic with friends might become "fellowship," and work might become "vocation" and an opportunity to minister to coworkers and raise support for the church's mission. One of Snow's interviewees remarked: "I had no concrete purpose in playing tennis. I used to think of all the troubles other people had and tennis seemed like a joke. But at those last two tennis tournaments I felt like I was playing for world peace."[77]

The relationship between language, thought, and action arises in complexity. Doctrinal language influences thought but only thought can determine doctrine's concrete application to life's circumstances, and action (the convert's way of embracing the new role) both confirms doctrine (where doctrine gives actions a greater sense of purpose) and

---

75. Starbuck, *Psychology of Religion*, 29.
76. Snow, "The Sociology of Conversion," 174.
77. Snow, "The Convert as Social Type," 277. This mark, much like master attribution is obviously not exclusive to converts, though Snow would probably say that converts are more conscious of it.

influences thought, where certain actions prove thought's doctrinal application to be correct or not. Doctrine's value system influences all dimensions of the convert's life. Though idealistic in tone, Snow's research has turned up many cases to back the claim. Converts, like all religious believers, require ways to practice their faith. The church uses mission trips, social work, and fellowship in part to inspire its own members to follow Jesus in all areas of life. Though longer term believers many times internalize their ethical orientation and live it as second nature, the convert has not yet learned this subtlety and strives to draw obvious connections between faith and life.

These four markers of transcendence complete the scientific description of religious change. Not all of these marks will appear in all converts as Snow seems to imply, but they do describe how doctrine functions. Theology cannot use the marks to define conversion, but in explaining how theology is taken to heart, the church can use them to teach converts to embrace their new identity.

Conclusion

This chapter proposes that the scientific study of religion is a valuable conversation partner with theology, specifically that a description of religious change informs theology's task to understand and minister to converts. Through psychological forces, the universal capacity for religious faith becomes focused in a specific way. Peripheral ideas take central place, and the person begins a new life with a new identity. If that identity is formed by Christ, which includes resigning self-serving motives for trusting in him, then theology recognizes conversion. Though the psychological account cannot ground conversion's theological validity, it expands our knowledge of human nature and explains the material through which salvation appears.

This chapter asked what change looks like up close. Even through its descriptive tone a few notes sound to help theology. 1) Universal religiousness implies universal idolatry, and theology's task is less to prove God's existence but to expose idols and redirect its audience to the need for grace. 2) With Starbuck and BSV, religious change cannot be forced but must arise through converts' struggles and the church's perseverance in ministry. 3) With BSV, Ullman, Travisano, and Snow, cognitive and affective (cf. the problem solving and falling in love dynamics) communication of doctrine is equally necessary. The need for converts to study doctrine, carry out service assignments, or receive affection depends on individual personalities and faith's maturity at different points. In all cases doctrine's life embodiment is essential, but theologians must discern if a convert's best medicine is formal instruction, church work tasks, or simply compassion. The next chapter begins to detail the material causes of religious change. The more important question of causality, of *why* people change, holds richer implications for theology's task.

3

Transformation of the Individual

WITH A DESCRIPTION OF religious change's dynamics and effects in hand, we can begin to explore the kinds of cognitive and emotional influences that might position people to change religious beliefs. These influences cannot *cause* conversion (theologically defined), but they might cause people to enter an ecclesial context where faith is possible. The central argument is that people shift beliefs when they are challenged by doubt. Three observations will outline this challenge. The first shows how religion provides a meaning system that, when challenged, might need more adequate tenets. The second discusses cognitive challenges to faith, focusing on research into the active religious seeker, and the third section discusses emotional crises that influence belief.

Mind, Will, and Heart: An Introduction

To follow our theological definition of conversion as a spiritually-inspired change in mind, will, and heart not only connotes that these elements of personhood feel religious change's effects but that they are the very matter through which change is possible.[1] As last chapter's problem solving dynamic demonstrated, sometimes change occurs as a cognitive struggle for truth; but as the falling in love dynamic added,

---

1. Chapter 1 stated this definition. See Formula of Concord II (FC) in Kolb and Wengert, *Book of Concord*, 560.83.

sometimes change comes through affective allure. "Mind, will, and heart" is not a systematic breakdown or psychological analysis of a human being but rather a way of expressing that conversion influences all aspects of our personhood. However, it is helpful in this chapter to view the will as caught between the mind and heart, the cognitive and affective. In its central place, the will is the practical force of a person's identity. When the mind's cognitive input and the heart's affective draws settle at a given moment, the will or resultant *desire* best describes a person's spiritual character.[2] If we view the will as the core of a person's spiritual character, then it is the part of humankind that needs the Spirit's intervention most. At social science's level of observation, secular minds and hearts can accomplish great cognitive feats and have heartfelt compassion, which shows that the Spirit does not change physical capabilities in an empirically discernable fashion. But without the Spirit directing the will, none of these human potentials can please God. The Spirit's presence does not necessarily change our levels of mental or emotional power but he directs our desires to holy ends. Though mind, will, and heart are all fallen and conversion is doubtless a change in them all, the mind and heart can be viewed as more obvious elements of this change and hence more observable than the will as the innermost core of spiritual character. On these presuppositions, the "spark of faith" in Christ that signifies conversion is possible most expressly as the Spirit heals the human will. Yet this healing action does not become manifest without the more external influences on the mind and heart. Indeed, the magical power of Cupid's arrow and Zeus's lightning bolt makes them poor analogues for the Spirit's healing power that happens through people's emotional and cognitive capacities. These influences on the mind and heart are points of close correlation between theology and social science that are worth exploring in more detail to see how they might inform theology's concerns to address the mind and heart within its own framework.

---

2. 1 Pet 1:14 is especially attuned to this theme: "As obedient children, do not conform to the evil desires you had when you lived in ignorance," and 2:11, "Dear friends, I urge you, as aliens and strangers in the world, to abstain from sinful desires, which war against your soul."

Religious Change Motifs

	Conversion Motifs					
	1. Intellectual	2. Mystical	3. Experimental	4. Affectional	5. Revivalist	6. Coercive
1. Degree of social pressure	low or none	none or little	low	medium	high	high
2. Temporal Duration	medium	short	long	long	short	long
3. Level of Affective Arousal	medium	high	low	medium	high	high
4. Affective Content	illumination	awe, love, fear	curiosity	affection	love (& fear)	fear (& love)
5. Belief-Participation Sequence	belief-participation	belief-participation	participation-belief	participation-belief	participation-belief	participation-belief

Source: Lofland and Skonovd, "Conversion Motifs," 3.

Doubt as a Fundamental Challenge to Religious Meanings

Though dramatic human changes inevitably involve both cognitive and emotional adaptation, social science's accounts of religious change tend to emphasize one or the other as demonstrated in the two change dynamics. The table of "conversion motifs" highlights the variety of affective and intellectual forces that might inspire change. Intellectual or experimentally driven changes have much stronger cognitive draws, whereas revivalist experiences occur under heightened emotions. A comprehensive correlation to conversion needs to consider both sides, but this chapter's sequential accounts of cognitive and emotional change will benefit from first asking the broader question of how faith systems, as systems of meaning, might be challenged by pressures of cognitive and emotional origin and forced to change.

To ask religious people why they confess their faith is probably to elicit an answer concerning their conviction of doctrine's truth (e.g., I believe in God because he *is* the Father almighty). However, there is a more personal character to faith's tenets than the assertion of fact. I also believe that Kalamazoo is south of Grand Rapids, that leaves turn color in October, and that Dante wrote the *Inferno*, but I do not confess them. Theological assertions have a special quality of relating to existence, supplying life's most important values and meaning itself. Psychologists have generally argued that religion's importance is not its factuality but its function to provide meaning: "Religion more than any other human function satisfies the need for meaning in life."[3] A correlational approach to psychology cannot allow doctrine's meaning function to eclipse the question of facts, but viewing religion as a meaning system complements the last chapter's discussion of humanity's universally religious nature and explains how religious beliefs might be challenged to change.

The topics of death, suffering, and service will serve to illustrate. Biblical faith cannot see death as an annihilation of existence and conclusion of life's ultimate meaning. "If we live, we live to the Lord; and if we die, we die to the Lord. So whether we live or die we belong to the Lord."[4] Life and death are connected to Christ, meaning

3. Clark, *Psychology of Religion*, 419.
4. Rom 14:8.

that the redemption from meaninglessness and discovery of true life are exhausted in him. A similar angle appears for suffering. The epistle of James says: "Consider it pure joy, my brothers, whenever you face trials of many kinds, because you know that the testing of your faith produces perseverance."[5] Suffering becomes meaningful in drawing the church closer to Christ. Finally, all levels of church work (e.g., apostle, evangelist, teacher, and pastor) are significant for building the church. "From him the whole body, joined and held together by every supporting ligament, grows and builds itself up in love, as each part does its own work."[6] This analysis of meaning shows that one of theology's major psychological impacts is to grant life *purpose*.

Religious faith brings order to existence, a function without which it tends to shift or dissolve. A helpful account of shifting meaning systems comes from psychologist Raymond Paloutzian, who follows James Fowler's definition of faith as an "orientation of the total person."[7] Given that faith provides a worldview, an ethic, and a set of expectations for life, Paloutzian inquires into what conditions might cause reorientation. Forming the question thus, he builds on Max Heirich's work that challenged conventional research to ask: "What circumstances destroy clarity about root reality? The conventional social science wisdom turns immediately to arguments concerning individual or collective stress, but religious tradition suggests a wider range of circumstances that might be at work."[8]

The meaning system analysis of religion predicts that a loss of meaning precipitates change, making the more accurate question: What causes faith to lose meaning? Paloutzian's gruesomely turbid passage summarizes: "(1) input pressures prompt (2) internal change in one or more components of the meaning system that (3) shows expression as altered outcomes that are connected to those internal components of the meaning system that have been affected."[9] Though most people live in relative balance, not suffering major challenges to their faith systems, converts face "input pressures" that challenge their religious beliefs.

5. Jas 1:2–3.

6. Eph 4:16.

7. Paloutzian, "Religious Conversion," 335. This view is consonant also with Travisano, Heirich, and Snow in chapter 2.

8. Heirich, *Change of Heart*, 674.

9. Ibid., 335–36.

Because faith is systematic in nature, strain at one point can potentially unravel or at least shift the whole system. This claim is interesting to the systematic theologian who is especially intentional about doctrine's internal logic. Paloutzian appears to argue that humanity is filled with systematic theologians who achieve doctrinal clarity by organizing "input pressures" into a stable "altered outcomes" better suited to handle the pressures. Of course, people are quite capable of believing contradictory things and perhaps compartmentalizing their lives so that each role has an autonomous set of rules.[10] But psychology counters that living in contradiction creates mental tension sometimes called "cognitive dissonance,"[11] that can prove too tense to bear. Certain circumstances demand that the old worldview give way to a new, more systematic view that relieves the pressure. The new system suffices so long as it does not encounter overbearing input pressure to force another reevaluation.

Heirich suggested three challenges to root reality.[12] If we encounter a problem that we cannot solve within our current explanatory framework (cf. Archimedes and the problem solving dynamic), then our basic assumptions about reality might need editing. If we see inevitable, dreadful circumstances arising, they might be fully comprehensible within the old faith system but nonetheless force us to reconceive them in a more favorable way that perhaps provides a better response. Or if a respected religious leader causes a falling out with his or her followers or changes theologies, these things can cause people to question their grounding assumptions.

From there, Paloutzian arranges the discussion around the concept of doubt: "A key element to any [religious change] or transformation process must be some element of doubt, pressure, or motivation to change: there is no reason to change one's belief system or worldview if one has no doubts whatsoever about them or if life circumstances have not confronted the person's religious beliefs or practices sufficiently for them to be called into question."[13] This principle of religious change brushes the difficult question of theology's subjective authentication.[14]

10. Berger, *Invitation to Sociology*, 49–50.
11. Festinger, *Theory of Cognitive Dissonance*.
12. Heirich, "Change of Heart," 674–75.
13. Paloutzian, "Religious Conversion," 336.
14. Here "authentication" means "to appear true and meaningful." Philosopher

For the believer, doctrines are authenticated in experience. For example, depravity doctrines are meaningful, in part, because they describe the world's fallenness. Other doctrines such as the resurrection are authenticating because of their existential meaning of inspiring hope: "he has given us new birth into a living hope through the resurrection of Jesus Christ from the dead."[15] Other kinds of validation might exist also, but Paloutzian's point is that sometimes problems in life can cause a doubt capable of severing the connection between a doctrine and its personal significance for the convert. His example concerns prayer's efficacy. If I pray for a dying loved one to be healed and she dies, then the tension between my belief in prayer and the evidence can cause disequilibrium in my belief system. If disequilibrium surfaces into consciousness and the problem begins to trouble me, the result is often doubt in the old views and their modification if not complete revision.

Paloutzian's description is not complicated in principle: people's faith systems tend to be stable unless vitally challenged. Actual cases are less predictable. The challenge could be suppressed,[16] it could only nuance faith's system, or—if sufficiently dramatic—it could completely uproot the old system. The concept of doubt is general enough to encompass many types of changes pressured by intellectual or emotional inputs, but its wide applicability sacrifices the ability to explain the positive apprehension of a new faith system. As Snow, Machalek, and Travisano demonstrated,[17] converts' disillusionment with their past lives shows doubt's role in the process, but it is only the beginning of their change.

Theological Observations on Doubt

Theologically evaluated, doubt's object is idols or penultimate comforts that become exposed when compared with Christ. When truly sensing

---

Alvin Plantinga, in *Warranted Christian Belief*, provides an authoritative defense of faith that ties into this issue of subjective authentication.

15. 1 Pet 1:3.

16. Festinger, *Theory of Cognitive Dissonance*, 248, explains how even in the face of failed prophecy, such as William Miller's nineteenth-century predictions of the world's end, religious groups will not necessarily lose their faith.

17. See chapter 2.

one's fallenness, no choice remains but to doubt the wayward previous path and turn to grace. Paloutzian's account can help to apply this doctrine. If all people are created to have faith but are misdirected, then they continually worship idols. Worshiping idols such as people, nations, or money can be very satisfying, but they are ephemeral things that can redeem neither from sin nor death. One important theological task is to expose these idols, that is, to create doubt in our reliance on temporal things, a task equally applicable in preaching formally or evangelizing in many contexts. If theology can create sufficient doubt about temporal securities, then it can open room to offer a new root reality: "the grass withers and the flower falls, but he word of our God stands forever."[18] Conversion begins only in the annihilation of any idols humans might use to defend their preferential place in God's eyes, and God's law is thus theology's greatest resource for opening the way to grace, which is first learned through doubt of self.

However, Paloutzian's argument has another side, one more daunting for the church. If doubt spurs people *into* faith, it could also cause apostasy *out of* faith. Though this is not a book about apostasy, it is worth addressing briefly. Often apologetics is the discipline of defending the faith against attacks from the outside. This approach is salient in Friedrich Schleiermacher's famous work that persuades religion's despisers to see Christianity's reasonableness.[19] Though this apologetic function has a certain merit, research on apostasy indicates a more primary function. One study in particular demonstrated that many apostates tended to leave Christianity because their faith stopped cohering with the adverse worldview they learned in school.[20] To the extent that this problem appears, apologetics's actual audience should be *the church itself* and its function should be to defend doctrine's perennial meaning, not necessarily to improve Christianity's image in scientists' eyes. While too much discussion on this point will distract our inquiry from its central focus, it bears mentioning that the apologetic spirit here represented is concerned with maintaining the church's faith regardless of

18. Isa 40:8.
19. See, Schleiermacher, *On Religion*.
20. One apostate in Altemeyer and Hunsberger, *Amazing Conversions*, 45, remarks: "When I ask people who are very religious what keeps them believing, and all those people say is that they have faith, I can't understand for the life of me what faith is. How can you believe in something that is completely intangible?"

the method's employed. Such a commitment does not dictate the kind of apologetics, whether, for example, it is a defense of God's existence, biblical historicity, or explaining theology's ethical significance. It dictates only that apologetics (defined as any faith-defending theology) always begins as an in-house discipline. Based on the social scientific data, defenses of Christianity's reasonableness[21] appear to be secondary to a more holistic apologetics in which theology communicates its doctrines meaningfully by explaining their ethical force in life.

Concerning doubt as a way into religious change, the task to expose idols and focus apologetics internally are some of the most pressing assignments psychology gives to theology. Doubt is only the beginning of religious change's motivation, however, and the discussion of subsequent motivations will require several angles of inquiry. The discussion begins with so-called active religious changes to address the cognitive side.

The Intellect and Active Changes

The Background and Insight

Cognitive motivations for change are well represented in the active change motif. This sociological theme has roots in existentialist philosophy such as Jean Paul Sartre's, who denied a universal human nature (knowable and predictable by science) because he thought it would preclude humans' ability to fashion their lives' paths through creative (productive and innovative) choices.[22] When America saw a rise in new religious movements in the 1960s and '70s, many sociologists determined that a self-creative explanatory framework best explained people's rapid affiliation (and disaffiliation) with these groups. People had "conversion careers" in which joining many groups throughout their lives was typical.[23] When parents began to prosecute religious leaders for allegedly brainwashing their children, sociologists reacted by explaining that "coercion" is a distorted interpretation of religious affiliation; converts' wills, they countered, are not *forced* by religious pres-

---

21. E.g., Craig, *Reasonable Faith*.
22. Sartre, *L'Existentialisme est un Humanisme*, 9–95.
23. See Richardson, *Conversion Careers*.

sures. Rather, converts' own decisions and personal choices are actually primary causes of change.[24]

Robert Jay Lifton was the first sociologist to lay definite groundwork for this active paradigm.[25] His cultural analysis parallels Peter Berger's, whose idea of *alternation* posited that individuals in modern society operate within several conflicting ideologies. Lifton proposed the "Protean Man," after the Greek god Proteus, who could change shapes at will. Due to society's lack of central symbolic organization (both in the West and Japan) and the flooding of diverse imagery typical of the information age, people tend to be fickle in their commitments, he argued.[26] They change roles, ideologies, and thought structures with relative ease. The result, as Erik Erikson and Berger also noted, is that many moderns are confused about their identity, having no definite sense of tradition or coherence to the world. Though they find many adequate expressions of meaning, they have no ultimate loyalties except to the ongoing pursuit of meaning, something Lifton saw reflected in Erikson's eight ages of humankind. In Paloutzian's terms, the protean has no meaning system invulnerable to input pressures, and he or she might even seek out new systems due to the inherent instability of all. "He is starved for ideas and feelings that give coherence to his world," Lifton writes, "but here too his taste is toward new combinations."[27] The flood of imagery in this technological age is portrayed as a flash flood that rushes quickly over terrain but does not sink in. Though his essay elicited much conflict, Lifton maintained that without symbolic depth, society produces generations of shape-shifters.

Though Lifton's insights are broadly applicable outside of scientific religious study, he unwittingly set groundwork for the academic study of the *religious seeker*, a denominationally particular version of "Protean Man." Religious searching is a timeless phenomenon, and in sociology the *pursuit of meaning* has long been recognized as explaining

---

24. Cf. Long and Hadden, "Religious Conversion and the Concept of Socialization," 1–14.

25. As early as 1978, Robert Balch and David Taylor cite Lifton as explaining active seekership's social roots. See Balch and Taylor, "Seekers and Saucers," 51–53.

26. Lifton, "Protean Man," 318.

27. Ibid., 324.

affiliation with ideological groups.[28] The seeker has a special place in America's sociological tradition, however, because of the new religious movements and ensuing brainwashing controversy. The central question was whether or not actively achieved religious changes were on the rise empirically or if sociology was newly sensitized to the active understanding of conversion. Both claims are probably true. Perhaps the rise in seekership caused methodological sensitivity in sociology, causing researchers to see active elements even where they could not previously. A change could appear active at some points in its process and passive elsewhere just as research can find these varying elements at different places depending on the researcher's method.[29]

Roger Straus was one of the first researchers to document the activist tendency. In studying diverse religions (including Jehovah's Witness, Christianity, Buddhism, and Scientology), he discovered a syndrome in which seekers would actively join and participate in groups for purely selfish reasons, namely to change themselves and remedy their problems. Straus called it "creative bumbling," as people felt out potential groups in their quest, and "instrumental exploitation" if they chose to use the group for their own purposes.[30] Surely part of his sensitivity to active seekership came from his own experimentation with Scientology, a group emphasizing this-worldly benefits to its followers. This sensitivity produced the raw data of his early research, where he documented how seekers transform themselves by first learning to act like believers and follow rituals, in effect, to try out a theology and determine if it has the seeds of positive change. Straus's early work consisted mostly of organizing sources of creative exploitation. In a later essay he developed more abstract conclusions about the group being reducible to individuals as autonomous agents of creative activity. The humanistic dogma in the activist paradigm appears vividly: that groups exist to serve individuals' needs for meaning, and individuals are responsible to appropriate groups according to their needs. This approach, he says: "allows us to best capture the full texture of the dynamic [religious change] phenomenon in both its individual and collective aspects, and

---

28. See Zurcher and Snow, "Collective Behavior," 450.

29. Lorne Dawson gives philosophical ground for the possibility and recognition of an active religious change in "Self-Affirmation, Freedom, and Rationality," 141–63.

30. Straus, "Changing Oneself," 253.

to treat the human beings performing this drama as the complex, interacting, striving and creating social actors they happen to be."[31]

Sociologist James Richardson is less confident than Straus that the activist theory can function as a metaphysic to prove existentialist notions of freedom of self-creativity. His work concerns method, or the adequacy of sociological paradigms for describing religious phenomena.[32] Traditional research beginning in William James and E. D. Starbuck unconsciously adopted St. Paul's Damascus road conversion as the template for religious change, but many late modern researchers have begun shifting their paradigms. Due to the pressures discussed above—the brainwashing accusations, rising philosophies of freedom, and new religious movement research—social researchers have begun to discuss religious change as an active and multifarious process. Richardson is skeptical of any researcher's ability to know *what really happens* in these changes because converts tend to color their stories according to newly adopted theology and scientists consistently reflect their dogmas in their methods and conclusions. The new paradigm is not necessarily better, he would say, but it tends to find favor because its explanation is congenial to current sociologists' values. This point is important because the values have not changed drastically since Richardson's writing,[33] and the activist model continues to gain followers, such as social theorists C. David Gartrell and Zane Shannon.

In studying the Divine Light Mission (DLM) in Victoria, B.C., Gartrell and Shannon illustrate the cognitive side of Paloutzian's explanation for faith system shifts.[34] They follow "balance theory" (a development of cognitive dissonance theory), stating that people strive for balance (harmony) between their beliefs and actions.[35] Like the problem of doubt discussed above, inconsistencies between beliefs and

---

31. Straus, "Religious Conversion," 165.

32. See Richardson, "The Active vs. Passive Convert," 163–78. Also Kilbourne and Richardson, "Paradigm Conflict, Types of Conversion, and Conversion Theories," 1–21.

33. E.g., Zock, "Paradigms in Psychological Conversion Research," 55. This essay discusses how an even newer paradigm that focuses on individual narratives and conversion processes is on the rise.

34. Gartrell and Shannon, "A Rational Choice Approach," 32–46.

35. On balance theory see Pitt, "A Balance Theoretical Approach to Religious Conversion," 171–83.

actions cause tension and discomfort that people seek to balance. Gartrell and Shannon's research indicated that many recruits to DLM suffered socially or cognitively and therefore used DLM's theology and social network to balance their deficiencies (e.g., counteracting their lack of purpose by finding new meaning in religion or loneliness by gaining friends). Even though some of these converts were set searching because of emotionally grounded concerns, Gartrell and Shannon emphasize that they processed these needs with shrewd rationality.[36] The important aspect of this study is its claim that converts were not sucked in through forces they could not control; on the contrary, they shopped for a means of balancing their cognitions much like in Straus's idea of instrumental exploitation. Weighing DLM's cognitive and social rewards together, their decisions to join the group were based on rational choices much like considering and buying a car.[37] Potential recruits were initially attracted either to the theology or the members. So long as their external social networks were not extremely determinative over their actions, an inclination toward either DLM's beliefs or people could lead the way to both (e.g., liking the members caused recruits to view their beliefs more positively). In most cases the recruits tended to monitor their choices and degrees of affiliation critically.[38] In so contending, Gartrell and Shannon emphasize that religion does meet human needs and that it is rational for humans to seek meaning and security in doctrines and communities of faith.

Specific Evidence and Forms of the Activist Paradigm

As much as the activist paradigm demonstrates sociologists' viewpoints and individual religious choices, it also shows society to be a marketplace of competing ideologies as Berger and Lifton perceived. A few

---

36. The active change paradigm is not limited to purely cognitive motivations, but it fits this study's section on cognitive roots of change largely because much of the research under this paradigm's auspices covers cognitive searches for meaning.

37. Gartrell and Shannon, "Contacts, Cognitions, and Conversion," 45, say: "A theory of conversion might be devised that considers the members of such audiences as 'buyers' and religious groups as 'sellers' in the marketplace of religious affiliations."

38. Dawson, "Self-Affirmation, Freedom, and Rationality," 160, concludes: "I am suggesting that an active conversion might profitably be conceived as a rational conversion, which in turn should be thought of as a reflectively monitored conversion."

studies demonstrate different ways that active changes might occur in today's world while giving specific evidence for this paradigm.

The mildest form of this phenomenon does not qualify as religious change in a strict sense, but it nevertheless exemplifies the religious marketplace. *Switching* is evident where individuals change denominations. Researcher Matthew Loveland's statistics on religious switching show that up to one-third of Americans switch faith systems at some point.[39] Though denominational distinctiveness (such as Catholic tradition) tends to inhibit switching, Loveland has demonstrated that childhood religious instruction is not definitive for adult religious affiliation. His explanation follows rational choice theory, that "human behavior results from individuals seeking to maximize benefits and avoid costs."[40] If a change in denomination does not cause too much disruption in life and if change includes tangible benefits (e.g., the church is closer to home), then switching is probable unless people are enthralled by their denomination's particular doctrinal expression. Though rational choice is not the only explanation, Loveland sees it as the best account and thereby shows his alliance with the current momentum of sociology.

Another study that documents the motives of French adolescent converts to Islam provides a more extreme example.[41] The French researchers attempted to catalogue varieties of religious changes and motives that cause them. They used Lofland and Skonovd's typology (cited above) but also added the possibility of other motives such as opposing one's family, fighting for the poor, and sharing possessions. They concluded that the majority of motives were very conscious, intentional, and personal. "This overall pattern of results is completely consistent with Richardson's and Dawson's views, indicating that the convert is much more frequently an active, purposeful person who willingly chooses the new faith, rather than a passive person conforming to social pressure or being the victim of uncontrollable psychological forces."[42] The vision represented here makes converts appear as activists who change for a social good.

---

39. Loveland, "Religious Switching," 147.
40. Ibid., 149.
41. Lakhdar et al., "Conversion to Islam," 1–15.
42. Ibid., 13.

The last piece of evidence is the most bizarre. University of Montana sociologists Robert Balch and David Taylor went undercover in a cult to study its practices and processes of affiliation.[43] In 1975 over thirty people disappeared in Oregon after attending a lecture on flying saucers, the kingdom of heaven, and the ability to transcend humanity's level of existence. Balch and Taylor explain that, though these people did not convert in a strong sense, they decided within only four hours to leave their past lives behind. This study is challenging to competing social theories because it does not leave time for specific psychological pressures to work on a person—pressures such as those represented in the religious change dynamics—or for social bonds to form with the group's insiders (as chapter 6 will discuss). Balch and Taylor concluded that the only explanation for this rash decision making is a kind of religious seekership in which people actively search for groups and messages that they are predisposed to favor. The cult leaders in this study combined elements from Eastern mysticism, Christianity, and science fiction, making their message sound familiar despite its peculiarity.

In Paloutzian's terms, the active seeker best exemplifies the cognitive struggle for meaning. These people do not wait for doubt to creep into their heads and pressure their system to change; they actively doubt and seek ways to transcend it. Though some of the research is far removed from mainstream Christianity, studies like Loveland's apply directly, and Gartrell and Shannon suggest their study's broad applicability. If Berger and Lifton are correct that there is a protean impulse in late modern society, then active religious seekership will continue to be a challenge to the church. Given the recent strides in information technology and flooding of imagery (cited by Lifton already in 1961) active changes will not likely decline, raising the question of how a church that believes that salvation is a divine gift should handle the active seeker.

Theology for Addressing the Activist Phenomenon

The active conversion is probably sociology's most direct challenge to monergistic theology which holds that conversion is not, as Straus

---

43. Balch and Taylor, "Seekers and Saucers," 43–64. This cult later called itself "Heaven's Gate" and became famous for its mass suicide in San Diego, CA, coinciding with the Hale-Bopp comet's appearance in March of 1997.

called it, "a personal accomplishment." Humankind's distorted nature renders the will unable to choose God. Though deciding many things, the will is unable to sanctify its desires by a creatively spontaneous act, which is why conversion's ultimate explanation must always lie in the Spirit's re-creative intervention. When sociologists begin saying that converts create their own realities by choosing groups to exploit instrumentally and thus satisfy their own existential cravings, their method and evidence seem to cut directly across theology's portrayal of the passive convert.

At this contrast's border the correlational method is helpful, first, in determining that the contrast has a border. Theology cannot deny that many self-serving motives lead people to affiliate with religious groups, nor is its task to sift through them to determine the better or worse. Its task is rather to expose the impurities that everyone has, to reveal their dependence on God, and ultimately point them to grace. Even if theology grants that active seekers could decide to affiliate with a religious group out of free choice, this philosophical interpretation of the social research is not ultimately an affront to salvation's gift-quality but applicable only in explaining a possible means through which someone could be drawn into the church and encountered by Christ. Theology should not be threatened by human freedom or any other supposed cause of conversion other than God's Spirit and word because freedom and material factors explain causality on a different level of explanation.[44] As science and theology operate on two different levels of concern and explanation, they avoid a logical contradiction and rather work to explain different kinds of assertions.

The greatest possible discrepancy I perceive between theology's agenda and that of the active seeker is whether active seekers could think that they have chosen the gospel out of a pure act of will and still have the gospel at all. This question is complex and should not be answered with an absolute yes or no. Theologians would be wise to remember that though doctrine necessarily points people to Christ, there

---

44. Free choice has, at best, an indirect influence on a person's acquiring of faith. Theologians from both Protestant and Catholic traditions have nevertheless insisted that free choice somehow has a direct effect, arguing that human responsibility explains how a person converts. While it is a separate discussion, it is worth mentioning that the correlational method interprets this synergistic approach as a confusion of theological and philosophical values that should not be conjoined.

is a distinction between having doctrine and having Christ, a distinction that leaves room for the active seeker with blurry doctrine to find Christ truly, albeit unclearly. God's saving action is not caused by the degree of doctrinal purity, making it incorrect to limit God's saving potential and will even over people who are caught in this mode of thinking. However, the church cannot view active conversion as a normative viewpoint for its members and must continually offer its corrective, especially if this trend is widely influential. The sociological research assists theology by defining this challenge, not only on an academic level but as a societal trend. Theology's task is to explain seekership's larger context, namely that people seek God because they were created for him yet are fallen, that free choice applies potentially to civil righteousness but is the wrong category to view conversion, and that salvation is God's action not because of but despite human efforts.

If Lifton is right that the protean impulse is widespread and Loveland's statistics on religious switching are accurate, then the church now comprises many people who are weakly committed to their particular denominational body. The active seeker provides many opportunities for theological instruction because he or she is by nature open minded to hearing various viewpoints. The church's challenge is not to get people with these tendencies in through the door, so to speak, but to *keep* them there. Sociology has intimated that strong commitment to faith involves a sense of its pervasive meaning for life (Paloutzian) and that denominational distinctiveness prevents switching faiths (Loveland). If active seekers are not taught these things, research predicts that they will not maintain their affiliations. Of course, sociology cannot determine theological truth, but if theologians desire to preserve commitment to their particularity, the social research helps to determine which resources within theology's own tradition might best cultivate faith. A starting point could be to teach church history from a church's particular perspective (to protect distinctiveness) and a christological ethic of love and forgiveness (to embody faith's life significance).

Discussion of active religious changes highlights a specific part of Paloutzian's model where the *mind* is the primary means through which change begins (though such change ultimately affects the will and desires). Though affective and cognitive causes can never be divorced, research on the seeker looking for a compelling worldview explains an intellectual aspect of religious change's process. Other studies focus more on the affective means through which people change. Considering them will complement the discussion of cognitive motivators just as last chapter's falling in love dynamic brought coherence to the problem solving dynamic.

Affective Powers of Change

Paloutzian designed his model broadly enough to capture motivations of many kinds. Anything from studying philosophy to enduring natural disasters could pressure a system change. His consideration of the affective side relies greatly on Peter Hill, who offers an account of emotions and spiritual transformation.[45] Hill argues that both negative and positive emotions significantly influence religious change's process. Classical Protestant theology has acknowledged this same kind of dynamic in prescribing the law as a cause of anxiety and the gospel of comfort.[46] Hill's account is useful, then, for explaining the psychological underpinnings of the traditional law/gospel dialectic.

Negative Emotions

Negative emotions, he explains, tend to narrow and focus attention. They center on specific problems and motivate action to alleviate those problems. Like a rabbit perceiving a wolf, the event inspires anxiety around a certain problem and focuses attention completely on escaping. Most people can recall a time when negative emotions caused by angry interchanges, hazardous driving conditions, or worry about a loved one's late return tended to cause obsession on a single problem. Religiously, these negative emotions are important to the process of change because they strand the individual in a momentary state of helplessness when problems appear spiritually irresolvable from their current meaning system, a state that might be part of the problem

---

45. Hill, "Spiritual Transformation," 87–108.
46. Pieper, *Christian Dogmatics*, 2:459–60. Pieper states that any conversion must have a "terror of conscience" and "trust of the heart" as its inner motivations; however, through he prescribes these two states as necessary he still recognizes that there is no fixed degree of either contrition or faith.

solving dynamic's preparation stage. The tension of negative emotion pressures individuals to find new answers to their problems, and sometimes religious change results. We will see that theology can translate emotional crises into helplessness before God, a state that prepares a person to hear the gospel. Theology's task is to address these negative emotions and place them in Christianity's redemptive framework, but to understand the psychological context will show specifically what theology must address.

Specifically, Hill discusses four kinds of crises that produce negative emotions and thus leave people in need of spiritual illumination: crises of meaning, value, efficacy, and self-worth. Though not exhaustive, Hill's list gives a helpful framework for exploring crisis's role in religious change. The crisis of meaning is similar to the active seeker's problem, a restless need to find meaning and even identity in life, a large part of which is deciding which things and values are important to orienting one's life. Above, this problem had a cognitive form that portrayed an intellectual search for superior doctrine, but the intellectual component also has an emotional side that is sometimes more influential and unpredictable. The feeling of meaninglessness often drives intellectual pursuits where life's current state proves disappointing and current values come up short. For example, according to psychologist D. J. Levinson, people in their thirties often derive meaning from their employment, but by their forties these goals become either unattainable or lacking in their original attributed value.[47] According to Hill, this kind of state causes many people to reevaluate their philosophy of what is important in life. Theologians will see that the negative emotions of boredom and pointlessness characterize the experience of placing ultimate trust in penultimate things, those material structures that can never address problems as great as sin and death. If the sense of meaninglessness becomes too acute, negative emotions motivate a sense of helplessness, leading the concern for a more perennial ground of meaning.

The crisis of value is a version of theology's *convicted conscience*. In a word, the value crisis is a feeling of guilt in failing to uphold an ethical ideal. This crisis was important to Martin Luther in his concern to find freedom from sin: "It is the nature of the divine light and truth

---

47. Hill, "Spiritual Transformation," 99.

to comfort consciences, cheer the heart, and establish a free spirit, in the same way as human doctrines naturally depress consciences, torture the heart, and extinguish the spirit."[48] Medieval Catholic teachings spurred Luther's crisis and led him to rediscover justification by faith. Hill emphasizes that a value crisis does not take place in philosophical discussion as a metaphysical search for truth; negative emotions rather focus it around a singular feeling of guilt that motivates the person to alleviate this pressure. As chapter 5 on ideology addresses, sometimes the alleviation begins in cognitive form, illustrating how religious changes are always a mixture of cognitive and emotional factors, but the powerful negative feelings are an inextricable beginning to many changes such as Luther's.

The crisis of efficacy could start as a value crisis but it is not so much the feeling of guilt but of hopelessness to escape a particular quandary. The mark of an efficacy crisis is powerlessness, that is, to alter life circumstances for the better and overcome problems. This crisis's most important manifestation is tragedy.[49] In our country's recent history, church attendance spiked in the months following the September 11, 2001, attacks on the World Trade Center, demonstrating how the nation's overwhelmed feeling drove many people to seek spiritual solutions. Psychologists warn: "Transformations from the meaninglessness of such traumatic events into happiness and fulfillment are rare. Today, when even the North American continent is the target of large scale traumatic events, wariness and fear are palpable."[50] The 9/11 attacks show how severely people feel this psychological correlate to the fear of God, but the lack of heightened church attendance in 2002 shows that negative emotions only potentially begin a process of religious change that often fizzles out. Like the active seeker in and out of religions, the fearful are as easily in and out of churches.

Another type of efficacy crisis bears mentioning for its interest alone. Neurologists Warren Brown and Carla Caetano discuss epileptic

---

48. Luther, Sermons 2, in *Luther's Works*, 52:274.

49. Altemeyer and Hunsberger, *Amazing Conversions*, 165, quote Ken, a convert to Christianity: "Several relatives, friends, and acquaintances died in accidents, and two grandparents passed away all in the space of about a year and a half. 'Death was becoming a reality' and as a consequence Ken started wondering 'What is there after death? Where does God fit in?'"

50. Oatley and Djikic, "Emotions and Transformation," 112.

religious experience and the relationship between brain seizures and mystical perception.[51] They explain: "Because of the brain system in which the seizure activity begins, the aura of these individuals is characterized by dramatic mood changes (euphoria, anxiety, fear), dreamy states, feelings of familiarity or strangeness, hallucinations, delusions, and a 'crescendo' feeling of rising emotion."[52] Probably the most dramatic form of efficacy crisis, the source is within the convert's very mental apparatus. Brown and Caetano aver the possibility that feelings of what Rudolf Otto called "the Holy," or Schleiermacher called "absolute dependence," or mystical states of any kind could be caused by abnormal brain functioning. The range of emotions in this type of religious experience is potentially vast, from hopelessness to extreme cheer, but it is clear that epileptic firings render people powerless in controlling them. No convert is more helpless than one whose brain decides, in effect, to change itself.

Finally, the crisis of self worth is a more personal version of the meaninglessness crisis. The question of meaning asks about the value of things and actions, but the self worth crisis questions *my* very life's worth. Negative emotions associated with imbalanced self esteem factor into many personal changes that discover self worth in religion. The parable of the lost sheep in Matthew illustrates that "your Father in heaven is not willing that any of these little ones should be lost."[53] The shepherd's unshakable devotion presupposes his value of his sheep. In many cases, however, the sheep must undergo a self worth crisis before the shepherd can find them, so to speak.

Negative emotions explain many changes' initial motivators, but negativity alone is like law without gospel. Positive emotions offer a constructive way to explain the emotional basis under which new theology is believed even if the emotions themselves are not conversion's spiritual significance. Hill argues that where negative emotions tend to

---

51. Also see Wootton and Allen, "Dramatic Religious Conversion and Schizophrenic Decompensation," 219, who say that "The similarities between dramatic religious conversion and decompensation to schizophrenic psychosis are evident from the review of the literature. Each of the two phenomena proceeds in a series of characteristically identifiable stages."

52. Brown and Caetano, "Conversion, Cognition, and Neuropsychology," in Maloney, *Handbook of Religious Conversion*, 151.

53. Matt 18:10–14.

focus attention, positive emotions often broaden attention, which helps to describe the convert's ability to trust in theology's broad and ultimate assertions.

Positive Motivators and the Upward Spiral

For his work on positive emotions, Hill draws centrally on Barbara Fredrickson's research, which shows how positive emotions such as interest, contentment, and love are not polar opposites of negative emotions but a completely different emotional class. Where the negative often focus attention on a particular problem, the positive tend to "broaden people's momentary thought-action repertoires and build their enduring personal resources, ranging from physical and intellectual resources to social and psychological resources."[54] Positive emotions can dissolve the negative because they facilitate the mind's broader perceptive abilities to qualify a problem's direness by placing it in a greater context. In popular language, the "big picture" frees us from "tunnel vision." Fredrickson hypothesizes that positive emotions not only broaden perspectives but also build and compound to produce emotionally resilient people better able to handle crises. She is not referring, I think, to euphoria or happiness bordering on giddiness but to those emotions associated with a positive attitude. Positive thinking creates an "upward spiral," building a mentally tougher person tempered to recover from negative turns.

In spiritual transformation, this upward turn parallels the problem solving dynamic's illumination and verification stages of finding a new solution and the falling in love dynamic's positive attachment to God though a faith community. Hill suggests (quoting Starbuck) that religious change's process eventually becomes "less a 'struggling away from sin' and more a 'striving toward righteousness.'"[55] The emotional concomitants of "striving toward righteousness" counteract the four crises (meaning, value, efficacy, and self worth) discussed above. Positive emotions in a religious context help, respectively, to support the convert's sense of newfound meaning, to encourage a sense of moral

---

54. Fredrickson, "The Role of Positive Emotions in Positive Psychology," 219.
55. Hill, "Spiritual Transformation," 102.

value without conflict, to give a sense of spiritual efficacy even if the world's cruelties are not abolished, and to undergird people's feeling of self worth in God's eyes.

The psychologist is trained to observe religion's positive value for life such as these emotional benefits of change, but a correlational approach suggests that these emotional patterns are useful primarily in showing how people become prepared to listen to the gospel. The following evaluation of emotion gives specific theological correlations to the negative/positive emotional pattern of religious change. It provides some of this research's implications for theology's task by suggesting how the gospel might be presented to people undergoing emotionally driven changes.

Correlation to the Four Emotional Crises and Positive Emotion

This research on emotions opens a field ripe for theological harvest, but it must be a discerning one. Even from a psychological perspective, Hill's assertion that negative emotions narrow focus to a single object is not completely accurate. Paul Tillich has shown that fear has a definite object that courage can overcome if it is strong enough to absorb it, but humanity's deeper dilemma is anxiety: the threat of non-being or the negation of objects.[56] This nuance implies that negative emotions spurring change will not always corral people away from a definite problem if the threat is indefinite anxiety. Cases of chemical imbalance also prove that negative emotions are not always rooted in a specific crisis but a depressed or anxious feeling attributable to non-conscious factors. These issues show the affective life's complexity in which the classical guilty conscience is but one manifestation.

Theology is not required to prescribe a spectrum of negative and positive emotions around conversion but only to recognize that the diversity of emotion does not have a direct bearing on conversion's validity, which is known through the gospel rather than religious experience. The classical guilty conscience, we have seen, is but one form and does not exhaust the other negative emotions associated with meaninglessness, helplessness, and existential anxiety. Often negativity inspires

---

56. See Tillich, *The Courage to Be*, 36.

movement away from a dreaded object, but sometimes it has no object. To raise these possibilities is helpful to clarify that theology's broadest task is to give negative emotion the right object by placing it in a biblical framework. Theology interprets crisis from Scripture's independent authority so that if the crisis has no feared object it will obtain one in the convert's acknowledgement of creation's fallenness, but if the crisis has an object, then theology translates it into the Bible's terms.

As research demonstrates, negative emotions arise from subjective crises such as self worth and external crises from terrorism or losing family members. Though theologians should not attempt to know divine reasons for permitting tragedy, theology must interpret tragedy in its biblical context. Paul wrote: "Scripture declares that the whole world is a prisoner of sin, so that what was promised, being given through faith in Jesus Christ, might be given to those who believe."[57] This concise statement applies in innumerable ways, interpreting crises as resulting from creation's fallenness and the human heart's captivity. To address the variety of possible applications is a further exploration for pastoral theology; the point here is that theology gives meaning to negative emotions and begins to narrow the convert's focus to tragedy's spiritual root. If a crisis has no object, then theology supplies the object, but more often when a crisis has an object, then theology places that object in a broader perspective to show that the ultimate tragedy is a fallen creation. Other times theology might inflict a crisis itself where it exposes human helplessness before God and the human tendency to cling to idols. Because theology concerns believing and hoping in certain things—objects of thought and reality—its means of addressing emotional crises is irreducibly cognitive. It could be expressed that the object of belief validates the experience of believing it. But even if theology's truth is not dependent on the hearer's emotional state, certain states of emotion such the guilty and comforted conscience are inextricable from the process of developing faith. In all cases, interpretation of crisis is the most valuable contribution theology can supply to negative motivations, and undoubtedly positive emotions will arise from this message's comfort.

By placing a crisis into the context of a Christian theological system, the crisis is set up as struggle away from the right problem to find

---

57. Gal 3:22.

the right answer. Theology, of course, addresses humanity's spiritual nature and ultimate end; it cannot be expected to solve all of counseling's problems or chemical imbalances. For the convert, theology either adds or hones the spiritual side of problems by placing them in the biblical narrative of redemption. "Consider it pure joy," we recall, "when you have trials of many kinds, because you know that the testing of your faith develops perseverance."[58] To ask whether these trials are good or evil in themselves is to imply a direct theological mandate either to counteract or encourage emotional crisis. James ignores this question. Trials come from many sources, and God's attitude toward them (whether he desires them for a greater good or only permits them but does not desire them: theodicy) is unknowable. Theology should rather interpret whatever trials arise to increase trust in God's ultimate provision and to inspire the church to take care of people's physical needs as part of this task to communicate God's care.

By focusing people's attention and setting them searching for relief, negative emotions are a significant material cause through which people begin to believe and consequently interpret their crises through a theology. This reinterpretation of the world and of self fits chapter 2's description of the convert's social type; that converts are recognizable by their need to reinterpret their past and to live according to a master attribution scheme in which God grants significance to human actions. This reinterpretation will not stabilize however, if theology does not eventually inspire the positive emotions that broaden and build people's confidence in their new faith, traditionally the theme of the gospel's comfort. In this study, the discussion of positive emotions represents the "striving toward righteousness," falling in love (Ullman), or building trust (Erikson/Fowler) half of religious change.[59]

With theology's general method of addressing crises of religious change outlined (viz. that it reinterprets crises in scriptural light and eventually inspires a positive comfort), we can look again at Hill's four crises (meaning, value, efficacy, and self worth). The meaninglessness crisis is important for theology to address directly. If church doctrine is a meaning system tempered by time and tradition, then it offers a

---

58. Jas 1:2–3.

59. See Starbuck, *Psychology of Religion*, 64; Ullman, *Transformed Self*, xvi; Erikson, *Childhood and Society*, 247; Fowler, *Stages of Faith*, 119–21.

stable corrective to meaning systems thrown off balance by negative emotions. If the convert's life seems meaningless, the Scriptures encourage a certain attitude applying even to the most mundane things: "Whatever you do, work at it with all your heart, as working for the LORD, not for men, since you know that you will receive an inheritance from the LORD as a reward."[60] Works, duties—these things can never achieve ultimate meaning by virtue of having been performed because their righteousness is limited to the civil realm. But if works are inspired by an eternal reward already guaranteed, then they have ultimate meaning not by being performed but by being inspired. Conversion, for its complexity, is perhaps no more complicated than receiving a Christ-like spirit in tasks glorious or mundane. If the acquisition of meaning causes positive emotions, then this feeling of contentedness will subjectively authenticate new faith and (with Fredrickson) build positive momentum that can broaden and deepen faith and strengthen it against doubt.

The moral value crisis requires little summary, being the express target of law and gospel. The benefit of looking at law and gospel psychologically is to recognize that the corresponding conviction and comfort might take diverse forms. A guilty conscience might cause a crisis of meaning or self worth, not only guilt and obsession over one's sordid past actions. Likewise, comfort has innumerable expressions depending on the person and circumstances of forgiveness. The important correlational insight is to avoid making any one set of emotions a pattern for salvation's certainty. The church trusts its means of grace and confession of faith for security, not religious affections.[61] A sophisticated understanding of law and gospel will expand the emotional and cognitive possibilities through which God works, yet focus solely on the gospel's presence as conversion's mark of truth. After all: "the Holy Spirit's activity is often hidden under the cover of great weakness." Neither eccentric religious experience nor spiritual despair negates or confirms the gospel directly.[62]

---

60. These instructions to slaves are in Col 3:23–24. Also see Prov 16:3; 1 Cor 10:31; and Col 3:17.

61. The supreme account of this thesis is Jonathan Edwards's *The Religious Affections*.

62. FC II in Kolb and Wengert, *Book of Concord*, 554.56.

The efficacy crisis is theology's most difficult task, in part because it involves addressing physical suffering with spiritual alleviation and the irresolvable problem of theodicy (God's permission of evil). Though theology cannot cure epilepsy, chemical imbalance, or change violence's history, it places these problems in a broader perspective to make their ultimate impact less dire. Though theology cannot explain God's reasons for allowing gratuitous pain, it can point to the resurrection's transcendence of pain: "He will wipe away every tear from their eyes. There will be no more death or mourning or crying or pain, for the old order of things has passed away."[63] This eschatological hope can inspire positive emotions that condition a person better to handle grief and tragedy. Rituals such as burial rites and last rites as well help people to cope with their lack of efficacy facing death and grant meaning to mortality. It is important for theologians to remember that gospel-inspired positive emotions are not the goal of giving the gospel. Positive emotions rather form a basis that supports human belief and can continue to broaden and deepen as people are exposed to God's word, even if God alone gives the faith marking conversion.

Finally, theology addresses the self worth crisis by recognizing the created dignity of human life. As "all things were created by him and for him,"[64] there is no human life created inherently worthless. Scripture's bold statements of God's love for the world and desire for all people's salvation proclaim a person's redeemable status no matter how beaten down self esteem is. The doctrine of election also speaks to converts amid this crisis because it proclaims that God desires everyone's salvation but chooses by grace through faith in Christ, meaning that God desires *your* salvation and that your own appraisal of self worth is irrelevant to God's appraisal of you in Christ. The positive emotions associated with discovering the root of self worth in God's love are a powerful motivator of change and, indeed, an authentic turn to Christ because this kind of turn naturally avoids pride.

Though change dynamics have innumerable emotional patterns, they almost always follow a negative/positive pattern. The net of research outlined above cannot catch everything, but it provides a contemporary account that expands the affective possibilities classically

---

63. Rev 21:4.
64. Col 1:15–17.

associated with law and gospel. The psychological research helps to suggest which resources the theological tradition has to apply to specific crises and their spiritual resolution in the gospel, even if this account is not exhaustive. Though a clean cut system for addressing every convert's negative and positive motivators is impossible, the work accomplished emphasizes the major themes and gives theology a useful methodological starting point.

Conclusion

This chapter has introduced intellectual and emotional factors in change's process. Paloutzian's broad interpretation of religious change as a meaning system shift is useful to explain how input pressures of many kinds can begin a cognitive reorganization process that results in acquiring new faith. The prime case of intellectual pressures was the active seeker, and the prime emotional case was Hill's four crises. Though treated separately, the intellectual and emotional are never isolated from each other in life, and no psychological or theological rule prescribes one side as the dominant motivator in all cases. The Spirit works through both in unknown ways that only glint to human perception so far as faith in the gospel sparks. In all cases, theology's central task for addressing religious change is to supply meaning and grant significance to temporal events in the biblical narrative's light, but which meaning exactly depends on the nature of one's intellectual seekership or the kind of crisis a potential convert undergoes. Now that we have a description of religious change and an account of pressures influencing it, we can turn to a specific form of these pressures in discussing parental influence on faith development, the next chapter's theme.

4

The Individual and Parental Influences

ONE WAY OR ANOTHER, our parents influence our religion, but the kind of influence depends greatly on the stability of the relationship. Here we explore religious change motivations specifically from the context of parental influence, stable and unstable. The first is catechesis, the familiar process in which children develop faith gradually. Catechesis's lasting development is common in stable families in which their religious ethos is authenticated to children in a way of life formed by doctrine. However, many children are raised amid instability (e.g., negligent or hostile parents), and many cases of sudden religious change occur in these circumstances. The second section explores how familial instability (negative influences of the father and mother) might create a different religious profile that requires different theological treatment.

The Difficulty of Sensing the Spirit

The previous chapter discussed influences on the mind and heart as a way into changing the will and thus orienting the whole person to Christ. Whether focusing on intellectual or emotional factors, both appeared under scrutiny of the conscious struggle for religious answers. To confess that the Spirit is only discernable from the word is, for theology's purposes, to value the conscious struggle as the most important aspect of conversion's human side because only the conscious side is able to recognize the word's effectiveness. If "faith comes through hearing the message,"[1] presumably the convert's attentive listening, responding, and ultimately believing the faith is theology's means of finding the gospel criterion that marks religious experience's validity. Historically, Protestant theology has been compelled to chasten its recognitions of the Spirit's presence with the word, lest human speculation misattribute the Spirit for unholy purposes.[2] This principle means that we should not try to detect the Spirit outside of the gospel's presence to faith. Though this epistemological delimitation is necessary to inhibit abuse of divine authority, it can only be understood as a limitation of human knowledge and not of the Spirit's power. The Spirit is free to work in inconceivable ways even if human discernment of him is always subservient to the word. Thus, I cannot claim to know *how* the Spirit operates, but in a limited way I can know *where* and *when*. In exploring some of religious change's non-conscious factors in this chapter, this rule is especially important not only because of this research's already speculative nature but because the word consciously known cannot be pinned to non-conscious antecedents of conversion. That is, the Spirit's operation through non-conscious forces can only be known (if at all) in retrospect of faith's conscious appearance. Nevertheless, parental relationships have a significant impact on religious affiliations in ways not always obvious to consciousness. To neglect these considerations is to forfeit a realistic understanding of faith development, and though these non-conscious factors cannot reveal the Spirit directly, they reveal a change process that will be validated as true religion if it ends in conversion.

This chapter features two parts: stable religious socialization, and psychoanalytical factors (unstable relationship cases). Though they represent opposite poles on the spectrum of gradual versus sudden changes,[3] they are related as parental religious influences. In effect, this chapter asks, in sequence, what kind of changes familial stability predicts and then the same question when stability disintegrates.

1. Rom 10:17.

2. Luther's Smalcald Articles in Kolb and Wengert, *Book of Concord*, 323.9–10 state: "Everything that boasts of being from the Spirit apart from such a Word and sacrament is of the devil."

3. It might help to clarify that psychoanalytic factors do not necessitate sudden change experiences, but the psychoanalytic studies featured in this chapter have concentrated their research most on sudden awakenings, which are indeed the most interesting variety.

The Role of Catechesis

The church has long recognized that formal ministry is insufficient to preserve people's faith without a broader social infrastructure supporting its creed. For children, this social support begins not so much in sacramental encounters or Sunday schools but in their trusting relationships to their parents.[4] The church's symbol for the parents' role in childhood faith development is *catechesis*, a term usually referring to catechetical instruction. In his *Large Catechism*, Martin Luther provides a sense of catechesis's importance by explaining the result of neglecting it: "Think what deadly harm you do when you are negligent and fail to bring up your children to be useful and godly. You bring upon yourself sin and wrath, thus earning hell by the way you have reared your own children, no matter how holy and upright you may be otherwise."[5] Though catechesis is often narrowly defined, this education takes place in a broader matrix of instructing children to be "useful and godly." Parental instruction transcends the classroom by inculcating children not only with knowledge but with a trusting relationship and a specific way of life. The faith and theology awakening in children is very distant from last chapter's active change motif because for children theology is validated through a relationship that leaves very few religious options. I call this path to faith "non-conscious" because choice is not only absent at this stage but many aspects of childhood socialization are not even remembered in a way that they could be consciously monitored. As Batson, Schoenrade, and Ventis (BSV) emphasize: "You are free to choose only the religious stance that your particular social background dictates."[6] Like learning our native language, we cannot recall when we learned the vast majority of our vocabulary; its presence indicates social exposure of which we are no longer conscious.

In social psychology, parental influence is a specific manifestation of the *social womb* that nurtures and bears all people of a locality.[7] Because parents are the most immediate influence on children during

---

4. Cf. Erikson, *Childhood and Society*, 249.

5. Large Catechism in Kolb and Wengert, *Book of Concord*, 410.176.

6. Batson et al., *Religion and the Individual*, 25. Obviously, the non-conscious elements of catechesis can be overstated and cannot take formal instruction's place, but I intend here simply to call attention to this influence.

7. See Barnhart and Barnhart, *The New Birth*, 71–82.

their most impressionable developmental stages, they obviously have significant power to color the social womb's formative influence in a child's early life. Research shows that parental religion is especially transferable to children, even more than political values. A study of 203 Stanford students, for example, presented correlation coefficients for students and parents of 0.57 for religion, whereas politics was 0.32 and other categories such as sports and entertainment preferences were 0.16 or lower.[8] This study demonstrates parents' preferential position in determining their children's religious outlook, especially when religion correlations between the students and their friends were only 0.20 across the board.

If parents are a child's primary reference group and "a major source of social rewards and punishments,"[9] then children have very little choice but to socialize into their parents' religion. In young children, this claim holds very strongly. Once a child grows up and perhaps moves away to college or employment elsewhere, the correlation coefficients for parent/child religion generally dip because the original reference group changes and the rules for social reward and punishment differ. In youth, social rewards abound from children's ability to follow their parents' stipulations and mimic their theological speech. In college the stipulations tend to change, and adhesion to particular religious language is often challenged by a more pluralistic religious outlook. Many parents anticipating disparity between educational and family values thus send their children to parochial schools that will better unify their reference world. But even if children do broaden their exposure outside of their family's community, the surest predictor of religious denomination is still parental influence. If choice is involved in childhood socialization, the research suggests that it is the parents' choice to teach their children. The parents who value religion most influence their children the most.[10]

BSV explain this influence in terms of positive and negative reinforcement, that the social bond between parents and children is too strong to allow nonconformity. Non-consciously influencing, parents do not necessarily have to instruct with strict moral codes whose adherence earns and incurs rewards and punishments. Parental approval

8. Cited in Beit-Hallahmi and Argyle, *The Psychology of Religious Behaviour*, 100.
9. Batson et al., *Religion and the Individual*, 43.
10. Ibid., 43.

of unspoken behavioral rules can be an equally rigid form of social reinforcement that is, for its subtlety, less likely to provoke rebellion. More specifically, Beit-Hallahmi and Argyle (BHA) found that religious activity at home such as praying and Scripture reading helped children to value religion as a way of life. Mother and father agreement is another important factor in socializing children into a pervasive religious outlook over all of life's spheres. If the mother and father lack agreement in this educational purpose, children have more often followed their mother's viewpoint.[11]

The important question, I think, is to ask *why* parental influence predicts children's religion so strongly while other categories are predicted weakly. The studies do not recognize often enough that religious doctrines have a different nature than other categories such as politics, sports, entertainment, and food preferences. If taught in particularity, doctrines' very claims presuppose their eternal significance and their significance for making sense of the world around us, suggesting that parents influence their children by emphasizing religion's importance and demonstrating it in life. When this importance is inculcated to children at a young age and mediated indecipherably from an attachment to the mother and father, so that basic trust latches onto the parents themselves and their vital words, then the religion often takes a strong hold on the child. If the child can be shown through practices (such as going to a Christian school, praying, reading, and developing Christian friendships) that religion is a self-authenticating way of life as well as the truth, then the parents' initial influence tends to have a lasting effect.

This claim has a common sense quality and requires little expansion, but there is a noteworthy counterpoint that nuances the common sense understanding of parental influence. Conventional social-psychological wisdom has always treated religion as a social phenomenon whose manifestations, at least on a material level, are largely reducible to social causes such as parental influence. In later research, however, scientists have begun looking for biological explanations for religion, especially in the University of Minnesota studies of twins who have been separated at birth and reared apart. Because genetics in these individuals is a constant, this research helps clarify the boundaries of socialization in the nature/nurture relationship. One particular study

---

11. Beit-Hallahmi and Argyle, *The Psychology of Religious Behaviour*, 100–106.

tested fifty-three pairs of monozygotic (identical) and thirty-one pairs of dizygotic twins with standard religiosity tests such as the Wiggins fundamentalism survey and the Allport-Vernon-Lindzey religious values test.[12] It concluded that genetic predispositions explained about 50 percent of the survey results. Because genetics influence personality and personality influences religious attitudes (e.g., levels of fundamentalism), biological factors proved to be much more influential than researchers previously imagined. A "Christian gene" has not been discovered—human behavior is complex and is not simply determined by genes—but these studies show that some people are, in their genetic potential, more open to the unseen than others.

Commentary

This section requires little commentary because catechesis is the norm of Christian practice dating back to the church's origin and continuation of Old Testament religious instruction.[13] The most important element highlighted by social science is that doctrine is inseparable from a trusting relationship, and though children are the immediate focus here, this aspect of faith does not tend to change in later life. The "spark of faith" (signifying conversion) is faith not merely in a *fact* but in Christ the *person*, as mediated through the church. If parents neither demonstrate love for each other nor catechize their children lovingly, then the child's attachment will likely be compromised and catechesis's effectiveness with it. As the twin studies demonstrate, children's ability to believe in various levels of comprehension and commitment varies over time, partly according to their genetic potential, which suggests that if catechesis strives to produce clones it will be disappointed by non-conscious factors that neither parents nor children will ever fully comprehend. Because "all things were created by him and for him,"[14] no one is born without the potential to believe, but the personal seat of faith and even people's attitudes toward doctrinal particulars are subject to great diversity.

12. Waller et al., "Genetic and Environmental Influences," 138–42.
13. See Acts 18:25; 1 Cor 14:19; Gal 6:6; (Deut 6:6–7).
14. Col 1:16.

Though conversion happens in a single divine act, catechetical faith-development happens gradually over time and under stable parental relationships. The more interesting religious changes happen more suddenly and tend to be associated with parental instability. Though this brand of research is speculative, it can minimally show that people might compensate for parental instability with religion's stability, an insight that helps theology to address these converts.

Father Hatred

If an historical template exists for the dramatic religious changes discovered by clinical psychology, it is St. Augustine, who turned rather suddenly away from his pagan father's profligacy and toward his Christian mother's godliness.[15] Humanity's created religiousness explains why, even when parental influence fails, individuals have no less a need for faith. Due to the material means through which all faith develops, however, the religiousness of unstable families is quite different than that of stable catechesis. This section covers the scenario when parental religion goes wrong and results in the dramatic changes that clinical psychologists have analyzed. Regarding the change dynamics in chapter 2, this section takes a close look at the problem solving dynamic's incubation stage or love deprivation preceding the falling in love motif, except that it considers how subconscious (rather than consciously monitored) forces might come into play. Though the Freudian dogmas pervading this research should not have free reign, these accounts are at least fundamentally helpful in showing that familial instability can cause people to seek stability in religion. Though far from a Freudian, William James commented that: "*if there be* higher spiritual agencies that can directly touch us, the psychological condition of their doing so *might be* our possession of a subconscious region which alone should yield access to them. The hubbub of the waking life might close a door which in the dreamy subliminal might remain ajar or open."[16] A rather intriguing correlation to James's viewpoint is the Formula of Concord's statement that "the presence, effectiveness, and gift of the Holy Spirit should not and cannot always be assessed *ex sensu*, as a person feels it

---

15. See Kerr and Mulder, *Famous Conversions*, 11–14.
16. James, *Varieties of Religious Experience*, 198, italics original.

in the heart."[17] Both sources leave open the possibility that the Spirit may and does work subconsciously, encouraging the investigation to proceed.

Progress from Freud to Ullman

Probably the best starting place is Sigmund Freud's own contribution to religious psychology. Though Freud personally rejected religion, it still fascinated him, and his ideas influenced clinicians well beyond his time. He did write one short article on religions change. In 1927 he had received a letter from a journalist acquaintance who, upon seeing a "sweet-faced dear old woman" dead on a dissecting table, was struck with the sensation: "There is no God: if there were a God he would not have allowed this dear old woman to be brought into the dissecting room."[18] This sudden suspension of faith, however, led to a searching process whereby the journalist found an inner certainty of Christianity's truth after a few days. This event's interpretation was so clear to Freud that he dedicated only a couple pages to it. Applying the Oedipus complex analytic tool,[19] he concluded that seeing the lady reminded the journalist of his own mother, seeing her dead caused him to hate God for abusing her just as the subconscious perceives the father's hostility to the mother. The journalist's father hatred at first became directed at his notion of God, which he had not yet distinguished from his own father (i.e., to hate one is to hate the other), but his religious experience split this perceived God/father identification and allowed him to acknowledge a loving heavenly father even amid his hostility to his biological father. Due to its speculative nature, this interpretation is valuable more for historical reasons than contemporary validity, but it shows concretely how clinical psychology would begin to address religious change and improve on Freud's method.

Where Freud tended to impose an Oedipal construct directly onto religious experiences, later researchers were more careful to factor in converts' family histories. Though the mid-twentieth century

17. Formula of Concord II in Kolb and Wengert, *Book of Concord*, 554.56.

18. Freud, "A Religious Experience," 169. Freud did write about religion more broadly in works such as *The Future of an Illusion*, but he did not discuss conversion.

19. After the Greek myth of Oedipus, Freud's well known theory contends that men have an unconscious desire to kill their fathers and marry their mothers.

witnessed, for the most part, a lull in religious psychology, a rare essay by Leon Salzman bridged the psychoanalytic tradition from Freud to the later twentieth century.[20] Salzman recognized two kinds of changes: the progressive/maturational, and the regressive. As discussed above, the progressive denotes a typical process of learning and adhering to new ideas, while the regressive refers to more emotionally extreme and sudden changes. Salzman's psychiatric work led him to focus on regressive conversions; they are, after all, the more interesting type anyway. He saw patients for various neuroses and only later began to realize the high number of religious converts among his patients. In reviewing their stories, he discovered "a common thread" running through them. In last chapter's terms, these converts entered treatment for conscious emotional crises,[21] but upon further examination, Salzman found them to have deeply rooted conflicts with their fathers. "Occasionally in adults and often in adolescents, the inner struggle with the problem of hatred toward the father or toward father symbols—that is, toward authority—results in overwhelming anxiety and can result in conversion experience." For Salzman, regressive changes are "the acceptance of a new and higher authority, one that cannot be hated and must be loved,"[22] regardless of the disruptive interpersonal relationships from which they arise. Because regressive changes occur under high strain between conscious and subliminal tensions, they can happen quickly like flashes of insight. The rapidity of change can inspire extreme clarity, but it can easily misfire. Often, because of regression's quickness, it cannot transcend the problem completely, especially those problems that take time to resolve. Salzman was therefore not surprised by E. D. Starbuck's early observation of *backsliding* among converts, though he felt Starbuck overlooked the continual problem solving process as its cause.

About a decade later Carl Christensen improved on Salzman's study by examining a sample of twenty-two adolescent mental health patients. Christensen found similar results to Salzman's. His patients had hostile relationships with their fathers or none at all. Some of the patients also had abnormally strong dependencies with their mothers,

20. Salzman, "The Psychology of Religious and Ideological Conversion," 177–87.

21. Discussed elsewhere in chapter 3 with Hill, "Spiritual Transformation," 87–108. The types were crisis of meaning, value, efficacy, and self-worth.

22. Salzman, "The Psychology of Religious and Ideological Conversion," 186.

which evinced the Oedipus complex in Christensen's eyes. Because of disruptive family life and because their mothers tended to treat them as children into their teens, these patients were unable to develop a strong sense of self as they grew into adulthood.[23] Christensen explains that his patients' troublesome upbringings left them with a weak sense of self and security. Tormented by anxiety, guilt, and the normal adolescent pressures, these people developed weak egos that were especially susceptible to sudden change. When pushed to despair by a conscious conflict, sometimes caused by hearing a sermon, Christensen found a notion of giving up or relaxation associated with the despair. This pause, he figured, allowed the subconscious to provide a solution in religious terms. All of the cases discussed involve hearing voices of God such as "Why have you forsaken me?" or seeing visions of the cross. These findings led Christensen to define sudden religious change as "an acute hallucinatory episode," but he recognized that this point, where the ego tries to reintegrate itself, occurs in a larger context. All of his patients "found in the church the acceptance and approval they felt lacking in the home," and conformity to the church "was essentially ego supporting and contributed to a sense of security."[24] These hallucinatory episodes functioned not to produce a lasting commitment to Christianity but they spurred people into a relationship with the church that fostered their young faith and simultaneously compensated for previous trust insecurities. Like Salzman, Christensen believed that primal father hatred was the deep root of religious change in his case studies.

Freud's influence over clinical research is remarkable in that, though the various doctors have different focuses, they all appear to agree on the essential dogmas surrounding oedipal conflict. Yale psychologist Joel Allison performed case studies of divinity students and expanded Christensen's previous work.[25] His token study interprets the sudden change of an anonymous divinity student ("P"), son of a fundamentalist mother and a profligate father. Though the mother grounded P's moral sense, she also tended to be domineering toward him and her husband. P's father's weakness of character in front of his family and extra-marital affairs threw off P's moral education. Allison improves

23. Christensen, "Religious Conversion," 207–16.
24. Christensen, "Religious Conversion in Adolescence," 24.
25. Allison, "Recent Empirical Studies of Religious Conversion Experiences," 21–27.

on earlier studies by showing the mother's role more clearly. Following Freudian terms, he interpreted religious change as wanting both "to curtail sharply and also to realize and gratify an intense longing to fuse with the maternal figure in an undifferentiated matrix."[26] Change's lasting effect depended on successfully balancing the ambivalent desires to fuse with the mother and yet to separate into one's independence. For Allison, the father has a crucial role to prevent complete fusion by providing a secure masculine identity. In P's case, then, Allison believed that a return to Christianity symbolized regression to his mother in terms of reassuming her value system, and his love and respect of God replaced his obsequious earthly father. Like Augustine turning away from his father's ways and toward his mother's, P was able to attach healthily to his mother and find the security of a father who could not be tempted by carnal desires or weakness of character. In Allison's words: "The conversion experience forges a new psychological organization in which the early ties with the maternal wellsprings of faith, hope, and wholeness, and union are maintained and a strong, guiding paternal figure with clear, organized values and firm judgments is also acquired."[27]

These psychoanalytic interpretations depend greatly on faith in the Freudian method. Though their specifics are subject to question, doubters should remember that they at least expose aspects of familial life that correlate highly with change experience. The instability of a rocky upbringing causes many people to find a more secure basis of trust, and sometimes the church's resources, both its theology and its people, fit this need. An important study by Chana Ullman corroborates this point.[28]

In this area of empirical research, Ullman's study is perhaps the best ever produced. Unlike Salzman and Christensen, who studied people from their lists of mental health patients, Ullman began by finding actual converts. In the Boston area during the early 1980s, she interviewed and surveyed forty converts, ten each to Judaism, Catholicism, Bahai, and Hare Krishna. She selected only people of similar age who

---

26. Allison, "Religious Conversion: Regression and Progression in an Adolescent Experience," 24.

27. Ibid., 38.

28. Ullman's work appeared already in chapter 2 for the falling in love dynamic as a complement to the problem solving dynamic.

Converts' versus Controls' Perception of Parents

Characteristics		Absent	Passive	Hostile	Unstable	Overprotective	Neutral	Positive
Category	Father							
	Converts (n = 39)	28.2 (11)	20.5 (8)	23.0 (9)	2.6 (1)	2.6 (1)	2.6 (1)	20.5 (8)
	Nonconverts (n = 30)	3.3 (1)	6.7 (2)	13.3 (4)	0 (0)	0 (0)	23.3 (7)	53.4 (16)
	Mother							
	Converts (n = 30)	2.6 (1)	5.3 (2)	10.5 (4)	13.3 (5)	10.5 (4)	15.8 (6)	42.4 (16)
	Nonconverts (n = 30)	0 (0)	3.3 (1)	0 (0)	3.3 (1)	0 (0)	23.3 (7)	70.0 (21)

Source: Ullman, *Transformed Self*, 31. The first number is percent; the parenthetical number is the actual number of participants in that category.

had made a decisive commitment to an entirely new faith, and she excluded religious re-affiliations suspect of social advantage (such as for marriage). She not only found the most authentic converts possible but also correlated their data with thirty controls.[29]

Ullman found that nearly 80 percent of the converts had unhealthy relationships with their fathers next to about 23 percent in the controls. As the table above shows, negative qualities abound in the converts' perceptions of their mothers as well.[30] About one third of the converts had little or no contact with their fathers at all, which was three times higher than the national average. These statistics, coupled with Ullman's personal interviews, led her to believe that troubled relationships, especially parental, are the axis of religious change.

About 80 percent of her converts reported extended periods (two years average) of anxiety and depression that often could be traced (from interviews) back to developmental deficiencies.[31] Ullman began to think of religious change in terms of falling in love because so many of her subjects seemed to compensate for parental affection by turning to a religious community. For the theologian who cherishes doctrine, it is painful to hear Ullman report that: "For most of the religious converts I interviewed, the actual conversion experience focused on newly found protection, attention, and acceptance by another or by a group of others, which rendered superfluous and unnecessary an examination of the beliefs or of the actions involved."[32] Ullman cautions that her statistics are correlated such that causal explanations cannot be derived directly from them, but combined with her interviews, they provide convincing evidence that deficient parental relationships predict radical religious change in certain cases where potential converts are exposed to a religious community's warmth and security. For troubled souls such as those Ullman studied, the spark of faith signaling conversion was indistinguishable from faith in a religious leader or body. Ullman helps to illustrate how the theology that matters most in transforming

---

29. This study is best summarized in the original article: Ullman, "Cognitive and Emotional Antecedents of Religious Conversion," 183–92.

30. Ullman, *Transformed Self*, 30–31.

31. Ullman, "Cognitive and Emotional Antecedents of Religious Conversion," 190.

32. Ullman, *Transformed Self*, 20–21.

people's lives cannot be separated from the church's communal attitude in supporting each other.[33]

This psychoanalytic approach defines religious change best as a process of reattachment. Although Christensen saw it as a hallucinatory episode, this observation's larger context concerned the converts' efforts to attach to their mothers and fathers in a healthy fashion. These classically oriented studies focus mostly on attachment to God as a superior father figure, but they tend to overlook the mother's role in this process. Recent research into attachment psychology has uncovered more data focusing specifically on the mother, which helps to complement these classic studies and provide a clearer illustration of religious trust's material basis.

Mother Love

Religious psychology did not easily escape Freud's emphasis on the father figure, but in the last twenty years social scientists have finally begun to research the mother's role in shaping children's religious futures. Mothers have a definite place in the above section on catechesis, no doubt, but this late research investigates the mother's less intentional influence as an attachment figure. The original insights into attachment were developed by John Bowlby (from 1969–80), who sought to explain children's maternal care and hence survival. Biologically speaking, if infants had no psychological apparatus for seeking parental care, they would not survive long in this vulnerable age; obviously the human race's survival depends on successful child rearing. This attachment apparatus is similar to Erikson's basic trust concept, except that Bowlby was interested less in faith development or even child development and more on the capacity to form stable relationships that sustain the human race.

Attachment Backgrounds

Attachment theory's starting place is the same as Erikson's basic trust. The infant quickly develops an affective bond with its attachment

---

33. Chapter 6 on social networks will develop this theme.

figure, defined as its primary caregiver (typically, but not necessarily, the mother). In caring for the child, the attachment figure is responsible for providing a secure base and a haven of comfort.[34] The secure base is the child's impression that, even in the mother's absence, someone will provide a haven of comfort should the child become troubled. The secure base grounds the infant's need to explore its new world without fear, but the inevitable deprivations and pains that accompany this exploration elicit *attachment behavior*, essentially the infant's call back to motherly care. The underlying premise is that the development of healthy relationships is influenced heavily by this element of upbringing including the attachment behavior and the attachment figure's responsiveness to it. It predicts that emotional soundness (the ability to regulate emotion and use it for rational ends) will be correlated consistently with the quality of maternal care.

Because not all maternal care is equally sound and because children do not perceive this care with equal accuracy, there are various levels of perceived attachment quality. This research has discovered three different patterns of attachment that are necessary to understand because of their correlation coefficients to different religious outcomes. *Secure attachment* is the most common. It means that the mother has provided for the child sufficiently to establish what Bowlby calls "confidence" and "assurance," terms similar to "trust" in Erikson and Fowler. When the child feels threatened and elicits care, the securely related mother addresses this care with sufficient consistency to merit the child's confidence. In contrast, *insecure* (mistrusting) attachment's two categories of anxious (or ambivalent) and avoidant relationships indicate a compromise, however severe, of this basic trust. *Anxious* attachment predicts excessively dependent adult relationships. It indicates that the infant is unsure whether the caregiver will be available for terminating the pains that cause it to cry for relief. Though it expects motherly care, the child mistrusts its consistency and therefore is afflicted by uncertainty-based anxiety. *Avoidant* attachment predicts hostility and defensiveness into adulthood. The infant is so often denied a response to cries of pain and deprivation that it ceases to expect consistent care and instead develops a more self-reliant attitude. Psychologists have tested these attachment levels by surveying respondents according to their perceptions of how

---

34. Oksanen, *Religious Conversion*, 27–28.

their mothers (or caregivers) related to them. The following descriptions illustrate these categories:

> Secure: "She was generally warm and responsive; she was good at knowing when to be supportive and when to let me operate on my own; our relationship was almost always comfortable, and I have no major reservations or complaints about it."
>
> Anxious: "She was noticeably inconsistent in her reactions to me, sometimes warm and sometimes not; she had her own needs and agendas which sometimes got in the way of her receptiveness and responsiveness to my needs; she definitely loved me but didn't always show it in the best way."
>
> Avoidant: "She was fairly cold, distant, and rejecting, and not very responsive; I often felt that her concerns were elsewhere; I frequently had the feeling that she would just as soon not have had me."[35]

These categories were originally intended for research into maternal influence and relationships to discover the degree to which insecurely attached individuals might compensate for their childhood lack of care. In the late 1980s, however, psychologist Lee Kirkpatrick began to consider their implications for religion. If, following Freud, God serves as an exalted father figure, could he not also become an attachment figure? As discussed last chapter, crises of various kinds cause many people to reevaluate their worldviews and turn to God for comfort. To psychologists, this action looks fundamentally the same as a distressed infant's attachment behavior, seeking the safe haven of its mother's embrace. The comforting aspect of religion, though only narrowly understood from psychology's viewpoint, still warranted research into attachment history and religious change.

The flagship study resulted from Kirkpatrick's and Phillip Shaver's collaboration. Rather than the typical testing of college students, they issued a newspaper survey and collected 670 responses inquiring into people's attachment history and their religiousness (specifically Christianity). The most striking finding was that sudden turns to Christianity occurred in 44.4 percent of those who had an avoidant attachment history, whereas only 8 or 9 percent of secure and anxious individuals reported religious changes. The majority of converts reported emotional

---

35. Kirkpatrick and Shaver, "Attachment Theory and Religion," 323.

turmoil preceding their change, and for the older respondents divorce and marriage difficulties pervaded the accounts.

Kirkpatrick's initial research helped to clarify the central question about whether or not God could compensate for a lacking secure attachment. The hypothesis is difficult to prove in part because cases of insecure attachment and change are exceptions where the rule is what Kirkpatrick called the *correspondence hypothesis*, as covered above, that children tend to follow their parents' religious instruction to a high degree. Support for *compensation*, Kirkpatrick suggested, is best discovered in cases where children are raised amid turbulent family life and minimal religious instruction. He cited studies such as Ullman's in support of this basic notion that if comfort is impossible to find on earth, it might be found in heaven.[36] If shown to be credible, the compensation hypothesis demonstrates that in these cases, conversion's spark of faith is not only adherence to doctrinal tenets but rather, for conscious and subconscious reasons, a grasp for ultimate comfort.

Fortunately, researchers in Uppsala, Sweden, have corroborated some of Kirkpatrick's research and added credibility to attachment studies of religion. Sweden proved a very complementary milieu for testing Kirkpatrick and Shaver's results because, while Christianity is still the majority religion (90 percent are members of the state church), less than 10 percent of the population are confessing Christians.[37] Because high maternal religiousness tends to predict gradual (correspondent) faith development, Sweden offers a context to determine how maternal influence can impact religion unintentionally. Pehr Granqvist of Uppsala University drew samples largely from the community's religious population, surveying 203 individuals on their perceived attachments to mother and father, their parents' level of religiousness, and their own attitudes toward religion. Of his discoveries, the most germane is: "Support for the compensation hypothesis emerged in a relatively straightforward way in that insecure respondents in the maternal relationship had experienced a major religious change during adulthood to a larger

---

36. Kirkpatrick, "An Attachment-Theory Approach to the Psychology of Religion," 16–18.

37. Granqvist and Hagekull, "Religiousness and Perceived Childhood Attachment," 259.

extent than secure respondents."[38] As expected, these converts were the exception rather than the norm, and Granqvist found that high parental religion predicted the same in children about 85 percent of the time, which is higher even than BHA's results above. These findings led Granqvist to conclude that attachment research uncovers two distinct religious profiles paralleling the correspondence and compensation hypotheses. Correspondence faith, he predicted, would arise from gradual socialization through parental and cultural influence; compensation faith would happen quickly under an attempt to regulate emotional distress. These profiles have a precedent in Salzman's maturational and regressive profiles above.

Granqvist and his partner Berit Hagekull largely validated these hypotheses in a study of 156 students.[39] They developed methods for testing the two convert profiles and then employed them on actual subjects. Like Snow and Machalek's social type for converts (chapter 2), these two profiles (correspondence and compensation) give patterns for change experience, except in this case focusing specifically on parental factors. Reviewing Granqvist and Hagekull's tabulated data, a clear picture emerges that avoidant and ambivalent attachments correlate positively with emotionally based religion and secure attachments correlate negatively. On the scale of gradual religious socialization the insecurely attached, as predicted, demonstrated negative correlations and the secure positive correlations.[40] This data, though representing only one study, falls soundly in line with BHA's and BSV's work on parental catechesis (for the secure) and with the psychoanalytic material through Ullman, who proved that familial instability caused converts to find a more ideal family in religious community. These studies demonstrate that to join a religious group and take up a new creed can be influential in regulating negative emotions and producing positive thinking. If one's natural family and identity lead to despair, a spiritual family and identity can lead to alleviation.

38. Granqvist, "Religiousness and Perceived Childhood Attachment," 361–62, chart on 358.

39. Granqvist and Hagekull, "Religiousness and Perceived Childhood Attachment," 254–73.

40. Pehr Granqvist suggests that these two profiles are useful for dividing the classic versus contemporary change paradigms on the issue of gradualness or suddenness. See Granqvist, "Attachment Theory and Religious Conversions," 172–87.

The Validity of Attachment Research

More than fifteen years after his first study, Kirkpatrick worked together with Granqvist to produce a meta-analysis, or summary of attachment research's contribution to religious change.[41] Looking at eleven total studies (over 1400 participants) from the United States and Scandinavia, they determined that the most important hypotheses revolved around compensation, or the relationship between insecure attachment and sudden change as a means to regulate negative emotions. Though the results were not shocking regarding any one conclusion, the original hypotheses stood confirmed. Secure attachments tended to predict gradual, socially-inspired faith, and insecure attachments predicted more emotionally driven, sudden religious changes. The authors summarize: "By showing that sudden converts and nonsudden converts differ, not only on perceived attachment history with parents, but also with respect to the functions and individual origins or their religiosity, the results of this study seem to suggest that sudden converts and nonsudden converts represent two relatively distinct religious profiles."[42] The authors note that this interpretation of religious experience goes back at least to William James's notion of the "healthy-minded" and "sick soul" kinds of religion in which the former accepts faith naturally without having to win it in existential battle and the other turns to faith or grows in faith, many times, as a last resort.[43] By reaching back to James they offer a bridge between early religious psychology and very recent insights; while corroborating their hypothesis with James, they also further his work with greater depth into discovering why some people are naturally healthy-minded and others are sick souls in need of spiritual medicine.

The ultimate question of causality (i.e., if weak attachments cause sudden change) is impossible to draw with certainty because of the complexities in human experience and the correlational nature of these studies. There might be other significant factors explaining the correlations such as converts' tendency to reinterpret their pasts better to

---

41. Granqvist and Kirkpatrick, "Religious Conversion and Perceived Childhood Attachment," 223–50.

42. Ibid., 240.

43. James, *Varieties of Religious Experience*, 165.

serve their present redeemed status.⁴⁴ Taken together and with the classical psychoanalytic studies, however, attachment research at least explains the minimal thesis that I have emphasized throughout. Familial instability causes restlessness in many people who turn to find rest in the church. Non-conscious desires for peace and acceptance increase religious change's probability and lead some people to begin exploring a faith network.

The Correlation: Theology for the Non-Conscious

Strangely, one attachment researcher was brave enough to include implications for pastoral theology in his psychology book. The Swede Antti Oksanen recommends that because religious changes typically happen amid an emotional dynamic of distress and relief, the church should emphasize the comforting aspects of doctrine in all cases.⁴⁵ Though this prescription explains a possible avenue of praxis, it is surely the theology of a psychologist. The correlational method never allows theological validity to rest in the scientist's hands; it rather allows the scientist to help clarify which of theology's own resources might best speak meaningfully to people in different contexts of faith. If Oksanen is correct in prescribing a comforting message, the convert's distress must first be placed into the biblical narrative and offered alleviation on theology's own terms. Emotional distress is not a theological evil *per se*, nor is comfort a theological virtue in itself, but so far as these modes of being have the potential to focus individuals' attention on the deeper realities of sin and redemption, they can serve as a way into religious change that offers an ultimate kind of comfort.

Perhaps the greatest challenge regressive/compensation converts pose to theology is that an immediate psychological payoff accompanies their belief in God. Scripture consistently points out that focus on this-worldly benefits cannot lead to eternity, and though theology does provide benefits in this life, they can easily become an idolatrous foundation of faith.⁴⁶ The church's solution is to lead a liturgy of repentance

---

44. See the discussion of this factor in chapter 2.
45. Oksanen, *Religious Conversion*, 165.
46. Matt 10:39 ("Whoever finds his life will lose it, and whoever loses his life for my sake will find it"); 16:25; Mark 8:35; Luke 9:24; 17:33; John 12:25.

and absolution because these impure religious motives pervade the entire church along with sudden converts. Theology's continual task is to expose the church's domesticated and mythologized uses of God and lead it to its own annihilation and resurrection, the only context where idolatrous uses of divinity can be held in check.

So long as theology is not transformed into a therapeutic device, this chapter offers useful insights into conversion's human side. The discussion of parental influence, both positive and negative, clarifies one theme especially: people are created to live in trusting relationships. The most powerful predictor of faith development is parental nurture because this platform of trust validates catechesis in children from an age before they are able to separate their parents' authority from doctrine's. Though children later develop the ability to distinguish theological authority from their parents', this research demonstrates that theology's meaningful impact, if not its truth, is dependent on its bearers. I would not say that truth is "personal in nature" whatever that might mean, but the meaning of truth is always mediated through interpersonal dynamics. Especially in Ullman's study, the relationship aspect appeared to eclipse doctrinal particularities. Broken and hostile homes serve this point in the converts' experience of turning to God as an attempt to overcome the disintegrated mediums of trust that they had previously known. In these cases, low parental religion and disruptive family life brought people into the church only through obscure and reactionary paths such that Christensen began defining religious change as a "hallucinatory episode."

It might be tempting to perceive the Spirit's work in sudden (Pauline-like) changes like those covered in psychoanalytic and attachment research, but the material causes of this profile rule out, in correlational theology, the possibility that both Spirit and matter explain these events on the same level. If psychology gives an adequate account of the process, spiritual attribution only stands to lose in direct competition. But even if it were legitimate to detect the Spirit as directly causing sudden changes, it would probably be unwise to assume that radical changes are spiritually unique such that they need little further ministry. The Spirit, as discussed at the start of this chapter, is known only in the gospel's light. The event or pattern of change reveals nothing of the Spirit in itself, but if this experience deepens the convert's immersion in the gospel, then the Spirit is know in terms of this awakening to the gospel. The most valuable insight of these particular scientific insights is that a sudden change displays much more a need for the gospel than the gospel's definite presence.

This chapter concludes our express study of individual converts and the psychosocial pressures that motivate religious change. Though future discussion cannot leave these pressures behind, it will develop them in terms of broader ideological and social conditions of faith development to a particular religion. Chapter 5 discusses these pressures and their alleviation though religious doctrine, and chapter 6 discusses the role of social networks.

5

The Lure of Ideology

AT THIS POINT IN our trek into the science of religious change it is helpful to remember that conversion experience has three constituent parts: a convert, a creed, and a social group. This chapter begins to take on the second element: the creed, or doctrinal influences on religious change. After a brief discussion about how theology is self-authenticating to believers, this chapter introduces deprivation sociology as a means of understanding how ideologies of religious groups attract people. Deprivation sociology attempts to detail the tensions people suffer when they lack some contentment in life that they feel they should have, be it love, money, health, or something else that they desire. Focusing on tensions, it fits within Paloutzian's notion that change is caused by pressure on thought systems, but in discussing deprivation it narrows the question to a form of pressure that has been useful in explaining why people assume certain ideologies. Because ideology and its practice cannot be cleanly divided, the last section demonstrates how a new religious lifestyle might further explain how theology creates new converts.

Beyond Individual Pressures to Change

The last three chapters have outlined various motivational layers through which religious change is possible. These layers are not competing paradigms but various factors that work together or separately in a process. Someone restless from familial insecurity might become an active seeker scouring various religions but only finding rest once one worldview appears most adequate amid an emotional crisis. The ongoing argument about religious experience's validity has been that no single experiential pattern makes conversion true because "the LORD looks at the heart."[1] Only religious change's *theological orientation* can grant validation in the church's eyes, yet this element is underappreciated in most social research. Perhaps social scientists feel that their jurisdiction runs out at this point, or perhaps the entire field is biased toward more impersonal explanatory means than actual beliefs. But whatever forces explain religion, change itself is meaningless without finding a theology.[2] Though a minority, a few sociologists have researched ideology's role, how its interpretive power over life supplies its own allure as a motivational factor in religious affiliation. Their accounts will expand our focus outside of change-inspiring tensions alone and provide an important conversation partner for theology.

Doctrine's Self-Authentication as Its Appeal

If conversion's validity is known most specifically in a moment of faith, then a theological definition helps to clarify this moment. Fortunately chapter 1 has accomplished the legwork on this question to suggest that faith is experienced in some way as despair of self and trust in Christ as known through the gospel. This faith is ultimately not in doctrinal phrasing, like a password for heavenly access, but is a trusting disposition toward a person. However, a trusting disposition toward Christ is impossible without a certain idea of his identity theologically. The relationship between primary theology[3] (e.g., proclamation) and secondary theology (e.g., doctrinal tenets) demonstrates how crucial doctrine is to direct people to Christ while at the same time conveying doctrinal

---

1. 1 Sam 16:7.

2. In *Transforming Worldviews*, anthropologist Paul Hiebert consistently emphasizes that assuming a worldview is crucial to conversion's lasting effect.

3. Here "primary theology" is intended to convey the church's liturgical rehearsal of the sacramental encounter with Christ. The term "primary theology" does not capture so much the church's doctrinal statements but the specific experience of conversion's original conviction. The church's conviction will not be directed rightly, however, if it does not understand doctrine's claims that ground the reason for primary theology's action.

statements' limitations in being unable to manipulate the Spirit. Secondary doctrines outline the church's theology and worldview, what is believed in the head and followed in action, but as theological positions, they work rather as something for faith to latch on to rather than as faith's direct cause. Though secondary doctrines cannot communicate Christ directly, they direct the convert to the sacramental context in which faith arises. They give faith a path to follow that directs it once it has been sparked by the Spirit's gift of Christ in primary theology. This chapter suggests that sociological work on ideology offers a useful parallel to secondary theology by demonstrating how doctrine, speaking to various needs, draws people to a new religious environment and thus becomes a precursor to conversion.

A way into this issue—how theology motivates conversion—is to acknowledge the self-authenticating nature of religious belief. Our late modern milieu is sensitive to the subjectivity of religious belief, meaning that though doctrines have absolute referents, their truth is unable to be demonstrated (or discredited) by repeatable scientific proof.[4] Many theologians and philosophers today contend that faith cannot be based on universal canons of reason because scientific or rational foundations for faith are actually bet-hedging moves to eliminate having to be "certain of what we do not see."[5] But faith's lack of philosophical grounding does not compromise its existential significance, especially when the choice humans face appears to be between faiths and not between belief and unbelief.[6] Subjectively considered, religion grants meaning and order to life. Because this meaning-granting function serves the continuum of human existence from within, both informing and being tested by ethical action and religious experience, it is self-authenticating as an important element of human life.[7] Faith, that is, provides an irreplaceable fulfillment to believers. Even on materialistic assumptions, sociologists recognize that belief's content is not a product of unconscious social forces. In some cases ideology attracts people to join a religion because of its value in shaping their life's meaning

---

4. See Gogarten, *The Reality of Faith*, 9.
5. Heb 11:1.
6. See chapter 2 on universal religiousness.
7. For a robust defense of self-authentication see Evans, *Subjectivity and Religious Belief*.

and providing ultimate significance. Theology's self-authentication is the very character of this drawing power because it asks less of objective factuality and more of personal significance. Though an incomplete area of research, sociology has discovered definite trends in which ideology has captured converts. The accounts will illuminate conversion's theological content (i.e., what is believed in the turn to faith) from a real life context and explain how the gospel might apply to different needs.

Sociological Functions of Belief

Marx on Religion

Sociological appreciation of doctrine goes back at least to Karl Marx's early Critique of Hegel's *Philosophy of Right*, though "appreciation" might be the wrong word! The popular history tells how Marx became enthralled with Hegel's view of dialectic in history but quickly demystified the theological aspects of Hegel's thought via Ludwig Feuerbach's anthropological reduction of theology. Marx was only twenty-five when he wrote his famous statement: "*Religious* suffering is at the same time an *expression* of real suffering and a *protest* against real suffering. Religion is the sigh of the oppressed creature, the sentiment of a heartless world, and the soul of soulless conditions. It is the *opium* of the people. The abolition of religion as the *illusory* happiness of men is a demand for their *real* happiness."[8]

This statement's hostile tone seems to taunt theology's defensive response, but to take an apologetic stance is to miss Marx's insight into religion. He made his famous assertion from the premise that "*man makes religion*,"[9] and to the extent that religious belief and practice is irreducibly human, it will always be subject to illusion and false attempts at happiness. Christian television programming continually demonstrates Marx's point by promising the multiplication of wealth for donors or certain knowledge of imminent apocalypse. He could not believe, however, that the Spirit works even through religious folly to give God's grace to people despite their theological mistakes. The opium metaphor is more descriptive than it sounds. In the nineteenth century

8. Marx, "Critique of Hegel's *Philosophy of Right*," 12.
9. Ibid., 11.

it was a common pain killer whose hallucinatory effect at least provided temporary alleviation. In this sense Marx does not say that that religion is pointless but that it impedes the true path to happiness by furnishing an inauthentic happiness, something like sleep on an airplane compared to sleep in a comfortable bed. He did not deny religion's ability to address suffering and protest against it; he only doubted that religion holds the possibility of true redemption because it does not reliably end labor alienation. Marx saw clearly, though critically, that spiritual values are meaningful and that people who suffer are especially attuned to them for their alleviating effect.

Deprivation Seeking Ideology

Though Marx's analysis of religion receives few direct citations in modern sociological texts, his influence is clearly present. Sociology, at least through the twentieth century, has honored the essential premises of Marx's early thought by pairing theology's allure with general unhappiness.[10] Though Marx did not develop a doctrine of relative deprivation, a condition in which people desire to attain the relatively unattainable, he clearly proposed that economically deprived people (those alienated from their labor's fruits) turn to religion for happiness when life's conditions primarily bring misery. Turned into a theory, Marx's insight would predict that relatively comfortable people (viz. the middle and upper classes) would not turn to religion for its ideological appeal. If life offers sufficient material satisfactions, then the perceived need for divine blessing and otherworldly redemption would proportionally decline.[11]

Marx's string of thought threaded through the eyelets of German theorists Max Weber, Ernst Troeltsch, and eventually through H. Richard Niebuhr, who brought distinctly American concerns to social

---

10. More recently see Bainbridge, "The Sociology of Conversion," 178–91.

11. Though a wider level of analysis, this principle coheres with the previous discussion of emotional crises, insecure parental attachments, and Paloutzian's thesis that change does not occur without a perceived need. Of course, many economically comfortable people remain strongly committed to their religion and its beliefs, implying that wealth does not clearly predict irreligion, only that their entrance into the faith is more likely a different route than deprivation seeking theology.

theory.¹² Though primarily a theologian, Niebuhr's early writing on society influenced secular sociology of later generations. He intended his insights into religious sect formation for use in unifying a church that he felt was too divided, but sociologists later applied his work to religious affiliation and religious body dynamics. Niebuhr saw that churches (religious bodies in low tension with surrounding society) tend to liberalize or compromise with external cultural norms to an extent that a minority will inevitably break off and form a sect over ideological reasons. "In Protestant history," Niebuhr explains, "the sect has ever been the child of an outcast minority, taking its rise in the religious revolts of the poor, of those who were without effective representation in church or state and who formed their conventicles of dissent in the only way open to them, on the democratic, associational pattern."¹³ Niebuhr theorized that the departed sect would only maintain its ideological fervor for one generation and would eventually liberalize, form a church, and then serve as a platform for more sects to break off. The important point for this study is that Niebuhr laid the groundwork for current deprivation sociology. Though in the quote above he mentions the "revolts of the poor," the more essential theme concerns those "without effective representation" so far as it communicates powerlessness in sectarian converts (before re-affiliating). Modern sociology has not significantly deviated from this general statement that powerlessness in life has, for many people, inspired them to seek power in religious faith and the hope of future fulfillment.¹⁴

From Niebuhr's early work on sect formation, sociology made little improvement in classifying types of deprivation and means of spiritual alleviation until Charles Glock's typology.¹⁵ Though the typology accommodates Marx's insights on economic deprivation that have survived through Niebuhr, it broadens deprivation theory outside of eco-

---

12. See Niebuhr, *Social Sources of Denominationalism*, originally published in 1939.

13. Ibid., 19.

14. Jürgen Moltmann's theological program is worth noting because it thematizes the concept of hope for oppressed people's liberation. Using Ernst Bloch's Marxist philosophy as a starting point, Moltmann specifically tailors hope theology as an inspiring reference point for deprived peoples and an impetus of social action. See Moltmann, *Theologie der Hoffnung*.

15. See Glock, "The Role of Deprivation," 25–36.

nomic reductionism and thereby accounts for many possible aspects of ideology appealing to people deprived of various powers. Discussion of these types will not only demonstrate theology's possible functions in life but help to determine what needs theology must address to communicate effectively to different social backgrounds. Though Glock organized his types differently, I have ordered them loosely according to their prevalence today. The types are: psychic (deprivation of meaning), ethical (outrage, or deprivation of moral right), economic (lacking material resources), social (deprived of a status), and organismic (suffering illness).

PSYCHIC DEPRIVATION

Glock defines deprivation as: "any and all of the ways that an individual or group may be, or feel, disadvantaged in comparison either to other individuals or groups or to an internalized set of standards."[16] He asserts that people will seek to overcome deprivation through either social action (e.g., peasant revolts) or symbolism, which is the more relevant avenue for this study. The first type, *psychic deprivation* is the sociological equivalent of the restless search for meaning discussed in chapter 3, but it could be more richly defined as the need for existential satisfaction. A simple example of this phenomenon is my own experience as a security guard. I once worked security for a summer resort community in Northern Michigan, a job that was little more complicated than recording the cars entering into the club and greeting the people. Glock explains: "The individual is not missing the material advantages of life but has been denied its psychic rewards."[17] The job satisfied life's material needs, but over time the repetition and perceived needlessness of such work drained the well of psychic rewards dry and spurred restlessness toward a better life purpose.

Though psychic deprivation can sometimes find alleviation through change in life circumstances, regarding religious change those circumstances are beneficial only so far as they mediate a better ideology. In cases of active seekership such as Leo Tolstoy's, for example, life circumstances were nearly inconsequential. Born into Russian

16. Ibid., 27.
17. Ibid., 29.

aristocracy and having secured a successful writing career, he was above the common social and economic deprivations but nevertheless lived unfulfilled: "During the whole of that year [1879], when I was asking myself almost every minute whether I should or should not put an end to it all with a cord or a pistol, during the time my mind was occupied with the thoughts which I have described, my heart was oppressed by a tormenting feeling. This feeling I cannot describe otherwise than as a searching after God."[18]

Tolstoy recounts how he ransacked theology and Enlightenment philosophy to secure his comfort of God's existence and religion's meaning but was repeatedly discouraged until he found an ethically-based theology that finally settled his soul. Tolstoy's case is perhaps the purest form of psychic deprivation/alleviation because his struggle occurred almost completely within an internal search for truth. He only found rest from his distress in discovering a subjectively authenticating theology, in his case an ethical derivative of Christianity.

Because Tolstoy is an extraordinary example, it could be tempting to think that he was a unique case. Contemporary sociology with its sensitivity to the active religious change, however, has generally argued that changes of the *intellectualist* sort are on the rise.[19] With the plurality of existing worldviews catalyzed by unprecedented communicatory means, individuals face enough options to turn many people into religious consumers searching for the most satisfying worldviews. Shopping in a limitless mall of religious products, the intellectualist consumer subscribes to the ideology that best supports and communicates to his or her cognitive and emotional circumstances.[20] Psychic deprivation, though not the only factor in religious change today, is common and becoming more important with the increase in communication technology.

---

18. Quoted in Kerr and Mulder, *Famous Conversions*, 134.

19. Lofland and Skonovd, "Conversion Motifs," 3. Intellectuals are those best representing the active seeker ("Protean Man") in chapter 3.

20. Over the short term at least, churches that market their theology for a religious consumer and advertise widely will have an advantage to win affiliates over churches that emphasize orthodoxy and tradition. Yet if converts are won as easily as VW advertising could win over a Nissan customer, then this change seems shy of a true religious change and better illustrates *switching*.

Modern documentation of psychic deprivation by Ali Köse, a Turkish researcher, helps to confirm this point. In studying seventy native British converts to Islam, he discovered that change into the Muslim faith occurred at the average age of 29.7,[21] a marked difference from conventional statistics (since Starbuck's day) that have placed the average age within early teenage years. Köse's participants were generally raised in culturally Christian homes, but they failed to continue in their faith in later years. Though the participants did have teenage affiliation with Christianity, they usually shifted out of its tradition and into a vague secularism characterizing modern British education. These participants eventually grew dissatisfied with secularism's lack of meaning, especially in its implicit avowal of hedonism, and entered a developmentally intermediate state. Köse links this state to Erik Erikson's moratorium stage of development out of which increased occupational and ideological commitment is common.[22] If this study completed in 1996 can mark any general trends, it perhaps shows that the moratorium stage of life is one best suited to brew psychic deprivation amid publicly secularized society. Upon espousing Islam, one convert noted: "Islam gives you the basis. It gives you personal hygiene, five times prayer a day, and so forth. There is no way you can avoid Islam during your day. You have to think about God, you have to think about your workmates, your family, and so forth."[23] To the Christian mind, these many rules cannot but appear as a burden, but the testimony provides clear evidence that some people are drawn to religion because society's ideological vagueness leaves them unfounded. Perhaps the Christian church has room to offer an analogous structure of conduct, so long as it does so under the notion of civil and moral righteousness (as opposed to achieving God's righteousness). The effects would then be similar to those found by Köse (essentially giving converts a sense of grounding) but would not impose the same burden because the conduct would be carried out in the knowledge of a Christian's freedom from sin and the law.

21. Ali Köse, "Religious Conversion," 255.

22. Ibid., 258. A moratorium developmental stage occurs in young adulthood and includes the person's effort to explore and experiment with various cultural inputs before settling on a perennial vocation and creed.

23. Ibid., 261.

These sociological insights confirm that if the church appeals to the psychically deprived and prevents deprivation from forming within its own ranks, it must proclaim theology meaningfully. In itself the assertion is plain, yet the complexity of communicating theology effectively to today's audience cannot easily be summarized. The issue is complicated by psychic deprivation's subjective nature that obscures a clear perception of how the church should alleviate it. Notwithstanding individual subjectivities and styles of learning, the methods and cultural metaphors used to proclaim the gospel depend as much on the local context. People will, of course, find satisfactions in diverse worship styles, and what one perceives as meaningful another will undoubtedly perceive as superficial. In cases such as Tolstoy's, orthodox Christianity was unable to end his religious search. Perhaps further inquiry into deprivation will clarify theology's task. In the mean time, a correlational approach to sociology and theology will hold faithfulness to the gospel apart from quantifiable success.[24]

ETHICAL DEPRIVATION

Ethical deprivation is similar to psychic in that both cases result from dissatisfaction with the status quo value system in an individual life. This deprivation has a distinct moral quality such that Tolstoy's question "does God exist?" might take the form: "What does God require?" The question of truth, that is, serves the question of righteousness.

The complexity in detecting ethical deprivation comes from its two distinct but related forms. One form explains deprivation as resulting from society's failure to provide a clear sense of right and wrong to guide us; the other explains deprivation from an individual's inability to find or live up to what Glock, in his definition of relative deprivation cited above, called an "internalized set of standards" (e.g., I do not know which ethical decision is right, or my current value system does

---

24. Chapter 2 has already argued, under the discussion of "embracing a convert role," that active responsibility is crucial to fulfilling converts' need to sense the importance of their new faith. Perhaps the beginning to addressing psychic deprivation is to give converts (and indeed anyone else) active duties inspired by the faith, or perhaps help them to discover a vocation. Some of these concerns will be covered below in discussing the "good hypocrisy." On the convert role see Snow and Machalek, "The Sociology of Conversion," 174.

not give me the strength to do what is right). The societal is the most common form used to explain the rise of social movements. Glock explains that ethical deprivation is often the product of gradual disillusionment with a societal value system.[25] A contemporary example of societally driven ethical deprivation is the struggle over food qualities. Mainstream grocers sell countless processed foods because they are highly demanded commodities. Though society at large values them, a minority of consumers have become ethically deprived, believing that these factory-produced products threaten society's health by overloading people with artificial ingredients and innutritious calories. Their disillusionment with society causes them to seek a new ideology and hence a new ethic in acquiring nourishment. The other, more individual form of ethical deprivation can be illustrated by again considering Köse's converts who reportedly embraced a new faith because without it they lacked the resources to be ethically at peace with themselves, and upon embracing Islam they found a code of living that they grew to appreciate. Of course, part of their ethical restlessness came directly from their culture's secularism, a point that illustrates how these two forms of ethical deprivation might be related. There is often an ethical failure on society's side that the convert reacts against, but there is also a subjective sense of failure on the individual's part, often because society is not offering an adequate ideology to quell this dissatisfaction.

This definition of deprivation is broad enough to account for most unresolved value conflicts that people suffer once a prevailing moral code fails them. This turn from conventional norms grounds sociology's concept of turning in religious change. When the conflicts are resolved, deprivation tends to be replaced by indignant or resentful attitudes toward the moral evil, as in converts' tendency to reinterpret their pasts.[26] To the Protestant theological milieu ethical deprivation needs little substantiation because, in its limited fashion, the concept interprets the Reformation itself as ignited by Martin Luther's dissatisfaction with the Roman penitential system. Glock comments: "Many great religious innovators, such as Luther . . . seem to have been motivated

---

25. Glock, "The Role of Deprivation," 28. See also Toch, *The Social Psychology of Social Movements*, 117–20. Toch found that the essence of religious change or social re-affiliation is disillusionment.

26. Travisano, "Alternation and Conversion," 601, notes: "The father sees his bachelorhood as youthful fun; the convert sees his as debauchery."

primarily by a sense of deprivation stemming from their ethical conflicts with society—an inability to lead their lives according to their own lights."[27] Glock overlooks, however, the intensely personal and even ultimate (i.e., life and death) form of this struggle as well as the struggle against prevailing norms. Specifically: "Biel's concept of a *synteresis* that preserved a spark of goodness—a foothold for human powers to move toward God—caused [Luther] to stumble over the demand to do his best."[28] This example again highlights the relationship between the two forms of ethical deprivation. Luther's struggle was certainly a personal one in which he struggled against his own ability to find and live up to an ideal, but it led to a struggle against the prevailing norms (e.g., the penitential system) that failed to supply adequate means to quell his deprivation. This example demonstrates the sociological principle that deprivation (especially ethical) is alleviated by a change in theology, that the theology plays a significant role in turning people, and that conversion is impossible without an adequate object toward which to turn.

Though an abstract social theory (that ideology causes change in the deprived), it does not detract from religious faith's richness but rather honors how rich faith's content can be, which in part explains its allure. To bring vividness, the American missionary David Brainerd illustrates the struggle between ethical deprivation and relief. In his case, the struggle is an extreme example of this deprivation's personal side, not resulting from inadequate societal values imposing themselves on him but of his inability to find righteousness before God. The inability is a result of the theology at hand that must be countered by a better theology. He eventually turns away from his picture of a wrathful God toward a merciful God:

> Sometime in the beginning of winter, 1738, it pleased God, one Sabbath morning, as I was walking out for prayer, to give me on a sudden such a sense of my *danger*, and the wrath of God, that I stood amazed, and my formerly good frames presently vanished. From the view which I had of my sin and vileness, I was much distressed all that day, fearing that the vengeance of God would soon overtake me.

27. Glock and Stark, *Religion and Society in Tension*, 248.
28. Kolb, *Martin Luther*, 64.

> It was the sight of *truth* concerning myself, *truth* respecting my state, as a creature fallen and alienated from God, and that consequently could make no demands on God for mercy, but must subscribe to the absolute sovereignty of the divine Being; the sight of the *truth*, I say, my soul shrank away from, and thus trembled to think of beholding.
>
> I felt myself in a new world, and every thing about me appeared with a different aspect from what it was wont to do. At this time, the *way of salvation* opened to me with such infinite wisdom, suitableness, and excellency, and I wondered I should ever think of any other way of salvation.[29]

Viewed from the convert's perspective, doctrine appears as a transforming power, evident in the quote's second paragraph in which Brainerd recounts his sight of truth. Change's motivational factors can never be isolated into percentages on a pie chart such that ideology should be expected to account for a specific slice. Rather, accounts such as Brainerd's demonstrate theology's multifaceted role in providing categories to understand ethical deprivation's cause and solution but also to cause deprivation with a certain concept of God's wrath against sinners. For him theology clarified deprivation, increased it, and then alleviated it in time.[30]

If Christianity is fundamentally about recognizing the world's fallenness and the christological means of redemption, then ethical deprivation is sociology's closest description of the redemption experience in which people sense their helplessness before God and turn to Christ. Glock's point that deprivation involves shifting ideology is helpful to show that God's word does not only convict individual selves but calls into question any theology that is not from Christ. It clarifies not only individuals' fallenness but the worldly structures or values that often serve as the idols that converts reject in embracing their new life.[31] This

---

29. Kerr and Mulder, *Famous Conversions*, 72–79. Quotes are from his journal from 1738–39.

30. George Lindbeck's influential thesis (in *The Nature of Doctrine*) that language forms thought is right, in part. We see theology forming Brainerd's religious struggle most definitely, but in this two year period to which he attributes his transformation, theology's interpretive power is many times subservient to his emotions. Theology's power to comfort him amid sin had no effect until he began to experience the "excellency" of salvation.

31. Note, for instance, 1 Cor 1:20, "Has not God made foolish the wisdom of the world?"

The Lure of Ideology

point catches the correlational tension that theology has not fulfilled its task simply by providing a better ideology among options. Theology indeed interprets ethical deprivation within its scriptural narrative (explaining moral outrage's root in sin and redemption in Christ), giving deprivation a better secondary theology, but ultimately conversion begins in realizing that no human-formulated ideologies or theologies can save (a realization effected through primary theology). So far as ethical deprivation helps to cancel human idols, then it cannot be considered unfortunate but a necessary moment in conversion's realization.

Because ethical deprivation most closely parallels theology's agenda, the other types of deprivation must, in some form, be treated in its light so that converts understand the ultimate sources of sin and redemption. Theologians will continually be tempted to address deprivation on its own terms, thus aligning theology directly with personal comforts and political kinds of agendas, but the correlational method distinguishes sociological relief from freedom from sin.[32] The church should recognize that theology's subjective benefits such as ethical satisfaction and the comfort of sensing meaning amid deprivations cannot ground salvation, but these social functions of theology still draw individuals into a community where faith is possible and begin to self-authenticate the church's message. When considered purely in terms of communicating the gospel, theology's job is thus to show the ethical dimension of all deprivation/ideology struggles and to address them via the biblical narrative of redemption history. Though assenting to a theology of ethical deprivation cannot save in itself, it will provide the gospel a contact point.

Because this book focuses most centrally on conversion and the salvation theology crucial to it, it is indeed biased toward soteriology, perhaps to the detriment of other spiritual needs. Though conversion itself happens as a single event, this phenomenon does not comprise the whole story of religious change, which is the process of deepening the human commitment to Christ and its implications for life. Part of the responsibility for religious change is personal, when individuals make efforts to learn and to seek a more Christian way of existing. But the

---

32. If theology addresses deprivations on their own terms, then gospel proclamation will lose out to particular agendas such as liberationist, pacifist, political, or "green" motifs. The ideologies that often intersect with Christian worldviews, though potentially good, are unable to replace the gospel.

other responsibility emphasized more here is the church's, to use whatever resources it has to care for its members.

In chapter 3 I noted that, in response to various emotional crises, the church should care for converts by employing the different resources from its theology that might best speak to each kind of crisis. In this chapter on deprivation, it bears mentioning that a similar rule might apply. Though Christ is the criterion of conversion (and in one sense converts will always have to sense the right problem to get the right solution), the specific forms of deprivation provide a clue as to which resources the church might employ to cultivate the religious change side of embracing a new faith.

With these considerations in mind (viz., that deprivations can be translated into ethical for conveying the gospel but can also be addressed specifically through the church's other resources to foster religious change) we can turn to economic deprivation and begin to ask how the gospel might address it and also consider which other resources in theology's tradition might care for the economically deprived.

ECONOMIC DEPRIVATION

Though the gospel demands an ethical deprivation/alleviation of sorts, this theological requirement cannot exhaust the reasons why people are drawn to Christianity. We have already seen the third type, *economic deprivation*, in discussing Karl Marx. This type predicts that converts will be members of a relatively low economic status, meaning that a lack of worldly satisfactions will create the desire to seek life's supernatural valuation. Naturally, theology's appeal is its esteem for the poor: "Has not God chosen the poor in the eyes of the world to be rich in faith and to inherit the kingdom?"[33] While earthly wealth is subject to ruin, the scriptures encourage the storing of "treasures in heaven, where moth and rust do not destroy, and where thieves do not break in and steal."[34] Though these passages do not reel impoverished people in like a fishing line, they show the Bible's appeal in granting the poor dignity as part of God's cherished creation even if many cultures devalue them on the rack of financial productivity.

33. Jas 2:25.
34. Matt 6:20.

Marx's thesis that economic strain between the rich and poor is the fundamental social force influenced twentieth-century sociology, and though Niebuhr did not accept Marx's materialism, he researched this strain in "the churches of the disinherited." Among them he named the Anabaptists, Quakers, Methodists, and Salvation Army—groups that grew dissatisfied with religion's mainstream compromise to culture and sought a more radical organizing ethos.[35] The commonality between these groups is not only their proletariat status but their formation around a countercultural message to which members ascribe because of conviction rather than inheritance. Naturally a transforming moment or experience becomes highly valued as a mark of new members' awakening to the group's ideals. The high cost of membership supplies a high sense of importance in the group's doctrine that unifies true believers in their attraction to the movement. Membership based on loose affiliation, a roster, or country citizenship cannot count; only community with the estranged margin and their beliefs can. And evangelism and recruitment of new members, finally, takes precedence over maintenance of an existing church body. Niebuhr thought that historically this path is the only one to vibrant religion and that the Christianity of his day had deteriorated to offer no high tension religion as early American sectarianism had. Glock explains the syndrome: "Thrift, frugality, and industry are highly valued. Over time their ideology helps to elevate sect members to middle-class statuses which in turn socialize them to middle-class values."[36] In sum, this early deprivation theory maintains that though tension between faith and society is hard to maintain, sects in tension with society's dominant values are most in a position to reach out interpersonally to society's marginalized.

Though the early theory can be improved, economic deprivation theory has helped to interpret religious changes that occur in the greater context of social friction between classes. In religious circumstances revolts happen that result in radical value reorientation (in the deprived members) even if people do not literally blow up factories or storm corporate offices. Their revolution is symbolic in which: "The latent resentment against society tends to be expressed in an ideology which rejects

---

35. Niebuhr, *Social Sources of Denominationalism*, 28.
36. Glock and Stark, *Religion and Society in Tension*, 244.

A Theology of Religious Change

and radically devalues the society. Thus, for those in the movement, the society is symbolically transformed."[37]

Pronounced cases of religious revolution or sect formation tend to attract study, but their salience need not imply that symbolic transformation of society is always revolutionary. Though little empirical research exists to broaden this topic,[38] a Gallup Poll expands the principle.[39] Testing people's responses to the question of how important religion is to their daily lives, Steve Crabtree and Brett Pelham found that in 143 countries where income is $2,000 or less, 92 percent of residents esteem religion highly as opposed to 44 percent in wealthier nations (salaries $25,000 or above). The poll included diverse religions, many from African and South Asian nations such as Myanmar and Bangladesh, showing that doctrinal particularity did not appear to matter more than social class. Because the survey allowed respondents to self-define religion, it reveals little about which ideologies appeal to impoverished peoples. The results express a minimal core of insight, however, that material comforts appear to have a distracting effect from religion so long as religion comprises a faith system offering intangible benefits. Though religion's appeal to the economically deprived is, as Niebuhr found, potentially revolutionary, it still need not have this volatile character. Whether or not the church should follow liberation theology in Gustavo Gutiérrez's style cannot be derived from the data, but the data show that radical revolution is not necessary to address economic deprivation.[40]

Another study clarifies the empirical status of this point because it demonstrates the relationship between economic deprivation and religious change for certain members within a church of mixed (low and middle) class. William Bainbridge encourages: "The Christian

---

37. Glock, "The Role of Deprivation," 29–30.

38. An early exception demonstrating deprivation in sect members is Demerath, *Social Class in American Protestantism*.

39. See Crabtree and Pelham, "Religion Provides Emotional Boost to World's Poor."

40. The charter text of liberation theology is Gustavo Gutiérrez's *A Theology of Liberation*. Gutiérrez outlines a political agenda to enlist the church's help in liberating the poor because of God's preferential choice of the poor. This point marks a contrast from this study, which does not prescribe action or agenda but fills out a theologically and sociologically informed basis from where the church must decide its own course of action.

The Lure of Ideology

tradition has been particularly strong in bridging the gap between the relatively deprived and the advantaged classes."[41] He and Rodney Stark researched Christian sects from four urban counties in Northern California that comprised multiple socio-economic representations. Bainbridge found that though the different classes worshiped together, there was a marked difference in how they came to join the groups.[42] Contrasting adult converts with socialized members who were raised religious, Stark and Bainbridge found that in categories of education, income, subjective perception of class, and occupational prestige (white/blue collar distinctions), the adult converts were consistently less economically successful in terms of actual income and perceived social status. Though this study cannot directly prove that economically deprived converts are drawn in by ideology, it empirically corroborates this principle while demonstrating that, contrary to Niebuhr, religious groups accommodating the poor need not be radical break-off splinters from a mainstream church.

What more can be concluded than: "it is easier for a camel to go through the eye of a needle than for a rich man to enter the kingdom of God"?[43] Though God redeems rich and poor alike, sociology indicates that to this day the poor are more open to religion than the rich. Perhaps material comforts cloud our sensitivity to spiritual realities. In either case, theology's task in communicating the gospel is to deprive and alleviate all spirits, rich or poor, by demonstrating humanity's need for grace. The caveat is that the poor might be more likely to begin listening, especially if they find the dignity Christ gives to all of his children regardless of social status.

It is also important to acknowledge here that this dignity (i.e., the poor's sense of value of their lives) need not come down to converts purely as a theological ideal. Part of the church's ability to minister to the economically deprived and instill Christ's dignity in them must come in caring for their concrete needs. As well as its spiritual value, theology should inspire help more concretely. Giving tithe money and

---

41. Bainbridge, "The Sociology of Conversion," 181.

42. The sect groups were Church of God, Churches of Christ, Nazarene, Assemblies of God, Seventh-Day Adventist, Gospel Lighthouse, and Four-square Gospel. See Stark and Bainbridge, *The Future of Religion*, 158.

43. Matt 19:24.

donating time to feed and care for people are perhaps the most common means in which the church reaches out to the economically deprived. Donating time and energy to help the poor find meaningful employment is an even greater way to convey Christ's love. Though instilling the gospel in its members is the church's ultimate purpose, this purpose might only speak to certain people if they witness the church's love in providing for their material needs. If the church shares the reasons for its care with potential converts, they will eventually be able to trust God as the church's inspiration and reason for existence rather than trusting in the church itself.

SOCIAL AND HEALTH DEPRIVATION

So far psychic, ethical, and economic deprivations have helped explain social reasons why people are drawn to a group specifically because of its message. In research past and present they are the most substantiated types. Glock mentions two other types of deprivation that broaden the definition, though they apply less to ideological resolution. *Social deprivation* involves religious re-affiliation to gain social advantage (e.g., prestige), and *organismic (health) deprivation* involves seeking to cure a psychological or physical malady.[44]

Social deprivation complicates a simple notion of ideological attraction because it predicts that people convert not because of doctrine's self-authentication to them but because of a social advantage in being affiliated with a particular creed. In cases such as ethical deprivation, converts often break away from the mainstream to higher tension sects that pit ideology against social status. In social deprivation the opposite might occur, that religious re-affiliation itself could furnish a more privileged social status. A common example of this syndrome is marriages where one potential spouse appears socially lacking next to the other family's religious standards. Full acceptance into the family requires the person's turn to the family's religion. In these cases, suspicion of motives is especially easy to sense because of the change's obvious material advantages. Though marriage is commonly social deprivation's context

---

44. See Glock, "The Role of Deprivation," 27–28. A more important type of social deprivation is the lack of a social network or friends. That topic demands its own consideration next chapter.

it need not be. One famous case is composer Gustav Mahler's change to Catholicism, apparently quite controversial.[45] In 1897, when he was offered the directorship of the Vienna Opera, he was unable to take the position as a religious Jew. Though he was not particularly religious, his change to Catholicism facilitated the transition to his new post.

Though religious change due to social advantage elicits suspicion of motives, it is helpful to balance this problem (and stay faithful to the correlational method) to recognize that social advantage resulting form religious re-affiliation cannot somehow disqualify a person's faith. All people who believe in Christ have motives for entering the church that are not always and only concerned with their relationship to God. Chapter 6 will discuss at length how the church's social manifestation is inextricable to its identity, a theme that will more fully explain the great importance of social deprivations and how theology addresses them. Until then we recognize this type of social motivation simply as a possible instance of deprivation that the church is called to address by loving its converts regardless of how suspect their reasons for affiliating are.

Like social deprivation, organismic deprivation spurs motion toward a specific end—healing. This category is the least substantiated from available empirical reports and therefore the most hypothetical. Glock found it in the rise of psychoanalysis and faith healing within the Episcopal Church, Father Divine, and Christian Science movements.[46] Obviously, use of psychoanalysis does not make converts in any dramatic sense, and even in a religious context Glock admits that organismic deprivation is a limited explanation for a movement's appeal. Nevertheless, if people experience healing from religious intervention either first hand or closely second hand, this witness would no doubt verify a group's claims to divine power and ground its appeal. In my experience with a Pentecostal school, some of the teachers and students had experienced radical healing in their transition to the faith. From their perspective, freeing oneself from unhealthy psychological or chemical dependencies and espousing a Christian theology were not particularly separable. The body and soul are redeemed together. Though Glock separated kinds of deprivation for analysis, he never claimed their purity. Organismic deprivation is one example that especially illustrates

45. See Steinberg, *The Symphony*, 277.
46. Glock, "The Role of Deprivation," 31.

A Theology of Religious Change

how different kinds could be linked so that people can experience them simultaneously (e.g., ethical and organismic) or one can become another quickly (e.g., illness can quickly become an ethical or psychic deprivation when seen in a religious context). What person in physical pain has not also been outraged at the universe for allowing it?

More types of deprivation and ideological response exist, but the evidence so far favors psychic, ethical, and economic strains as the most common, aside from the deprivation of a social network, which we shall discuss in the next chapter. The general principle is that ideological needs influence change, and the types show the varieties of these needs. Glock and Stark conclude: "We suggest that a necessary precondition for the rise of any organized social movement, whether it be religious or secular, is a situation of felt deprivation. However, while a necessary condition, deprivation is not, in itself, a sufficient condition. Also required are the additional conditions that the deprivation be shared, that no alternative institutional arrangements for its resolution are perceived, and that a leadership emerge with an innovating idea for building a movement out of the existing deprivation."[47]

This description fits this study's contention that religious change has several causal layers amid which deprivation plays a role. Though a necessary condition, it is not sufficient. To recognize that all people suffer deprivations at various times and few are compelled to join new religions cuts off the groundwork for theologians to construct a specific action plan for finding the most vulnerable potential converts. However, deprivation theory clarifies a human phenomenon that theology should address in its entire audience, converts and all. If theology transforms deprivations into an ethical type within the Christian narrative, showing how they draw our attention to the gospel, then it will use sociology's insight in the gospel's service. If people are drawn in because this message speaks to them, then it illustrates Glock's thesis. The important counterpoint to this gospel-driven effort is that the church overlooks sociology's usefulness if it relies only on an ethical deprivation.[48] Though the gospel is indeed the church's ultimate purpose, addressing individual deprivations on a human level (e.g., by supporting ill peoples' healing or giving social warmth) is inextricable from the

---

47. Glock and Stark, *Religion and Society in Tension*, 249.
48. I owe Dr. David Maxwell for this nuance.

church's ministry of the gospel itself. So long as the church continues to make known the inspiration of its actions, those actions themselves communicate Christ.

The next section, on religious practice, will help to illustrate this theme—how *real life interaction* with a church is a condition of religious belief. Though Glock did not presuppose that ideologies are purely cognitive in form, he underemphasized their practical manifestation in life. The next section adds this facet to our discussion of ideology: that a *behavioral dimension* is also important in religious groups' appeal. We have already seen in chapter 2 how embracement of a convert role is one mark of religious change. Here is an opportunity to revisit that theme in more detail.

The Sociological Function of Practice

A caricature of this chapter's claims would draw the convert as a frustrated person lacking purpose in life and possibly material comforts, who happens upon a group that provides a tract on which is printed a new creed that, if believed, will put frustrations to rest and provide life's purpose. A glancing view of deprivation/ideology might detect this wooden portrayal, but it would translate the story inaccurately. Western thought typically separates thought/action, belief/practice, ideology/ethics, and though the conceptual distinctions are legitimate, the real-time relationship between ideology and action is much less dichotomized. Ideology is never isolated thought, nor would a religious group want it to be. Pure intellectual assent to facts or ideas cannot produce a living faith. Faith tenets, after all, do not merely exist but take place amid action that forms and clarifies their meaning, and this belief/action relationship takes place in social movements organized around particular creeds. Obscure as organismic deprivation appeared above, it importantly demonstrates that sometimes a change in action (e.g., participation in healing rituals) precedes and forms change in belief.[49]

---

49. Among Lofland and Skonovd's "Conversion Motifs," four of the six motifs show participation in a religion as a precursor to belief.

A Theology of Religious Change

The Good Hypocrisy: How Living a Faith Might Precede Believing It

Christianity's theological tradition is not completely alien to the idea that behavior change precedes belief. Blaise Pascal, for instance, recommended that "behaving just as if [you] believed, taking holy water, having masses said, etc. . . . will make you believe quite naturally, and according to your animal reactions."[50] Similarly, when Dietrich Bonhoeffer confronted cheap grace, the problem of taking God's forgiveness for granted, he concluded: "faith is only real when there is obedience, never without it, and faith only becomes faith in the act of obedience."[51] Though God judges the heart, certain life practices are more conducive to faith development than others. For Pascal the ethical life begins to hammer the heart into shape and for Bonhoeffer obedience to Christ makes faith possible. Theologians would be right to sense danger in this thinking if it begins to ground the gospel in moral aspiration, but so long as the good hypocrisy is considered on the sociological level it helps to clarify the matter into which the Spirit breathes, so to speak. The mystery of flat, dead obedience is that though it cannot purchase the Spirit's indwelling into one's heart, it may place the heart in a sacramental context outside of which faith is impossible.

In this sparsely researched facet of religion a few sociologists have demonstrated a hypocrisy that can precede belief. During the high tide of new religious movements in America sudden religious change became common under certain groups' influence. New converts exhibited such drastic changes in speech and behavior that concerned parents and friends instigated a brainwashing controversy through the 1970s and beyond. The question revolved around how much cults could alienate people from their wills and control their thought. The controversy has not been resolved. Esoteric religious sects inevitably elicit brainwashing speculation from the mainstream. But some sympathetic studies have demonstrated that these sudden changes indicate much less a manipulated mind than a new religious role—new behavior but hardly a heart commitment. Role playing's influence would then be like learning a new game and behaving like a player but not undergoing a significant shift in values.

50. Pascal, *Pensées*, 156.
51. Bonhoeffer, *Discipleship*, 64.

Sociologist Robert Balch's undercover operation in an Oregon cult revealed to him that assumption of the group's theology was possible only if people associated with the group long enough to learn and process the leaders' teachings, but the behavioral change was quite sudden. "Sometimes," he notes, "dramatic behavioral changes occurred even before indoctrination began."[52] In his observations, the members refrained from games, music, smoking, and drinking, and they began to talk in the group's vocabulary. Because he and other members were continually deceived by behavior that was inconsistent with people's true beliefs and level of commitment, Balch determined that *role theory* best applied to his study of the Oregon group. Members were not brainwashed; if anything they were "behavior-washed." The group's prescribed role took over quickly for new converts but changed their minds only through continued socialization. "The boundless faith of the true believer usually develops only after lengthy involvement in the cult's day-to-day activities," Balch concluded. "Some members go for months without ever resolving their doubts, yet they may still appear fully committed because outwardly they are acting in the way they are expected to act."[53]

Around the same time University of Texas sociologists David Bromley and Anson Shupe produced similar results to Balch's in studying the mature Unification Church.[54] Testing role theory on forty-two converts helped them to clarify how people come to embrace a new ideology. They admit: "Concern with theology, the logical expectations of belief, and the consistency between ideals and actions have not characterized much of the psychological literature on conversion,"[55] however they believe that role theory clarifies theology's transforming role not just in attracting members (as Glock found) but in forming them. Unification theology taught that the world's end was near and only escapable through belief in the church's message in a messianic second coming. Though similar to Christianity, the group registered a strong

---

52. Balch, "Looking Behind the Scenes in a Religious Cult," 140.

53. Ibid., 143.

54. Bromley and Shupe, "A Role Theory Approach to Participation in Religious Movements," 159–85. By mature is meant that the church's evangelistic methods were more refined in its second decade of existence.

55. Ibid., 165.

sense of eschatological tension that grounded all members' vocation to be evangelists.

Bromley and Shupe found that converts were initially attracted to the group through what is sometimes called "social drift"[56] or searching around to fulfill certain deprivations of meaning, family, and friendship. Specifically, attractions to the group's theology, the community itself, or a particular person were the three biggest motivators.[57] However, attraction cannot fully explain change just as becoming a boxing fan does not necessarily explain how one becomes a fighter. The convert's formation rather occurred in becoming a deployable agent serving the church's message. Theology's importance is evident in determining both a dogmatic basis for specific action and the evangelist's message—a mission and a message.

It would be wrong to limit the church's role only to evangelism, however much they stressed it. The role extended deeper to communal and familial dimensions as well as the public missionary role. Together the church followed a rigorous schedule that began at 6:00 a.m. and ended after 11:00 at night. It included meals, chores, witnessing, discussion, and prayer. Like the military or the monastic tradition, the group cared for individual needs while limiting individual autonomy. In its family dimension, the group's theology inspired a fraternal atmosphere in which members followed strict celibacy rules and rather viewed each other as brothers and sisters, all of which fostered their communal faith.[58]

Certainly this role playing pressure tends to manufacture hypocrites, but sometimes religion's behavioral dimension can lead to a true change in heart. Bromley and Shupe found that the group's success was abnormally high simply because they expanded their role expectations for all members to the extent that the church's way of life became even the pretender's way of life. There was little room for the "Sunday

---

56. Long and Hadden. "Religious Conversion and the Concept of Socialization," 1–14.

57. Bromley and Shupe, "A Role Theory Approach," 171.

58. Ibid., 176, "It is apparent that new members acted out these feelings of sibling love to a far greater extent than their personal feelings could conceivably warrant . . . Such behavior can be interpreted as the result of normative expectations within the group and is better understood as role-connected rather than as spontaneously motivated."

Christian," because every day was Sunday in effect, and the church's doctrine and practice were very difficult to avoid once inside the door. Though the role demanded much, it returned much by bringing meaning, order, and friendship to members' lives.

Not everything that Bromley and Shupe discovered translates to Christian theology, but they do give an express view of faith and behavior's relationship that could be valuable in any religion. A church will better maintain its members' faith if it impacts many dimensions of their lives, which might turn out to be the best answer to psychic deprivations discussed above.

If Christian theology is to appropriate this insight for overcoming psychic deprivation (viz., that action grounds belief), the challenge is more complex than it is for the Unification Church because it must determine how to inspire the church to carry out concrete actions such as retreats, service projects, and evangelism without making their members' Christian identity contingent on doing these things. As mentioned above, theology calls these actions "civil" or "horizontal" righteousness, works inspired by faith but not determinative of salvation. The difference in the Christian church is that it tells its members, in effect: "We encourage you to participate in these works because they are spiritually nourishing for you and your neighbors, but if you do not want to, then neither God nor we love you less." If this horizontal righteousness is not confused with God's righteousness, then it frees the church to carry out belief-building actions in a different spirit than those religions that fail to live in the gospel's freedom.

Additional Theological Implications

These sociological insights into belief and practice provide definite glimpses of what religion offers to human life. In their theory of religion, Stark and Bainbridge develop the concept of religion as providing *supernatural compensators*, promises of intangible rewards that demand response in belief, ethics, and practice but cannot be realized in cash value.[59] They distinguished religious doctrine from *magic* that

---

59. Stark and Bainbridge, *A Theory of Religion*, 36; "Toward a Theory of Religion," 114–28. Stark later felt that the term "supernatural compensators" should be replaced with "other-worldly rewards."

seeks tangible benefits by manipulating the universe. Though Stark and Bainbridge did not write for Christianity's edification, their distinction is important to clarify that theology best serves its function when it centers on a lifestyle informed by the gospel and its hope. The more it emphasizes tangible rewards (e.g., social benefits, entertainment, therapy, prosperity), the less it functions as bearer of a divine word and the more as either a magical supplier of commodities or (from Glock's research) as simply another ideology among many, however satisfying.

Tension results in acknowledging that Christianity should not manipulate the universe for specific ends but also knowing that religious community always supports personal interests—religion does provide one's life with meaning, order, and friends. On righteousness's horizontal plane, these tangible rewards are not necessarily against the gospel, but the tension arises in that these things cannot ground faith and might even distract from it. Yet, as much as they distract the church from grace, they also bring people to the sacramental context where all idols die. Grace's very mystery is that it reaches people through their attraction to magic and social rewards, the very things that might cause them to pull away from it. To say that God works through means finally indicates that redemption cannot escape working through corrupt subjects who confess their fallenness in every liturgy. However, this cyclical repentance does not imply that all theologies are permissible so long as their errors are repented. The church can surely operate at different levels of theological and practical soundness. If it begins to neglect its primary theological identity, then it also ceases to function as the church and begins to compete in a market directly with secular organizations and therapists. But if it does not understand how theology appeals to people, then it will fail to speak. The central question arises: How can theology communicate soundly and effectively without diluting its message?

In 1932, pastoral theology professor John Fritz faced this same question, instructing aspiring preachers that proclamatory incompetence would impede the Spirit's efficacy,[60] and the task remains today for theologians to define and learn what he called "competence." The difficulty that pastors face now, as always, is to determine the meaning and limits of their responsibility in communicating the gospel. The

---

60. Fritz, *Pastoral Theology*, 97.

fundamental tension cannot be undone: that even though God acts monergistically (that is, his actions are not contingent on human cooperation), this monergism does not lessen the preacher's responsibility to communicate the gospel faithfully to the audience. Thus, the question remains to ask what proclamatory competence entails, so that the church can create an environment where faith is possible.

From a sociological perspective, competence would be a quantifiable result. The pastor would need to find the most effective way to reach deprived people and address their deprivations with a theology tailor-made to sparkle to them. A prosperity gospel might appeal to the economically deprived, or a message of social respectability might lure in the socially deprived. To take this angle with Fritz would be to say the Spirit himself is quantifiable in terms of the church's ostensible success in gaining numbers, something Fritz would surely repudiate. From this study's correlational method, immersion in the gospel message has to be the criterion of success. The mere fact of church growth might easily indicate good advertising. But competence much more concerns the gospel taking root in people's beings, and that cannot be quantified empirically, nor can it occur if the message is cluttered by ulterior messages that appeal to culture at large.

To say: "Be faithful to the gospel!" is not a platitude, however. The other side of competence is to influence actual lives by addressing them effectively. To stand in front of a congregation and dryly read sermons from a hundred years past might have the gospel, but it would not likely speak to the people or catch the fallen matter through which God works redemption. Sociology reveals definite needs that doctrine fills (especially ethical, meaning-providing, and roles), and the theologian must address these needs to convey the gospel successfully. The theologian must know what people need to hear, but theology must also translate people's desires into the biblical story so that it may communicate to deprivations from the broader narrative of redemption. If the reader takes nothing else away from this chapter: *Communication and faithfulness are less a matter of form or performance and more of finding content that especially reaches lives.*

The research into role theory also demonstrates that to develop lasting faith and commitment, people have to embody a theologically based role in the church's operations. Stark and Bainbridge's distinction between religious belief and magic needs this balance, that faith manifests itself not only in redemptive hope but also in ethical and even behavioral orientations. Self-authenticating faith cannot arise out of mere academic instruction but must germinate in pervasive life experience.[61]

Ultimately the church cannot take sole responsibility for changing minds, wills, and hearts, for these are the Spirit's task. The church's responsibility lies in caring for people's needs and proclaiming the gospel as directly to these needs as possible, recognizing that success or failure lie less in results than in its faithfulness to be a sacramental community. But because the gospel always falls on real lives and concerns, theology benefits from knowing its audience and the kinds of concerns discoverable by sociology: the need for meaning, an ethically satisfying theology, economic contentment, social wellness, and health. Though humans cannot manipulate the Spirit through doctrinal emphasis or nuance, theology's message will communicate more effectively if it speaks to deprivation.

The research to this point has given many reasons why people might join new religions or change religiously, but it has not yet covered the most important reason in social networks. The church's role has already appeared in discussing parental influence on children or role prescriptions for new members, but now we can focus directly on this most influential social mechanism and its importance for theology.

---

61. Festinger, *Theory of Cognitive Dissonance*, 158, notes, "It is very difficult to change an opinion that already exists if it is consonant with existing behavior or with an existing cluster of attitudes and opinions."

6

The Web of Social Ties

THROUGH OUR STUDY THUS far we have learned a variety of causes and consequences of religious change, but the most powerful factor has not yet received its due credit. Finally we can focus on the relationship building basis that underlies all religion. The central goal is to determine which sociological insights into social networks are the most enduring and thus valuable. The ultimate goal is to determine what theology should make of these insights.

The Church as Mission

When Jesus ordered the church to "make disciples of all nations, baptizing them in the name of the Father, and of the Son, and of the Holy Spirit" and teach them everything he had commanded,[1] he was not simply issuing ecclesial policy but was speaking of the church's very identity. The church is missional in nature, and if it fails to uphold its mission by neglecting to proclaim Jesus to all nations, then it begins to lose that identity.[2] Scripture gives no detailed blueprints for how this goal should be strategized but gives a straightforward theo-logic that God's love for

---

1. Matt 28:19.
2. Bultmann, "Jesus Christus und die Mythologie," 183. Bultmann helps to clarify that the "indicative" of Christian (or church) identity provides the ground for the "imperative" for life under this new identity. The church's missional actions and spirit are not arbitrary commands but stem from the church's very calling into existence, to reflect God's kingdom and glory and take care of his creatures.

the church, while distinct from inter-human love, entails loving one's neighbor.³ God's love is the motivation and the message of evangelism in whatever acts and words comprise it. If the gospel is the criterion of religious change that illuminates change with proper orientation and significance, then love is conversely a criterion of the church's role in shaping converts to a new way of believing and acting.

In order to spread the gospel and thus fulfill its missional identity, the church will benefit from studying the social context to which it speaks. The principle is simple: if people are to *teach* effectively then they must know something about how people *learn*. The sociological perspective of the church's role in cultivating religious change cannot determine the validity of its mission—that is theology's job. But it can help to clarify the human side of a religion's growth. The church's social influence plays a supportive role in every person's conversion, and though interpersonal bonds with Christians cannot ground anyone's salvation (i.e., I am not saved through my friends' faith), studying these interpersonal networks helps to illuminate a very basic reason why people begin to find themselves in a faith-enabling, sacramental encounter. In accounting for network sociology, the church can think more critically about how God's love speaks to converts though the community. Perhaps the purest brand of evangelistic wisdom is that which expresses the necessity of human outreach but the limitations of human action to take the Spirit's place, the vitality of proclamation yet our inability to manipulate the word. In studying the sociology of religious networks, this study will outline what ministry can and must accomplish but also that for which it must wait on God.

The Roots of Late Conversion Sociology

Sociology's most helpful insights into religious affiliation come from Rodney Stark and his colleagues, whose work in this area is broadly influential.⁴ A chronological approach will not only explain his view's endurance but also demonstrate which theoretical elements

---

3. Mark 12:31–33; Luke 10:27; Rom 13:9; Gal 5:14; Jas 2:8.

4. Shinn, "The Conversion/Brainwashing Controversy," 202, notes: "There are few articles on conversion published in the area of sociology that have wider readership or a greater number of citations."

have particularly withstood challenges and repeated tests in different contexts.

Lofland and Stark's Early Realization

The story begins in the early 1960s when Stark and his classmate John Lofland were graduate students at the University of California, Berkeley. By popular characterizations it would be difficult to imagine a richer environment for sociologists of religion to make their start than the San Francisco Bay area during the 1960s. Lofland and Stark sifted through the area's well-stocked variety of new religious groups to determine an adequate object of study, a group small enough to be monitored by a few students yet growing by recruiting new members. Their task was simply to determine why people would embrace deviant worldviews. Until that point sociology had relied heavily upon deprivation/ideology theory as discussed last chapter. Though this theory has a substantial sociological basis, Lofland and Stark doubted early on that it could exhaustively explain affiliation with esoteric cults because it places too heavy an explanatory burden on a single condition amid complex circumstances.[5] Research would soon prove this hunch, that conditions such as deprivation or its cousins *strain* and *tension* do not distinguish converts from controls and thus fail to predict religious change.[6] Lofland and Stark decided to see for themselves and began to affiliate with an early division of the Unification Church (UC) under leadership of Dr. Young Oon Kim, a former religion professor at Seoul, Korea's Ewha University.[7] By watching the process first-hand, they hoped to gain insights that previous studies had missed.

Their observation's results are summarized in what became a famous article.[8] The "world-saver" model of change as they called it laid

---

5. Recall this statement from Glock and Stark, *Religion and Society in Tension*, 249, at around the same time: "We suggest that a necessary precondition for the rise of any organized social movement, whether it be religious or secular, is a situation of felt deprivation. However, while a necessary condition, deprivation is not, in itself, a sufficient condition."

6. See Heirich, "Change of Heart," 653–80.

7. A detailed account of this group's attempts and failures to add to its numbers is available from John Lofland, *Doomsday Cult*.

8. See Lofland and Stark, "Becoming a World-Saver," 862–75.

out a *value added* scheme of seven steps in which each step increases the likelihood of change but only the process of undergoing all seven virtually guarantees a total shift in personal religious orientation. A person must: "1. Experience enduring, acutely felt tensions 2. within a religious problem-solving perspective, 3. which leads him to define himself as a religious seeker; 4. encountering the D.P. [UC] at a turning point in his life, 5. wherein an affective bond is formed (or pre-exists) with one or more converts; 6. where extra-cult attachments are absent or neutralized; 7. and, where, if he is to become a deployable agent, he is exposed to intensive interaction."[9]

At first glance the significance of these seven steps is not apparent. They are actually divisible into two, quite different prescriptions. The first set that discusses tensions, seekership, and a turning point (1–4) are all predispositional factors intended to outline a person's susceptibility to religious change.[10] The second set that begins with forming an affective bond (5–7) discloses situational conditions—actually being exposed to evangelists—without which joining a specific group would be impossible. This world-saver model became classic because it offered, though in embryonic form, a new level of sophistication to the question. Though virtually all of its steps are challenged from one angle or another, its focus on predispositional and situational factors within a context of radical change set a new research standard. Though Lofland and Stark bowed to traditional deprivation theory, they added that religious change becomes possible through specific affective bonds. After all: "no one in a Billy Graham crusade has converted to Buddhism."[11] Predispositional factors explain very little about attaining new religious life unless they have direct exposure to that life in others. Especially Lofland, who actually lived in the UC house for a time, observed that the greater exposure to Dr. Kim and other believers tended to predict

---

9. Ibid., 874. It is fair to ask if affiliation with cults is really comparable to affiliation in mainstream religious bodies. Indeed, there are some differences such as step 6 would not be as necessary to join a less exclusive religious body. In general, however, sociologists have valued this model for viewing diverse religious changes even to mainstream groups.

10. These kinds of predispositional factors are covered in chapters 3–5 using psychological research that provides more detail than is possible in the Lofland/Stark analysis level.

11. Jerome Frank cited in Ullman, *Transformed Self*, 84.

a greater chance of lasting commitment to the group. After the world-saver model's appearance it became impossible for sociologists to assume an abstract deprivation theory as a sufficient explanation for religious change.

But the world-saver model was based on the study of twenty-one people of whom only fifteen provided full data. Innovative as Lofland and Stark's research methods were, their small sample size and provincially limited study could not be assumed to explain change processes elsewhere. Fortunately several studies have challenged the world-saver model by determining its repeatability in other contexts, and the original authors have also revisited their early work to clarify its strongest aspects.

The World-Saver Model and Its Durability

An early attempt to test world-saver conclusions resulted from Brigham Young researchers John Seggar and Phillip Kunz's analysis of the Mormon Church.[12] They interviewed seventy-seven converts in an urban Kentucky area to determine how well the world-saver model could explain Mormon growth. Finding fewer than 60 percent of participants who experienced predispositional tensions of the kind that the world-savers had, they concluded that though personal crises are relevant to change, they are insufficient to predict it alone. A similar study by University of Michigan sociologist Max Heirich found that 277 Catholic charismatics of Ann Arbor reported stress with 83 percent frequency (23+ percent more than Seggar and Kunz), but at least 66 percent of the controls also reported stress.[13] Because Lofland and Stark did not use controls, their initial research was insensitive to the ubiquity of personal tension. Though it plays a significant role, later studies show its importance as secondary to situational factors. On a scheme of religious change's causes, the individual's psychological predisposition plays less a role than the group and its evangelism.

Seggar and Kunz noted: "It is interesting that our data include only one convert who sought the Church; all the others were proselyted by

12. Seggar and Kunz, "Conversion," 178–84.
13. Heirich, "Change of Heart," 664.

missionaries or other lay members."[14] Technically, 98.7 percent of the converts were drawn into their faith by developing social ties with missionaries formal or informal. The Mormon Church has emphasized evangelism even to the point of prescribing very specific steps to influence one's neighbor. Rather than emphasizing the distinctiveness of their message, many missionaries choose to concentrate first on developing friendships.[15] This emphasis appears in Seggar and Kunz's study, allowing them to disqualify the world-saver model as an adequate explanation. The result is not surprising, however, considering that early UC evangelists stressed their message to a fault (inviting potential converts to lectures, tape-recorded messages, and readings) and were therefore able to convince only an occasional self-defined religious seeker.

Research consistently demonstrates that the early process of obtaining new faith is usually more a matter of heart than of mind, even if intellectual aspects later grow in importance. Faith will always be a matter of committing one's whole being, making the intellectual assent initially sought by the UC appear lacking. More than a decade after the world-saver article Lofland revisited the UC and reported both on the shortcomings of the original publication and the UC development in the meantime. The group: "had learned to start [evangelistic] conversation at the emotional rather than the cognitive level, an aspect they did not thoroughly appreciate in the early sixties."[16] They employed several tactics to catch people at public places and universities and treated them with great hospitality. The UC even purchased a farm to which they took potential converts and "encapsulated" them to assure the influence of what Lofland and Stark called "intensive interaction" (step 7). Intensive interaction is different than, for example, the interaction of a soccer team that must work together to accomplish a goal. Though sports could indeed be one form of it, Lofland speaks primarily about

---

14. Seggar and Kunz, "Conversion," 182–83.

15. E.g., Eberhard, "How to Share the Gospel," 6–13, offers an extremely subtle plan for introducing potential converts to Mormonism. Stark and Bainbridge, "Networks of Faith," 1389, comment: "If we can assume the Mormons know what they are doing—and the fact that they are the most rapidly growing, large religious movement in the United States suggests they surely do—there seems compelling reason for sociologists to accept the theory that interpersonal bonds are the fundamental support for recruitment."

16. Lofland, "'Becoming a World-Saver' Revisited," 809.

"loving," granting each other positive assurance, or flooding newcomers with personal affirmation. "It almost didn't matter what they believed," one convert stated, "if only I could really share myself with them. I think that moment may be exactly the point at which many people decide to join."[17]

Around the same time as Lofland's reassessment, Penn State sociologist Roy Austin tested the world-saver model on nine converts to Campus Crusade and concluded similarly.[18] Of the original seven steps, not one of his subjects fulfilled all of them, but all subjects did succumb to intensive interaction. Austin located these people together because they were all living in a sort of half-way house for lawbreakers rented and run by Crusade. Clearly, predispositional crises/tensions played a role as these converts were formerly in legal troubles, but the most powerful influence in their "born again experience" was the close quarters with Christian evangelists. To live in the house they were required to participate in Bible studies, church services, and communal meals. Even if Austin dismissed the world-saver model's comprehensive explanatory power, he demonstrates its useful structure (to consider predispositional and situational factors) and the importance of its claims about affective bonds. Though a small sample size, Austin's study corroborates Lofland's revisions in a Protestant context and further clarifies the hierarchy of psychosocial influences. By 1980 the recognition of situational influences (viz. social ties) over predispositional was clear. Independently from Lofland, Stark, and his colleague William Bainbridge concluded similarly and began asking how ties and friendships mediate social value to converts and alleviate deprivation in an incarnate rather than purely ideological form.[19] The positive draw of close relationships appeared to be a more powerful factor in religious change than the negative motivations of deprivation. Continual examination of the world-saver model strengthened its best insights and clarified social networks' role.

Originally Lofland and Stark collected general traits of UC members and organized them according to a value added scheme in which

---

17. Ibid., 811–12. Lofland comments: "Indeed, we learn again from looking at the DPs [UC] that love can be the most coercive and cruel power of all."

18. Austin, "Empirical Adequacy of Lofland's Conversion Model," 282–87.

19. Stark and Bainbridge, "Networks of Faith," 1392.

each step was sequentially necessary before the next. The descriptive approach, when enhanced with the value added lens, could then become a causal explanation. But if Lofland and Stark had simply asked what is *necessary* for religious change (thus determining what is merely incidental), their model would be simplified. University of Texas researchers David Snow and Cynthia Phillips essentially asked this question in testing the world-saver model on a form of Japanese Buddhism known as Nichiren Shoshu.[20] They scrutinized the seven steps' presence in about 330 people's testimonies and found that most of them were potential influences on religious change but not in the inexorable sequence first posited of the world-savers. Step 5 (where an affective bond is formed or pre-exists between a cult's insiders and outsiders), however, appeared widespread. About 82 percent of the new Buddhists were brought into the group through relationships that existed independently of their religious association. The remaining 18 percent were recruited by street evangelists with whom they developed affective bonds.[21]

Snow and Phillips concluded that affective bonds are absolutely necessary for religious change and that the amount of intensive interaction significantly influences the chance of commitment. Their unique contribution, aside from expanding the world-saver's testing milieu, is their critique that the original model "ignores . . . that motives for behavior are generally emergent and interactional."[22] Though applied to Nichiren Shoshu, this insight highlights an aspect of religious change crucial to Christian salvation. If fallen human nature will never have a predisposition to love God, then the only possibility of salvation is the emergence of new motives according to the Holy Spirit's intervention. The best that old motives can accomplish is to lead a person into interaction with Christians under the church's sacramental presence, but the motive to trust Christ is an effect, not a preceding cause of salvation. Snow and Phillips's data show that if religious motives emerge, they do so most frequently amid pre-established social ties (friendship and

20. Snow and Phillips, "The Lofland-Stark Conversion Model," 430–47.

21. These numbers raise the question if there were another variable attenuating their predictive force, such as if converts were formed superficially because they were immigrants and religion was incidental to their deeper cultural ties, but as of 1980 the movement had 200,000 members from its evangelistic efforts and about 90 percent were reportedly Occidental.

22. Snow and Phillips, "The Lofland-Stark Conversion Model," 443.

kinship). Their data strongly support affective ties as necessary to religious affiliation, ties that ground the possibility of cultivating new motives much like associating with die hard Cardinals fans might interest someone in baseball's cardinal representation.[23]

While Snow and Phillips researched Nichiren Shoshu, University of Colorado sociologist James Downton studied the Divine Light Mission (a guru-centered Hare Krishna group) with similar aims.[24] He compared the world-saver steps closely to Krishnas and produced a very detailed account of their transformations through ten stages and twenty-seven steps. The attention to phenomenon description rather than theory makes the results questionable as general axioms, but his meticulous method was especially suited to underline the gradualness of religious change.[25] Even in a cult that emphasized immediate enlightenment or spiritual awakening, Downton saw that "spiritual conversion and commitment are very gradual in their development. While conversion does appear to be a sudden change of awareness which can transform a person's identity and perception of reality, radical changes of personality are rare."[26] These studies emphasizing change's gradualness help to distinguish it from theology's demand that God's saving action is "complete in the instant that it is accomplished."[27] The divine act is instantaneous, yet the human process of learning to follow a new theology will take years of interaction with people who are more fluent in it.

In examining the close detail of DLM indoctrination, Downton cast a vote for variety in experiences and predispositional tensions that he felt were classifiable under Lofland and Stark's seven steps. The variety of motivations that lead people to affiliate initially with a religious group are unlimited, but as the world-saver model states, they will

23. Zurcher and Snow, "Collective Behavior," 463, comment: "Just as successful businesses and corporations help create their own demand, so, it appears, do successful movements."

24. Downton, "An Evolutionary Theory of Spiritual Conversion and Commitment," 381–96.

25. In *Conversion in the New Testament*, Richard Peace makes a similar observation in comparing Paul's sudden road to faith with the twelve disciples who are in a constant trial and error process of understanding Jesus.

26. Downton, "An Evolutionary Theory of Spiritual Conversion and Commitment," 382. This point about personality change is strongly confirmed in Paloutzian et al., "Religious Conversion and Personality Change," 1047–79.

27. Meehl et al., *What, Then, Is Man?*, 251.

undoubtedly involve some kind affective bonds through a duration. The task remains for social science to develop a hierarchy to show more definitively which networks are most influential—be they with coworkers, neighbors, or club members, for instance—but the need for social interaction stands. A final study testing Lofland and Stark '65 helps to clarify networks' role. After hearing from these Dutch scholars, Stark will have a chance to explain his mature position thirty-five years later.

"Some twenty years of research have failed to yield adequate empirical evidence for the conversion model developed by Lofland and Stark,"[28] state this group of Utrecht sociologists. In reviewing our trek through the previous studies this claim's overstatement is evident, but these sentiments did motivate Willem Kox, Wim Meeus, and Harm 't Hart to test the model in the Netherlands, broadening its application. They interviewed converts and controls to Pentecostalism and the UC, selecting people who were similar to each other in age, gender, training, social class, and urbanization to allow strict comparison. In interviewing converts, they stressed objective events rather than recollection of past feelings. Step 4 about a life turning point, for instance, was tested by actual changes such as moving or changing jobs rather than remembered feelings. They used Richard Travisano's criterion of "radical change" to test converts who were not merely affiliates but true believers.

Kox, Meeus, and Hart's meticulous analysis is one of the better empirical studies to date. They discovered that in conducting interviews based on their interpretation of the world-saver steps they could predict change with 85 percent accuracy. Their major nuance was that the seven steps did not correlate highly to each other but operated relatively independently. Affective bonds appeared in 80 percent of the converts' path to faith, meaning that this element surely coincided with other conditions, but it was not the only or a necessary condition such as Austin or Snow and Phillips found. It could be that "intensive interaction's" popularity for explaining change is largely because it is easy to test. Though an important element, people's internal motives are far more peculiar than surface patterns of behavior belie, and while social science can never exhaustively explain humanity's meaning, Kox, Meeus, and Hart placed their bets with steps 1 and 3, enduring tensions and

---

28. Kox et al., "Religious Conversion of Adolescents," 229.

active seekership.[29] Testing the world-saver model has thus come full circle by demonstrating that predispositional and situational elements are *both* crucial but in different ways. The individual factors (crises, familial strife, and deprivations) stressed in chapters 3, 4, and 5 could all fall under Lofland and Stark's tensions, just as the active seekership of chapter 3 could fall under step 3. These personal motivations are the driving energy behind religious change and the human "stuff" that the Holy Spirit inspires, but they are potential energy that is not expended in a clear fashion unless a social network bearing a theology gives direction to otherwise restless searching.[30] Of course, exceptions are possible. As Snow and Phillips argued, sometimes religious groups create their own demand and socialize people very gradually, but even this process, though less extreme than Travisano's "radical change," is impossible unless converts sense deprivation (something lacking) in some sense amid continued association with a religious group.[31] To summarize, continuing research on Lofland and Stark's model has shown social networks to be absolutely necessary to religious change, while predispositional tensions are important in most cases.

Like the making of any Kung Fu master, Stark has known his place as apprentice and sage, sidekick and master. Whether joined as Glock and Stark, Lofland and Stark, Stark and Bainbridge, or Stark and Finke, he has worked fruitfully to hone his insights about religious commitment. The latest partnership with Roger Finke has yielded the definitive statement of the world-saver model, characterized not only by elegance but also by sympathy toward religious conviction. It deserves a place in this study's argument that social ties are essential for religious change and hence salvation itself.

---

29. Note that Lofland in "'Becoming a World-Saver' Revisited," 818, picked up on active seekership but only briefly.

30. As Kox et al. concluded in "Religious Conversion of Adolescents," 238, "It seems justified to suppose that religious groups have a twofold appeal: ideological, by offering a new perspective on life, and social, by providing a satisfactory social network."

31. Stark and Bainbridge in *A Theory of Religion*, ch. 2, state that everyone suffers deprivation in terms of possessing everlasting life.

The World-Saver Model's Mature Expression

Scientific inquiry into religion typically asks why people change. As demonstrated above, the sociological perspective has largely determined that people become influenced by their friends to think and act differently, especially under predisposing tensions. To use this question (why people change) alone is to focus on exceptions rather than the norm, however. Though perhaps the more fascinating question, it tends to distract our attention from a broader understanding of religion. Stark and Finke have turned the question around to ask why people *do not* convert, or what makes for steadfast religious commitment.[32] Their answer concerns the relationship between what they call *social* and *religious capital*. Social capital is the value people place on relationships and networks of friendship. The more people value their social network the more content they are, so that those with high social capital will not look to change their network significantly (whereas low social capital predicts change). Religious capital is not as much contentedness with religion but familiarity: knowing the language and rituals, knowing when to say "and also with you" or when to kneel and rise.

Stark and Finke ascribe to a rational theory of religion, which is perhaps the sociologist's best compliment to religious belief, though certainly foreign to theology. They mean most generally that all humans make decisions in favor of their self-preservation; they avoid pain and seek pleasure. Making religious choices, Stark and Finke believe, is no different. People choose the expression of religion that best serves their needs. Because faith is a basic part of human life and matters of faith cannot be proven or disproved they cannot readily be written off as irrational beliefs. A rational action for Stark and Finke is one that follows a person's beliefs, however bizarre. If I live in the mountains and believe that there's gold in them hills, then it is irrational for me *not* to start digging. If I believe that God speaks life into me in the church's proclamation, then I would be a fool not to participate.

Stark and Finke note that the church is a social and religious environment; people who have invested their time, money, and energy into it develop high levels of capital. They gain social capital from forming

---

32. Stark and Finke, *Acts of Faith*, 117. This method is a function of "control theory," they say.

affective bonds with other churchgoers and religious capital from being familiarized with their church's culture. For the committed, radical change is highly unlikely because, given the benefits of religion—social now and eternal beyond death—forsaking their religion would be irrational. When children are raised in a faith, the social networks and religious culture are so ingrained that they generally preclude radical shifts to a different faith (notwithstanding denominational switching). Acknowledging religious capital helps to avoid an oversight in previous research that, contrary to Snow and Phillips, new religious networks and personal tensions do not predict religious change when religious capital is well-maintained. For example: "Mormon missionaries who called upon the Unificationists were immune to conversion, despite forming warm relationships with several members."[33] Intensive interaction is not a magical formula for producing believers if it exists between people firmly committed to disparate faiths.

Presupposing that people act (rationally) according to their beliefs, working to preserve and increase their capital, the Stark/Finke model predicts that change into a religion will occur most often among people who have low levels of social and religious capital. "Thus, in the United States, the single most unstable 'religion' of origin is 'no religious preference.'"[34] Weighing the vast literature with their own observations, Stark and Finke argue that cases of pure seekership are rare. The effort to increase only one's religious capital is almost never a primary motive to change. They claim rather that change is initiated through social ties, in people's efforts to preserve and increase their social capital. As Lofland observed, the later UC immensely aided their evangelistic efforts by offering prospective converts extremely hospitable and loving social conditions up front. Religious capital—learning the religion—is mediated through social capital. It plays a different role by giving significance to the convert's new community and life, and the more it increases the more solidly it confirms a person's religious affiliation, hence the rationality of staying put in that religion even if a crisis in life or even social capital were to occur.

Though Stark and Finke use an odd language of economics, their claims are not fundamentally different from acknowledging that change

33. Ibid., 121.
34. Ibid.

A Theology of Religious Change

is unlikely without a need for friends and for meaning. Over thirty-five years of research have confirmed that social networks are the condition of change even if not its immediate cause. Rather than threading in the usual predispositional factors such as deprivation, tension, or crisis, Stark and Finke conclude that these conditions will usually cause recommitment to one's own religious background unless faced with a new and more appealing opportunity for religious and social capital.[35] Scholars can be found who disagree with Stark and Finke's model about ideology's role or their use of economic language,[36] but its fundamental insights into social networks stand. My greatest criticism of these studies is that they all claim the importance of social networks but they almost never organize the forms that networks can take when influencing people's religious commitment. Usually this information comes up anecdotally or is presupposed, but it would benefit us to define social networks before asking what theology can learn from this research.

The Form of Social Ties

The range of definitions I propose is not strictly scientific but rather a way to acknowledge that social networks operate in different dynamics. To understand them in terms of *life together*, *evangelism*, and *charisma* will clarify three types of relationships that appear frequently in religious change narratives.

1) Life together needs the least attention, being the most familiar network of social influence. Chapter 4 discussed catechesis, how parents instruct their children with direct teaching and by their lifestyle's more subtle assumptions. Though life together involves instruction, its influence is often less overt such as when one's spouse is a conduit into a religious group.[37] Especially if one spouse has a high level of religious capital and the other a low level, then the low level spouse will

---

35. Other studies corroborating Stark's general work are Bankston et al., "Toward a General Model," 279–93. This study especially supports intensive interaction. Malony, *Psychology of Religion for Ministry*, 105–7. Malony explains that the world-saver model is widely applicable for Christianity. And Halama and Halamová, "Process of Religious Conversion," 69–92.

36. E.g., Hak, "Conversion as a Rational Choice," 13–25.

37. Snow and Phillips, "The Lofland-Stark Conversion Model," 440.

be susceptible to the other's worldview. The essential principle is that to associate closely with people is to begin thinking like them, and in most cases influence flows from the firmest viewpoint outward. If I have little political preference but my workmates chatter nonstop about the wrongs of the system, then, if my nonchalance is not a firm position of its own, I will likely begin seeing the nation's problems in their terms. A good example of life together is Austin's study of the Campus Crusade half-way house. Though the former law breakers living there were required to participate in religious services, undoubtedly the lifestyle and order they learned was due largely to their constant exposure to Christian culture.

Though life together is a subtle form of influence it is effective in certain cases where people are intentional about sharing their faith. Other cases (such as college students living together in a dorm) might see very little transference of religion, especially under an implicit belief that religion is a personal matter to be respected but not shared. Religious groups seeking growth, however, will rarely place themselves in the vicinity of non-believers and wait to see what happens; they will make explicit efforts to evangelize.

2) An example of social networks and evangelism is the Mormon Church, which commissions its young members to carry out missions typically for a two year term. But even the older laity are encouraged to take extensive steps to build ties with their neighbors and begin introducing them to the faith. So heavy is the Mormon emphasis on evangelism that Seggar and Kunz had difficultly locating predispositional tensions in the converts they studied. The evangelists did not worry about finding the right kinds of people undergoing tensions but they diversified their message to all kinds and were able to elicit commitments from seventy-seven after building social ties. Contrasting networks built through life together, evangelism entails a more intentional agenda within the relationship and can never be purely spontaneous friendship, if such a thing is possible. Firm religious commitment entails believing that doctrine is absolute and applicable to the human condition, making the sharing of faith a part of believing it. Of course, not all theologies stress evangelism equally. Though Mormons and Mennonites might be equally strong believers in their respective faiths, their understandings of evangelism will be different. Sociology has

A Theology of Religious Change

often discussed theology's role in appealing to deprivation but would benefit from noticing theology's far more important role in defining a church's mission and thus inspiring evangelistic efforts.

3) The last form of social networks—charisma—is a more specific version of the evangelistic. Though seldom discussed in testing the world-saver model, it is still important to recognize.[38] Certain religious leaders elicit their followers' devotion through an unusual combination of gifts such as confidence, zeal, compassion, intellect, and elocution.[39] Charisma is an especially important element in sectarian groups that are in high tension with mainstream culture. Typically the high tension deters individuals from associating closely with a group (after all, who would want to know God through handling snakes?),[40] but a charismatic leader has the ability to legitimate the group. Strong leadership has such an influence on morale that it can many times establish a universe of language and action without reference to external standards. Admittedly, leaders such as politicians and television evangelists influence masses of people without any social bonds, but social research has demonstrated that the direct relationship between converts and leaders is an important form of the social network.

Chana Ullman, who likens religious change to falling in love (chapter 2), noticed that people's fascination with a particular religious leader could be a powerful draw, perhaps even more basic than theology (such that a termination of that relationship might also cause a crisis of faith). She cites the case of a convert to Orthodox Judaism named Meir, who quickly became attached to his rabbi. Ullman reports: "God was hardly mentioned in our interview, nor were the Jewish scriptures, the Torah, or the Talmud . . . His choice of Orthodox Judaism seems accidental. It is a by-product of his remarkable love at first sight. It is the powerful figure of the rabbi offering him guidance and acceptance, so clearly missing in his previous life, that transforms him."[41] Ullman interpreted Meir's adulation of the rabbi as compensation for his own

---

38. Max Weber was one of the first sociologists to recognize and study this characteristic. See *Grundriss der Sozialökonomik*, 140–48.

39. Rambo, "Charisma and Conversion," 100–101.

40. On snake handling see Hood and Morris, "Evaluation of the Legitimacy of Conversion Experience as a Function of the Five Signs of Mark 16," 95–108.

41. Ullman, *Transformed Self*, 36.

rather unassertive father, but even without the Freudian spin it still illustrates charisma's potential effect.

Research into The International Society for Krishna Consciousness (ISKCON) offers an even broader display of charisma. Though agreeing with Stark's fundamental emphasis on networks, sociologist Larry Shinn adds that for Krishnas the social network is theologically prescribed as a vertical, guru/disciple relationship.[42] Though hierarchy need not be a formal part of a religion to have a vertical faith network, it certainly is when a guru figure is instated to embody ISKCON salvation. Percentage-wise, Christianity will have fewer examples of charismatic leadership than those faiths organized explicitly around it, but the topic itself is potentially relevant to all religions marked by strong leadership, formal or informal. Shinn found that the guru/disciple relationship could be so strong that even a seceding guru could draw many disciples to secede with him. Perhaps the axiom to be drawn from this research is that for many people religious faith cannot easily be separated from the means through which that faith is learned, like children learning from parents. Once again the relationship is crucial.

This long trek in research history has helped to clarify social networks' importance. Though predisposing thirst for theology, tension, and crises are necessary in many cases of religious change, these factors are not sufficient without religious leadership to hone them into a specific theological form. Some scholars have even suggested that social interaction is the *only* condition for change. At least, it is the most important such condition.[43] This chapter's beginning stated that the church will better understand its missional role by studying the impact of social ties on conversion. With the sociology now substantiated it will be helpful to ask what service these varied accounts offer theology.

Sociology beneath the Cross

This topic more than others previously covered seems to tempt the church's hasty evangelistic action. Would it not be quite efficient to take

---

42. Shinn, "Conflicting Networks," 95–114.

43. Dr. Bruce Hartung has emphasized that this conclusion is natural and expected given the social nature of human beings as evinced in Gen 2:18—it was not good for Adam to be alone.

the best insights from the most successful religious movements and mimic them today? The church could organize cell groups around their most charismatic individuals and gather sociological data on people who have low social and religious capital, who have recently moved, divorced, or become unemployed, and use their most affectionate and encapsulating techniques to charm countless recruits into the faith. The paper by Eberhard Ernest on how to evangelize one's neighbors follows a similar-minded method, and if it works for Mormonism it could work for orthodox Christianity. Yet these approaches are temptations if the church begins to lose the correlational counterpoint that all of these calculating kinds of measures are only valuable to the extent that the gospel is their motivation. To make the practical outcomes of sociology-based evangelistic efforts the primary focus will neglect evangelism's true motivation in God's saving will, which extends to all people regardless of how their psychological profiles might predict religious change. Though evangelism always operates with a notion of society and its needs, this knowledge of human behavior best serves the church's ministry within the correlation's fine balance between caring for people's material needs (in this case, the need for relationships) without forgetting their spiritual needs. Part of academic theology's task is to explore how sociological data might serve the church without overstepping its bounds. Obviously missional churches wish to grow, but a correlational approach can encourage them that empirical measurements of growth are sociological concerns that, while serving a helpful role, can neither validate nor invalidate the mission that seeks in its conscience to do God's will.

The strength of a correlational approach to evangelism is that it accounts for the tension between God's grace that works despite human things and the human side of change that is redeemed rather than effaced in God's saving action. The Formula of Concord, for instance, emphasizes this point when it states that the human being is not like a stone in conversion even if salvation is a divine gift.[44] Part of God's converting action involves the passive reception and recognition of grace known in despair of self and trust in Christ. Faith is a personal, unachievable gift from God and as such its reception is passive, but the gift still informs a crucial human element that knows and feels unlike a stone can.

---

44. FC II in Kolb and Wengert, *Book of Concord*, 555.59, 518.12.

The Web of Social Ties

This human side of faith as the capacity to believe God's gift still has the ability to inhibit the gift and thus plays a significant role in salvation's outcome. Though unable to force God's gift, individuals are responsible to maintain the gift's human reception by exposing themselves to God's word. And as the social research demonstrates, the church is even more responsible for providing spiritual care for its members by maintaining a loving relationship. In their respective ways, the divine and the human roles are both fundamentally significant for conversion.

The sociological reports can help explain how the human capacity to believe is nurtured through converts' interaction with the church and how theology can inspire the church's responsibility to care for them. Sociology explains that religious change is a slow process in which the object that converts embrace in faith is inseparable from the social medium in which they learn it. Both change and relationship formation appear to operate within similar time frames. Above I suggested that evangelism, life together, and charisma were different social mediums that support faith development, all of which validate the convert's experience of new faith over time. The most important initial insight is that, though faith is God's gift, learning to believe in God and understand faith's significance happens gradually under exposure to a believing community. The above reports show that religious change is a very gradual process of forming relationships and learning a new religious and social culture. Early conversion psychology was fascinated with revivalist Christianity characterized by camp meetings, intense emotion, and high pressure to accept Christ suddenly. If the Apostle Paul's story in Acts is the only paradigm for conversion's divine and human phenomena, then these camp meetings were thoroughly accurate. But as Richard Peace argues, the Bible has a broad account of factors in its characters' roads to faith; the disciples in Mark's gospel apparently had a much different path than did Paul.[45] Paul, it seems, is an exception. The many people baptized into the faith and catechized by their parents show that no one receives the bulk of Christian identity in an instant. To recognize religious change's gradual development neither suggests that Christ's righteousness is incrementally obtained nor that God instills faith gradually. This gradualness refers to the human capacity to appreciate God's gift and take it to heart. But to know that God's

---

45. See Peace, *Conversion in the New Testament*, 1–16.

salvation is complete is a matter of hearing it proclaimed within the church's sacramental presence.

As the studies have demonstrated, religious change is gradual because it occurs through a relationship forming process without which there could be no entrance into the church. Theology does not need science to understand how crucial trust is to a convert's embrace of Jesus, but the accounts help to remind theology that this trust is never disconnected from the community that confesses it. There is no Jesus "in a vacuum," that is; loving relationships are crucial to converts' faith development. Relationship forming is perhaps the most difficult aspect of the church's mission to balance because true friendship is ideally spontaneous, but there is often a non-spontaneous agenda when church members focus on spreading their message. The most successful missionaries of the UC made converts through extravagant displays of love manifest in approving attitudes toward new recruits. From the outside this overt behavior seems disingenuous because it tends to objectify new recruits as things to influence but fails to treat them as people.

Above I stated that love, if defined biblically, is the criterion of the church's mission. The church has long realized that its faith spreads through social networks and that forming bonds with insiders opens converts to continued stay in the church. Considered alone this knowledge might foster disingenuous love, but a correlational approach to evangelism will provide a necessary correction. If the church concentrates on its own representation of love,[46] then its motivation will stem from its own calling to a certain identity. That is, the church should focus on being and acting according to God's criteria for the true church, including its formal ministries and individual members' actions. The church does not make converts, strictly speaking, nor should it focus on this exact outcome. It should not focus on how much it can influence people but how much it can influence itself to determine ways to show God's love to the world.

This principle, that the church must focus on its identity first, is difficult to test because it concerns a matter of the heart's disposition more than any outward actions or achievements that can be cited as proof. The sociological data indicates that if the church forms social

---

46. Phil 2:3, "Do nothing out of selfish ambition or vain conceit, but in humility consider others better than yourselves."

bonds with converts through mediums such as persuasive pastoral leadership, life together, and specific evangelistic efforts, it will address the human need for fellowship and further its growth; but the pressing question is: How can it fulfill these roles without making them the primary concern? Paul's words that "everything is permissible, but not everything is helpful"[47] apply in the admission that no particular evangelistic method that can be ruled out, but it must be carried out in the right spirit. As the gospel criterion is the test case for religious change, this criterion also judges the church's operations, by asking if the gospel is truly the focus of its efforts. In some cases (such as prosperity gospels or therapeutic appeals to potential converts) churches have forfeited much of their identity if they never distinguish that prosperity and therapy are not true indicators of Christ's love for their converts. But the physical comfort of social warmth, predicted by sociology to help religious change, is not an evil in itself, nor is the church wrong to emphasize this comfort so long as it continually reminds itself and its converts that Christ is the ultimate significance of their fellowship.

Part of manifesting God's love will undoubtedly involve forming social bonds with potential converts. But the church has the freedom of knowing that its efforts to establish social ties are not conversion's ultimate cause, and it need not take full responsibility for losing recruits simply because it failed to love (in the UC sense) people intensely enough or entice them though other material measures. A firm entailment of correlational thinking is that advertising people into the church through effective marketing is a victory foremost for sociology, not necessarily for the gospel.

Even if the church loves its recruits in good conscience, there will be cases where, though its motivations are pure, the recruits themselves will have impure motives. The impurity of motives for joining a faith pervades all religion; all have what Paul calls "selfish ambition." Therefore, if the church is truly to love converts, it does so not only through forming serving relationships but by teaching its community of God's justice, his promise, and the entire Christian worldview. This teaching involves revealing to converts their fallenness as a part of a fallen human race and explicitly that their reasons for associating with the church are flawed just as all churchgoers attend for imperfect reasons.

---

47. 1 Cor 10:23.

A Theology of Religious Change

But the wider context of these selfish ambitions is God's love as revealed in his Son's crucifixion and resurrection, and to concentrate on Christ is to find salvation from this fallenness, something much more powerful than the mire of impure motivations. By loving new recruits through an attitude of service and giving them the gospel, the church will expand its population without concentrating explicitly on expanding. The question of practical results, theologically understood, is not important next to the question of the church's faithfulness to God himself.

Stark and Finke help to show that part of that faithfulness involves not only developing the social bonds but, in their language, building people's religious capital, or teaching them a definite way of thinking and being. Anthropologist Paul Hiebert has likewise suggested that conversion is *both* sudden *and* gradual, *both* a point *and* a process.[48] He captures the divine/human tension in conveying the instantaneous nature of God's saving act yet the life-long process of learning salvation's meaning. The church that loves people will also teach them because it will desire to share its way of believing with them. The teaching about Jesus Christ's gospel is most important in the beginning of people's recruitment because it is the essence of Christianity's message, but it does not exhaust the necessity to expand converts' knowledge in a practically meaningful fashion. A recurrent theme in the research explains that people often enter a faith through emotional means such as through increasing social capital or, for Ullman, falling in love. Learning a worldview is not usually the first thing that attracts people to the church, but if the church is to maintain its faith, then it must address this cognitive side also. Apostasy often occurs through more cognitive means when people's religious expectations fail to hold meaning amid outside challenges,[49] the lesson being that people will be more apt to lose their faith if they are not taught a critical, meaningful worldview that can handle objections and keep secularism in its limited realm of meaning.

When Hiebert says that conversion is an instant and a process, his point is to emphasize that transforming worldviews is essential to religious change. However, worldview education is not important in the same way that most scholarly subjects are because the point is not to inform the church about facts and ideas but to explain God's lordship

---

48. Hiebert, *Transforming Worldviews*, 307–34.
49. See the discussion of apostasy in chapter 3.

of creation and its direct significance for faith. If faith's tenets are made to compete as mere facts competing on the same level as science, then they will be subject to the day's most popular science. But if a worldview is taught as directly conveying faith's meaning for ethics and hope of resurrection, then it will foster the church's religious capital and make apostasy unnecessary.[50] Even Hiebert, who wrote more than three-hundred pages on transforming worldviews, only says that this kind of transformation is crucial, but he does not attempt to paint a worldview that is the once-for-all Christian system. In this chapter on social ties I can do no better than to say with him that it is crucial to maintaining faith. The problem of finding meaning is that it must be discovered anew each day, making worldview education a continual task if theology is to offer spiritual care to its members.

Conclusion

This chapter ends our formal consultation with social science accounts of religious change. In examining the world-saver model I have outlined social networks' role in the church's mission and perhaps how network building can operate in good conscience. This broad-based sociology helps to complete the picture of religious change that began in chapter 2 that focused on the mind's internal dynamics. In retrospect, we can see the great variety of predispositional and situational influences that inspire change, all of which are significant conditions. But the insights on social ties have shown that situational conditions are the most important because without a religious group to provide leadership, personal crises and tensions will not find alleviation in religious form.

---

50. In "Religious Conversion and the Concept of Socialization," 1–14, sociologists Theodore Long and Jeffrey Hadden have documented this problem in the UC. The early UC of San Francisco emphasized their theology to a fault and had little success in evangelism, but the later UC compensated by excessively emphasizing the emotional level. The early UC made few converts, but those that they did make were die-hard whereas the late UC recruited many people and lost many. Long and Hadden suggest that this problem occurred because the late UC emphasized social bonding so much that they overlooked the necessity of teaching their new members a comprehensive theology. Without the social bonds working toward a stable worldview, the social capital without religious capital could easily be replaced. This point confirms Stark and Finke's general outlook that stable religious commitment is stamped by social *and* religious capital of which the late UC had lost track.

With so much emphasis on the human side of things my intention is still not to lose the divine. Has science eclipsed the Spirit's work? The answer is no, so long as we remember that the gospel is the criterion of religious changes that could be vastly diverse. It is not behaviors or neuroscientific data that distinguishes Christianity but the heart's condition, the inner orientation directed by God's love. The Spirit's work is known not because a convert has had a certain observable experience but because whatever experience he or she has awakens to the gospel. Religious experience motivates the dead (non-saving) act of placing oneself under the church's sacramental presence where faith is possible, and religious experience (viz. the human capacity for faith) latches on to God's promise and reveals, however partially, his will for humankind. But experience only serves God's saving act in passively receiving grace that saves despite experience's material workings, a salvation that begins, in fact, in despair of self. Thus, we must conclude that though the Spirit works mysteriously through creation, attempts to find evidence of him through the human side of faith ask the wrong question and should rather seek the Spirit's presence in God's revealed will to save and guide all of human life.

The final chapter will ask precisely the question about God's will and the nature of his workings in building his church. What has all of this research to say about grace and the human ability to receive it? This book began with a theological account of conversion, and it is now fitting to place that account into the wider picture of God's love for the world.

7

Conversion and the Divine Choice

THIS STUDY'S FINAL MOVE places the correlational accounts of religious change and conversion into their broader theological context, suggesting that though the church knows very little about God's ultimate plans to save individuals, it still knows its duty to respond to unbelief. Specifically, this chapter takes up the "theologians' cross" (i.e., the problem of why one person believes the gospel and another does not) to determine how a correlational approach to conversion might be helpful in addressing it. I conclude that though theology should not derive absolute reasons for belief and unbelief from ideas about God's decreeing decisions before time, the question of why certain individuals believe or disbelieve can be answered from a limited human perspective though use of the social sciences. This limited approach will focus theology's attention away from unsolvable mysteries and toward the question of how the church can communicate to people's needs, a theme that preceding chapters have continually emphasized.

Social Sciences and Means of Grace

That salvation comes through the Holy Spirit there can still be no doubt; however, our trek through empirical research has demonstrated the vast material conditions through which people attain faith. Though the correlational approach has helped to clarify how the gospel might speak to people changing under various motivations, the test of its lasting merit is its ability to deepen theology's comprehension of how God builds his church. Previous chapters have not yet made it obvious that these correlational accounts of religious change and conversion are well-suited to respond to the mystery of salvation's uneven dispersal, the final argument here offered. Because an ultimate theological comprehension of every person's final destiny is unknowable and impossible to generalize, the church should rather concentrate on speaking to unbelief in a practical fashion, suggested here as a correlational approach that focuses not on abstract/general statements to explain why people believe or not but on means of communicating the gospel in concrete instances and trusting that the gospel's manifestation in time and human lives is unquestionable evidence of their salvation. This chapter will offer an outline for theology that respects the predestinarian mystery, neither debating it in the contentiousness of classical terms nor avoiding discussion of it, but addresses it in action.

Classically, the question asking why some people (and not others) believe the gospel is called the "theologians' cross,"[1] known for its difficulty as a theological paradox precisely because it sets up an abstract problem implying that one of two things is true: either my capacity to choose Christ grounds my salvation or an unconditional decree does so, regardless of my conversion in time. The theologians' cross is something of a sucker's cross because it plays on the natural human tendency toward laziness and generalization that presupposes that there must be one easily conceivable abstraction to solve the puzzle: "It's ultimately one or the other, God or humans." It lures us into thinking that the Bible reveals more about salvation's initial and final horizons than it actually does, and consciously or unconsciously, it colors how we conceive of God's love and wrath applying to actual people.

Sensing this cross's danger, some commentators have refused to answer it directly, leaving its resolution to a realm of knowledge beyond humans. This attitude, presupposed here as the starting point, is clearly

---

1. Richard Muller, *Dictionary of Latin and Greek*, 86, offers a definition: "crux theologorum: *the cross of theologians;* i.e., the doctrinal question most troublesome to theologians, which cannot be solved in this life, viz., the question concerning the reason for the salvation of some people and not others; a term used by Lutherans to pose the problem of universal and particular grace and to point to the problem inherent both in Calvinism, which must qualify universal grace, and Arminianism, which must deny salvation by (particular) grace alone."

at work whenever theological formulations warn against excessive speculation about God's electing decree.[2] This warning against speculation fulfills the necessary task of keeping the theologians' cross at bay and preventing claims to knowledge about the unknowable. However, to heed against speculation is not to ignore theology's difficult matters but to address them in terms that limit their potential to cause error, especially those of such consequence as the theologians' cross that cannot but haunt those who have struggled with doubt or have witnessed loved ones cling to idols rather than to Christ.

My task is thus to give theology a correlational perspective for every time we consciously or unconsciously ask (and even answer) the question of why people believe or spurn the gospel. This final chapter provides a theological framework for understanding the material conditions of salvation not only as means to clarify theology's tasks but to handle the theologians' cross itself through altering its form. Though the problem's classical tension cannot be modified away by a new approach, the question itself can be altered to ask why actual people might believe or not. This question asks not if God loves one person more than another but rather inquires about whatever limited means are available to explain a person's belief or disbelief, including the sociological data discussed in chapters 2–6 that explain (in summary) how deprivations and crises become powerful motivators to change beliefs if potential converts encounter supportive social groups. To inform the question about why people believe on a social science basis directs the inquiry from the start toward knowable but limited elements that by their very nature disallow speculation into divine decrees and instead focus on goals within humanity's earnest potential. As stated, this approach does not erase the problem's tension, something theology will always endure, but it asks the question in a new fashion to give the church new energy for practice. By concentrating on religious change's material conditions, the church will hear the cross neither as despair nor as limitation—for limitation is already built into the inquiry—but as a call to action.

---

2. See Formula of Concord (FC) XI in Kolb and Wengert, *Book of Concord*, 642.9, "Moreover, no one should consider this eternal election or God's preordination to eternal life merely as the secret, inscrutable will of counsel of God, as if it had nothing more to it and nothing more to consider than that God perceived beforehand who and how many would be saved, and who and how many would be damned."

A Theology of Religious Change

The Context of a Concrete Approach

This approach has been significant in my own theological development, whose brief rehearsal contextualizes this essay. Before ever reading social science for theology, some primitive sociological observations helped me to find a way off of the theologians' cross, so to speak. Over a decade ago I was baffled by its fatal logic, wondering if I had to choose between God's love (in allowing creaturely freedom) and his power (to choose his elect). The idea of a double predestination in which God creates certain people that he never desires to save seemed clearly to contradict God's love, so I researched the theologians who resolve the mystery on the other side. Synergistic patterns of thought do not necessarily derive from egotistical motives but are honest attempts to preserve the earnestness of God's universal desire for salvation if not also his fairness in making salvation available to all people. By placing the mystery of evil and particularity of salvation in the human will, they reason, our picture of God will not include arbitrary elections and obsession with power. Two examples illustrate this thinking. From a Protestant-Evangelical perspective, William Lane Craig comments:

> Proponents of middle knowledge emphasize that God does not predestine persons because he knows they would receive Christ and persevere. Nor does he select a world because he knows that in it, say, Peter would be saved. Rather, God simply chooses the world he wants, and whoever in that world would freely receive Christ is, by the very act of God's selection of that world, predestined to do so. All the people in that world receive sufficient grace to be among the predestined. Their eternal destiny thus lies in their own hands. Everything depends on whether they freely receive or reject Christ.[3]

Craig has two PhDs, one from Birmingham under John Hick and one from Munich under Wolfhart Pannenberg. His book offers a sophisticated account of divine foreknowledge ultimately to demonstrate that salvation rests in human choice, predicating God's fairness on the relatively equal shot at salvation people have. From the Catholic side, Boston College professors Peter Kreeft and Ronald Tacelli argue similarly when explaining how people who have not heard the gospel have

---

3. Craig, *The Only Wise God*, 137.

the ability to choose God: "To summarize our solution: Socrates (or any other pagan) could seek God, could repent of his sins, and could obscurely believe in and accept the God he knew partially and obscurely, and therefore he could be saved—or damned, if he refused to seek, repent and believe. There is enough light and enough opportunity, enough knowledge and enough free choice, to make everyone responsible before God."[4]

Like Craig, Kreeft and Tacelli are committed to keeping the mystery of salvation's particularity outside of God's will, forcing them to perceive a relatively equal-opportunity standing for any person to believe and be saved. The strength that I found in these approaches was their regard for God's universally desired salvation. However, their tendency to leave everything up to the human will was a high price to pay for that advantage. The problem is that these abstract inquiries into predestination ask a question that cannot be resolved and thereby limit their helpfulness to address actual human circumstances.

Eventually, I began to examine the synergistic gospel in concrete terms. Having seen a documentary on children who grow up in impoverished and violent neighborhoods in American cities, it struck me that even though they live in a nation filled with Christians, these children are raised with such destructive perceptions of reality that to esteem their supposedly free choice as the final determiner of their unbelief is sociologically impossible to maintain. We must remember that a correlational approach to theology/sociology cannot use sociology to prove or eliminate a doctrine; however the closeness of correlation can compromise a doctrine's adequacy, and it seemed to me then—as it does now—that the synergistic gospel cannot have even potential meaning for many people who are raised amid animosity.[5]

Even in less extreme cases, chapter 4 of this study has already illustrated that parental religion predicts their children's religion far more reliably than their children's preference for other matters such as sports

---

4. Kreeft and Tacelli, *Handbook of Christian Apologetics*, 328. Also Pinnock, *A Wideness in God's Mercy*.

5. I discovered that doctrines that speak directly to human phenomena must inspire an experiential credulity to have meaning, which is partly why Pelagianisms and Christian perfectionisms, for instance, cannot maintain credibility through any honest confrontations with evil.

A Theology of Religious Change

teams or politics.[6] Likewise, chapter 6 showed that though predispositional tensions preceding religious change are significant and even necessary for the change to occur, it will be unable to take any definite form without a social relationship that addresses the problem with a meaningful theology and supportive network. Material causes of religious change are essential to any meaningful explanation of belief even if God's converting action alone orients hearts to Christ. It is far too simple to rest the explanation for belief and unbelief on a theory of free choice or even a notion of God's choice if that notion neglects the actual circumstances of belief.

If the theologian stands as a mediator between God's message and its audience, as stated in this study's opening pages, scholars such as Craig, Kreeft, and Tacelli tend to get lost in their notion of God's message such that they are blinded to actual people (audience) and possibilities within the horizon of human potential. Though their positions are philosophically defensible, they appear irrelevant when compared with actual contexts of religious choice discoverable by real-time observation. To say that the theologian is a mediator between God's word and its audience can never imply that the "God's word" side alone is worth studying, but those who solve the theologians' cross in a simple statement (that either God or humans choose) err in failing to consider the real-life correlation between religious change and conversion.[7]

This real-life approach can be called a "phenomenology of salvation" that pushes the question of salvation's causes beyond abstract solutions. Though it cannot make salvation's particularity seem fair, it has three crucial tasks: 1) to encourage salvation's certainty and thus comfort in time, 2) to allow the church to believe as earnestly as possible in God's will to save all people, 3) and to set the church on a course of action in sharing its message. Concentration on these tasks is intended to address more adequately the problems associated with the theologians' cross by asking the question in a form that focuses on actual individuals, and the preceding chapters have already enabled this new, concrete

6. Beit-Hallahmi and Argyle, *Psychology of Religious Behaviour*, 100.

7. For brevity's sake I am presupposing that an attempt to solve the theologians' cross on God's side, typically through a dual decree of his choice to salvation and damnation is not adequate. It tends to undermine the universality of God's call and the conversion experience's assurance, though it does not suffer the same incredibility as a fairness gospel.

form of the question to be asked with some of the best social scientific tools available.

As we have seen, the correlational method for relating science and religion has been the central organizing apparatus for the preceding chapters because it interprets religious change's and conversion's causes as close and interrelated yet essentially distinct. What I call the "phenomenology of salvation" is simply a way of referring to the data of religious experience, both of religious change, faith, and conversion that the correlational method interprets (i.e., correlates). Below I will explain that the correlational method filters the phenomena into "saving" and "non-saving" to set up the discussion of how the two might be related, ultimately asking what the social sciences can tell us, if anything, about how God works salvation in time.

The Phenomenology of Salvation

In constructing structures of thought we sometimes reach unsurpassable contradictions out of which there seems no escape. Sometimes the confusion is a limitation of cognitive power (e.g., a complicated physics problem), sometimes a limitation of time (e.g., only history will prove if the stock market is the safest path to retirement), and other times a limitation in logic itself (e.g., I cannot serve two masters fully). The difficulty of the theologians' cross comes from all of these. Though we trust God's promise, the human mind is not powerful enough to conceive an ultimate reason why salvation has universal and particular senses. As well, temporality limits our knowledge of the future when, we hope, final destinies and their reasons will be revealed more fully. And logic always asks: If God predestines some and destroys others, then how can his universal saving desire extend earnestly to all? Or: If he leaves destinies to free choice, then how can a fallen human nature find the power, however slight, to choose above itself? When posed abstractly, these questions elude a resting place. Like hitting the gophers in an arcade, one solved problem tends to elicit two more unsolved ones! At impasses such as the theologians' cross we have no choice, then, except to question the question's very terms. In a certain sense the question is not wrong, in so far as it leads us to the incomprehensibility of finding God's will behind the gospel's scenes. Yet it might also lead to a haunting sense that maybe, deep down, one side of the dilemma is right and that the gospel will always be contingent on a hidden decree or a subjective capacity to choose. If theology is to consider predestination in light of God's christological revelation rather than in speculative absolutes, it must push on to new conceptions that will eventually resist posing this question abstractly, thus falling back into the dilemma.

Philosophy's master synthesizer, G. W. F. Hegel, is helpful in this one respect because he understood clearly that sometimes, when we reach a contradiction, it is a problem of failing to see the whole context in which our particular issue functions.[8] The theologians' cross hangs theologians precisely because they are lured to perceive only a few responses, either God's choice or human choice.[9] Left in the abstract, these responses have never reached significant agreement or progress due to their narrowing form of presentation that tends to pit irreconcilable absolutes against each other.[10] Rather than setting out to find the mystery's edge they have rather sliced boundaries between schools of thought, pitting God's love against his power or freedom against providence. For progress to take root in this question, these viewpoints that, in fairness, arise out of legitimate concerns, must take shape as a "progressive evolution of truth," so to speak.[11] Hegel knew that abstract contradictions, when taken in themselves, will limit thought; but if they are viewed as phenomena within an historical continuum, then they spur thought on to conceive of the whole more richly. The proposal here offered is that saving and non-saving phenomena in human life cannot be pitted directly against one another (e.g., human vs. divine choice)

---

8. Hegel, *Phenomenology of Mind*, 68, writes: "The more the ordinary mind takes the opposition between true and false to be fixed, the more it is accustomed to expect either agreement or contradiction with a given philosophical system, and only to see reason for the one or the other in any explanatory statement concerning such a system. It does not conceive the diversity of philosophical systems as the progressive evolution of truth; rather, it sees only contradiction in that variety."

9. Sometimes theologians have insisted that there is a "broken logic" of God's choice of the elect and sinners' choice over their own non-election. See Wengert, "The Formula of Concord," 46.

10. Liefeld, "Saved on Purpose," 5, gives a concise historical account of Lutheran struggles with election, both Reformation period and in America. The abstract/absolute terms under which it was debated in America were intensely divisive such that "even now, the shape of American Lutheranism betrays the divisions provoked by it."

11. Hegel, *Phenomenology of Mind*, 68.

but should rather be viewed as different kinds of phenomena related indirectly and functioning differently within time. Though the human experience of salvation cannot be divided neatly into divine and human elements, this theological distinction preserves God's grace as unattainable by material causes while still admitting religious experience's great significance. Non-saving phenomena are everything that comprises that human side of religious experience, most especially the material conditions of religious change known through experience and empirical research, whereas the saving phenomenon is God's converting action known through the gospel, displayed externally in the sacraments and internally in despair of self and trust in Christ. The non-saving are perceived in sensation, the saving in faith.

The correlational approached developed throughout this book filters these phenomena into their respective manifestations as saving and non-saving so that God's action in granting faith cannot be mistaken for non-saving phenomena such as self-choosing of ideology or experiencing free decision. It might be helpful to recall again that the correlational method carries out this task by interpreting theological and material explanations as different levels of causality that, though they interact, never efface each other. The experience of free decision, for instance, can be recognized as a significant part of human life only when it is recognized as a material phenomenon unable to harness divine favor. Because this phenomenological approach resists making absolute statements about why God saves or destroys people, the phenomenology of salvation entails that our attributions to human or divine work (e.g., monergism, conversion, apostasy, rejection of grace) in time cannot be interpreted as timelessly valid but as elements within historical containment.[12] None of them can be considered any more valid interpretations of existence than what they appear through theology's means of recognizing them in time. And though this means of expression might seem odd, the gospel's comfort depends on this temporal vitality, its communicative ultimacy in the moment of its application that will only be compromised by thoughts of absolute (timeless) decrees to save or destroy. The most real security of eternal destiny is simply the promise and faith latching to it, which is where the phenomenology of

---

12. This historical relativity implies that phenomena cannot reveal a hidden, "absolute" plan of salvation behind that unfolded in the church's ministry.

salvation makes its departure. It implies, correspondingly, that theology can never feature a "once saved, always saved" position because abstract assumption of doctrine would trump a person's actual, future life history, nor, for the same reason, can apostasy ever confirm one's eternal reprobation.

To discover abstract causes of salvation or damnation has historically ended the discussion in polemical deadlock, but to ask why Ms. X believes and why Mr. P does not directs theology toward a deeper comprehension of belief's nature itself through every means available, including the psychosocial interpretation of each instance. Perhaps Ms. X is, in part, a product of "social drift," and her active seekership has led her to the church. And maybe Mr. P used to believe but has fallen away because his belief system was not constituted to endure secular challenges to faith, much like the apostates mentioned in chapter 3. The maturity of conceptualizing salvation is to recognize that religious change experience and the conversion known under God's word comprise the horizon beyond which humans dare not speculate. The saving and non-saving phenomena comprise the mystery's edge, as I have called it, but an edge that we may walk alongside of as time reveals ever more children of God. And to walk alongside this edge entails that theology—with its many resources—not only explain faith and unbelief but also seek further how the gospel might communicate to these specific instances. This is probably the correlational method's most fruitful insight.

When we inquire into the theologian's cross from the phenomenological perspective we discover that there is neither a single answer nor a complete void but that there are many limited answers comprising actual appearances of monergism, conversion, apostasy, and unbelief that an *a priori* conversion theology filters correlationally according to doctrine's prescription for differentiating saving and non-saving phenomena (or divine and human acts).[13] But to admit that the appearance of faith or unbelief within time is the limit of human speculation about individual destinies and that thoughts on salvation should be phenomenologically oriented rather than abstract is still only to begin

---

13. Immanuel Kant's general principle of knowledge holds today, that the mind imposes its categories onto reality; however, Kant did not fully appreciate the mind's malleability to adapt in its a priori perceptions. See Kant, *The Critique of Pure Reason*, Introduction, part 1.

Conversion and the Divine Choice

to conceive how God actually works in time and how time has constrained his desired universal salvation so far as time and phenomena reveal. The most important concept to understand God's means of salvation is the geography of divine action.

The Geography of Divine Action

The theologian's cross tends to force salvation to be considered either in terms of an existential decision or an eternal decree; rarely discussed is the geography of divine action, the acknowledgement that salvation is more possible in certain places than others. This geography's principle has already appeared under discussion of the *sacramental encounter* (chapter 1), the conveyance of Christ only possible in his church, through its preached word, sacraments, and laity influence. But we have also found the geography's material basis in exploring the social science of religious change, most notably in arguing that social networks (the spiritual geography's material basis; chapter 6) are nearly requisite to religious change so long as they bear a theology and practice meaningful enough to human life that it satisfies human deprivations such as the need for social, economic, and ethical stability (chapter 5).

The phenomenology of salvation considering the geography's saving and non-saving sides will inevitably discover that certain places and contexts are better mediators of faith than others.[14] "Geography" summarizes these places and contexts, but this term can only be a metaphor for the contexts in which faith is possible, presupposing that faith is impossible without learning God's word. It appears, then, that the geography is materially grounded, though spiritual in effect, because it comprises Christ's confession and proclamation in any faith-communicating medium. Though it might correspond to the floor plans of a sanctuary in a given duration, such is only while worship there communicates Christ.[15] Though it emanates from the catechetical mindset

14. Philosophers of religion talk about sacred and profane places or objects in all religions; however this analysis applies to the divine geography, it should be clear that the geography is not delineated by anything except people speaking and following God's word. Cf. Eliade, *The Sacred and the Profane*.

15. Ibid., 25, "For a believer, the church shares in a different space from the street in which it stands. The door that opens on the interior of the church actually signifies a solution of continuity. The threshold that separates the two spaces also indicates the

of parents to their children, it does so perhaps only while their attitudes are "the same as that of Christ Jesus."[16]

The divine geography is essential to conceptualizing the theologians' cross because it gives the best possible answer to explain faith and disbelief. Everything, however, depends on this little word "best," which elicits a re-visitation of this whole enterprise's motivations. The premise of this entire project is, analogically stated, to treat the world's spiritual sickness with the gospel's medicine. The best theology is that which best cultivates the gospel in the church's life and ministry, implying that the church comprehending the geography of divine action will be positioned to communicate the gospel in ministry. While theology has often valued the sacramental aspect, it has often overlooked the social underpinnings of religion that (from the material perspective) evince this geography as sociology's best explanation of belief and unbelief. The evidence clearly points to social ties as the greatest predictor of belief and though not the only factor, perhaps the only necessary social cause of religious change.[17] Even the arguments for so-called active or autonomous religious changes (chapter 3) do not in themselves contradict social networks' role, nor can they contradict religion's irreducibly communal infrastructure.[18] All of the arguments established on social networks' influence need not be repeated, though perception of their cogency is easily enough struck in remembering how often parental religion predicts children's religion, or that people would rarely affiliate religiously without any social warmth.

Social ties ground the entire science of religious change and so doing offer the non-saving phenomenological basis for all of salvation history and the geography through which it has been possible. Though lasting religious commitment must arise from faith's personal life significance rather than social benefits alone, the infrastructure supporting the possibility of this experience is still the church's communal practice and not isolated existential decisions. As individualistic as the

---

difference between two modes of being, the profane and the religious."

16. Phil 2:5.

17. Seggar and Kunz, "Conversion," 178–84.

18. Some works featuring the active perspective: Straus, "Religious Conversion as a Personal and Collective Accomplishment," 158–65. Balch and Taylor, "Seekers and Saucers," 43–64. Henning and Nestler, *Konversion*. Knoblauch et al., *Religiöse Konversion*.

"conversion experience" in James, Starbuck, and Batson, Schoenrade, and Ventis appears (chapter 2), it still presupposes that religious ideas toward which people focus come from *somewhere*. Behind all of these accounts stands a ministry, instantiating the divine geography and so opening the way for God's Spirit to act. Though the material conditions of religious change are diverse, they can now be seen as motivations causing individuals to enter this divine geography where they might begin to form a relationship with its affiliates and eventually be converted.

However, the geography of salvation's status as the best angle from which to address the theologians' cross is not its explanatory power but its built-in limitation. To say that the question of salvation's particularity must be addressed on a phenomenological level within time's constraints is to presuppose that abstract speculation into God's pre-temporal mind must itself be constrained, limiting the church's focus to the gospel's actual manifestations. Framed thus, the entire inquiry presupposes its limitation to find inductive patterns only, rather than deductive certainties. Though speculation must be limited, it is a liberating limitation that frees theology from the clash of absolutes in their abstract form. It rather focuses the church on creating an environment where faith in Christ becomes a live possibility, a context in which the embrace of Christ in time is not threatened by thoughts of a seemingly arbitrary but more real decree of predestination behind the gospel's actual manifestations.

Thus, we reach one approximation of the mystery's edge, that some people believe and others do not because some have entered the divine geography and others have not, although such a statement has very little significance in summary form and is rather intended to press toward actual particulars in each evangelistic milieu. Yet the geography helps in summary form to sort out saving and non-saving phenomena so far as saving phenomena by definition occur within the geography. The extra-geographical causes of religious experience discernable through empirical research are non-saving in themselves, even if, in retrospect, we descry God's work in precursory causes to a conversion recognized as such only in faith's spark. We now understand how saving and non-saving phenomena could be indirectly related. In this case non-saving phenomena place people into the divine geography, and saving phenomena cause their conversion. While material causes get people "to the threshold" and focus their attention on God's message, they do not find conversion until God's Spirit heals their minds, wills, and hearts. And I have emphasized the experience of despair and trust (chapter 1) as the surest theological pattern to conversion precisely because despair of self is that existential place where the idols that lure converts into the divine geography in the first place are cleared away so that their ultimate trust can then fall on Christ. The metaphor of non-saving phenomena getting people "to the threshold" is, of course, limited in its explanatory power of conversion and is rather meant to give one kind of illustration to show the indirect relationship between saving and non-saving phenomena. In actual religious life and worship, the material causes have a much more dynamic relationship in which they serve as a passive medium on which grace works and to which the Spirit reveals salvation. The discussion of change dynamics in chapter 2 illustrates how the mind's structures might rearrange as a person embraces a new faith. Though sudden awakenings are possible, they occur within a gradual process of the mind coming to terms with a new theology and often a new sense of leadership and friendship (chapter 6). The indirect relationship between saving and non-saving phenomena offers a conceptual device for interpreting the gradual process of how people come to and grow in faith yet without the ability to enact their own conversion. In actual human life, the saving and non-saving phenomena are much more difficult to separate, and perhaps it is unnecessary to try to separate them so long as trust in Christ is their effect.

The indirect relationship between saving and non-saving phenomena is no more complex than acknowledging that while I have no power to make the sun shine, I might still go outside to a place where sunlight is possible. "Although Peter cannot achieve his own conversion, he can leave his nets."[19] If some human choices are made in absolute indeterminacy, then even this so-called free will could be a possible material precursor of conversion, though always indirectly. As far as phenomena reveal, belief in God's monergism does not rule out an element of salvation's contingency on the human side, most obvious in the scriptural warnings against falling away from faith.[20] This human contingency is

---

19. Bonhoeffer, *Discipleship*, 65. I owe Bonhoeffer for this section's fundamental insight.

20. Marshall, *A Study of Perseverance and Falling Away*, 29–190. The very problem

perhaps the most difficult question in all of theology when formed in terms both of unbelief and apostasy, why a God who claims to want community with all human beings seems to overlook certain people or let people fall away, some of whom have even lived within the divine geography's borders for long periods. Though no satisfying answer might ever be reached, it is worth considering this problem from the phenomenological perspective to determine what advantages it might provide.

The Reasons for Unbelief

To ask why people fail to believe the gospel is relatively straightforward outside of the divine geography. The church must assume that if it brings outsiders into its community and communicates God's word to them, then its part in providing a place of conversion is fulfilled. But experience dictates that faith is neither equally maintained nor distributed. The dilemma resides in our attempt to understand why people fail to believe despite the church's efforts, or more so, why some people apostasize. The starting point to finding this mystery's edge is to heed the doctrinal rule stating that people disbelieve because of their own doing.[21] This statement serves the dual function of preserving a sin doctrine that implies individuals' tendency to turn away from God along with a regard for God's universal saving desire. Because individuals bear direct responsibility for their disbelief, the church may, in good conscience, insist that God does not decree the particularity of disbelief by necessity, allowing the gospel's universal call to be earnest. The sincerity of the gospel's universal call is essential to a phenomenology of salvation that takes its starting point from conversion's experience in time because conversion's assurance would only be threatened by thoughts of a hidden but more real decree of salvation that could

---

with synergistic theologies is their elevating of contingency to a level that it cannot handle. If human contingency is made the determining factor in every conversion, then this concept must absorb the theologians' cross's mystery as well as the theodicy questions concerning God's fairness in offering universal salvation while such is not realized in experience.

21. FC XI in Kolb and Wengert, *Book of Concord*, 518.12, "Instead, the reason for condemnation lies in their not hearing God's Word at all or arrogantly despising it, plugging their ears and their hearts . . . the fault lies not with God and his election but with their own wickedness."

A Theology of Religious Change

perhaps discredit the word's effectiveness in practice. But the subtler threat to salvation's comfort lies in the notion of the "responsibility" unbelievers have for their disposition and this concept's implications for the potential of belief.

The Reformers taught that regarding salvation, there are two total responsibilities—God's and the human creature's.[22] Broadly considered, this assertion acknowledges that in one sense God is the almighty creator who takes responsibility for ruling his creation. In another sense, God's lordship effaces neither human guilt nor responsibilities in life. Though these concepts are irreconcilable at points, they are presuppositions necessary for life under God's word. Their paradoxical nature does not rule out, however, clarification of human responsibility in terms of the gospel's universal call.[23]

The readiest source of confusion regarding human responsibility stems from two very different notions of the concept whose differentiation is philosophically crucial yet difficult to distinguish in everyday choices. Metaphysics has long recognized two possible kinds of responsibility based on the two broad strains of human freedom: compatibilism and incompatibilism (libertarianism).[24] Compatibilism holds that human choices can be free even if they are determined by unalterable causes, whereas incompatibilism holds that free choices are spontaneous such that they can come out differently in a given instant of decision. From these basic definitions different notions of responsibility follow, namely that for the compatibilist a responsible action is that which can be traced to a person's will, but for the incompatibilist responsibility is a function of indeterminate choice. For example, a sign in the park says "Do Not Feed the Ducks," but every time I walk by the duck pond I succumb to the temptation to share my lunch with them, and so one day a ranger catches and fines me. The incompatibilist will say that I am responsible for this infraction because, even though I have a duck feeding proclivity, I still made a free choice to act on it, and responsibility is traced to that choice. The compatibilist will say that I could not have

---

22. Kolb, *Bound Choice*, 6–10.

23. Theodore Dieter calls for continued work in defining the two total responsibilities, even if they are ultimately irresolvable in a meta-system. See Kolb, Review of *Bound Choice*, 691.

24. See Strawson, "Free Will," 745–53.

acted otherwise, but I am still responsible because the action resulted directly from my will without external coercion. One responsibility respects people's capacity at least to obey the law; the other, perhaps a *horrible* responsibility, is blind to counterfactuals, leaving people as responsible for their dispositions as a wolf is for chasing a rabbit.

This short visit in philosophy's office clarifies human responsibility regarding salvation. Though theology focuses on the heart's disposition more than moral action, the compatibilist viewpoint accurately summarizes how the will is responsible through its very disposition—not its potential to do otherwise. Regarding salvation, horrible responsibility rules, entailing that humans are incapable of turning toward Christ without the Spirit's intervention. It barely needs repeating that though this responsibility is horrible, the church valuing the gospel's comfort should not wish for another kind that opens up the decision for salvation, however slightly, and so places its burden directly on the human conscience. But the aspect of this responsibility seldom discussed is that the disbelief stranding so many people is not their fault such that they could do otherwise (as incompatibilism would hold) than reject Christ. The difference between belief and unbelief, that is, is not strictly a decision of *will* but *the gospel's presence* only possible by God's converting action. And if God is truly responsible for his creation, and he does not leave the particularity of salvation completely up to incompatibilist choice, then he too bears responsibility for unbelievers. Divine responsibility does not mean that God causes unbelief or sin but that he desires and works toward universal salvation. However, in working through the limitations of flawed agents he has constrained the means and method of spreading his salvation by depending on human responsibilities. The phenomenological perspective demonstrates contingencies on the human side showing that dead works (maybe even incompatibilist choices) sometimes lead people into the divine geography, furnishing the occasion of conversion; and sometimes baptized individuals manage to starve themselves of God's grace by choosing to avoid the geography. Though theology cannot deny God's ultimate control over his creation, these facts of experience are important for understanding belief and unbelief from the temporal perspective in which humans are meant to understand them.

A Theology of Religious Change

To approach the question phenomenologically is to admit that despite its best efforts theology has very little insight into God's monergistic acts in time. We know that in its converting capacity it overcomes the person, changing the mind, will, and heart, and that, in this moment, talk of simultaneously rejecting grace is meaningless. In this divine action the possibility of rejecting the gospel cannot apply because it would entail that a more powerful potential force than God's monergism exists, be it the human will or cosmic powers. Yet grace is often rejected when individuals turn away from or shut their ears to the divine geography, because grace does not work mechanically (*ex opere operato*), apart from hearing and understanding the word amid the church's network, nor does it allow us to take a "once, always saved" assurance for granted but acts rather like food that must continually nourish us (recall the Lord's Supper). The theologian's cross would be easier to address if God did manufacture Christians like a factory, but indeed he does not. People cling to the word at one point and fall away at another; some people build strong ties with the church but never believe. Thus, we are forced to conclude that the reason for unbelief lies in a shared mystery between God's inscrutable monergistic action strewn through time but also the contingency of non-saving phenomena that still indirectly affect salvation's appearance. This understanding leaves three hypothetical reasons for unbelief: 1) that at some points the human will indirectly causes unbelief by ignoring or choosing to cut itself off from God's word and sacrament. 2) Or perhaps the church itself causes unbelief by failing to preach Christ crucified. 3) It also postulates that, for unknowable reasons, God's Spirit does not change minds, wills, and hearts in every given instant, even if unbelievers are caught under the divine geography and listening to God's word proclaimed. Perhaps in any instant any combination of these three elements is possible. Even to mention them is to take theology out of its native environment, which is not to answer divine Rubik's cubes but to strengthen humans with the gospel.

These postulations demonstrate the mystery's furthest and most dangerous edge, the impossibility of knowing a simple root of unbelief, and the place traditionally featuring a citation of Rom 11:33. At this far edge, the only option is to turn back to communicate God's universally gracious will in each particular case of unbelief, knowing that even if God passes over an individual in time, that action neither rules out his desire for that person to be saved nor the necessary belief that, in his wisdom, he had reason for doing so, nor his future work to reach that person in the end.

The social sciences can help to clarify which doctrines or aspects of doctrine might best speak to each case. To review, chapter 3 discussed how people undergoing certain emotional crises might be theologically addressed by discussing God's election, giving them assurance of God's love. Chapter 4 discussed how a parental vocation is essential to children's religious upbringing and that the church itself might have to teach converts of God's fatherly love in cases where the converts have suffered unstable parental relationships. Chapter 5 listed some important deprivations that humans suffer along with their theological alleviations such as the dignity that God gives to all people regardless of wealth. And chapter 6 noted the church's imperative to evangelize and concentrate its own efforts on becoming a more loving community that will inevitably speak to the outside world. If the church faithfully learns its audience and proclaims God's universal graciousness and the law that clears away obstacles to it, then it has fulfilled its task.

The phenomenological approach to salvation is designed to inspire this effort to understand individual people in their particular spiritual and existential circumstances. By rooting salvation in faith's temporal manifestation it discourages thought of contrary preordained destinies while still upholding salvation's divine authorship. From here the task remains to treat the concept of predestination as separate from God's saving action in time to show that it can never threaten to overturn faith's temporal assurance or God's universal love. The next section can only be an outline for thinking about predestination afresh, but it serves the necessary task of finding a new departure point for this doctrine that resists the classically abstract formulations.

Predestination

"It is impossible for the human mind to take seriously the universality of grace if the particularity of grace is maintained with reference to the election of individuals."[25] This quotation from Hans Haug, more

25. Haug, "Predestination Controversy," 806. Liefeld deserves credit for finding this quotation.

than eight hundred pages into his dissertation on an American predestination controversy, highlights again the difficulty of addressing the theologians' cross abstractly. Constrained by similar categories that constrained the controversy, he opted for a dialectical approach that affirms both sides in existential tension. Indeed you could do worse, but while a dialectic is necessary to preserving the divine and human responsibilities in tension, I have proposed the phenomenological alternative to avoid an inherently unstable system that unravels the theologians' cross on God's account (weakening the universal call) or humanity's side (explaining salvation's particularity through the human will). The phenomenology's strength is its ability to uphold the gospel's temporal comfort and the universal call's earnestness because it roots out the threat of a deeper, contrary decree. The weakness of a phenomenology, however, is that in working to transcend abstract decretal theology, it does not naturally conceptualize predestination. Though a purely phenomenological approach might best serve theology eventually, the history of predestination controversy demands that this topic be addressed, especially if the phenomenology is to communicate to people who have never conceived of predestination outside of absolute decrees or absolutely conditional choices. This book can only offer an outline of how a new predestination theology might be feasible within a broader biblical and systematic theology.[26]

A crucial presupposition of biblical election theology, almost unrecognized in classic predestination theologies, is that the primary object of God's election is not individuals directly but a class.[27] God elects

---

26. Our inquiry will demonstrate its stable departure point by showing its biblical undergirding and tacit implications for interpreting Scripture's sticky language on divine and human acts. E.g., Paul admonishes: "work out your salvation" for "God works in you" (from Phil 2:12–13). A theology upholding monergism along with a realistic sense of human contingency (conceived as non-saving phenomena) naturally offers the conceptual tools to interpret this passage in an orthodox and useful fashion by explaining the meaning and limits of working out one's salvation, namely to place oneself continually within the divine geography.

27. Kaminsky, *Reclaiming the Biblical Concept of Election*, 185; Brueggemann, *Reverberations of Faith*, 63–64, "In the subsequent development of Christian theology, especially in the tradition of John Calvin, the notion of 'the elect' was hardened and perhaps unfortunately reified into teaching about predestination and double predestination. These formulations are attempts to root assurance of salvation in the inscrutable will of God. Such a formulation . . . turns the notion of YHWH's choosing in ways not intended or envisioned in the text."

Israel, or the *church*, but the Bible says nothing of a single, unconditional decree though which he chooses every person of all time for salvation.[28] When God singles out individuals (e.g., Noah, Abraham, Isaiah, Jesus, Paul) the narrative force is directed not to explaining their eternal heavenly security but their particular call to serve God's purpose. The selection of certain people for specific tasks is one manifestation of the general axiom that God elects the church, not in a heavenly vacuum but for its service in time.[29] The broad biblical concept of election's practical force furthers our concern to address the theologians' cross from a concrete and limited standpoint as opposed to abstraction. This view might be called a "corporate" or "communal" view of election because individuals are not chosen directly but by virtue of their incorporation into a chosen class of people.

The heavenly entailment of election's communal nature is that election (better stated here as predestination) derives from salvation's certainty in time. Just as the call to service originates in conversion (as someone becomes part of the chosen class), so does predestination itself: "Predestination is simply justification in the active voice."[30] The method of deriving predestination from conversion rules out speculation about God's pretemporal decrees, rather focusing on the eschatological aspect of salvation that points toward believers' final destiny. Pre-destination, to risk domesticating the concept, is like a train ticket. The destination is eternity, and the "pre" is now (or whenever the convert "receives the ticket"), but not God's inaccessible pretemporality. The train is predestined and individuals consequently by obtaining tickets (normatively in baptism). This viewpoint reveals vestiges of the "Theology of Hope" begun with Wolfhart Pannenberg and Jürgen Moltmann.[31] In this case predestination is an eschatological concept that grounds hope for those whom God justifies. We could even break down an anatomy of human faith and say that if justification grounds comfort and God's love grounds joy, then predestination grounds the hope that points to the

---

28. E.g., Rom. 9–11 will be misunderstood unless 9:30–31 is acknowledged as its center, explaining that Israel must recognize that God's elect are the class of people who have a righteousness of faith rather than the law.

29. Newbigin explains that election's very logic is that a select group is called in service to the outside world. See *Gospel in a Pluralist Society*, 80–88.

30. Braaten and Jensen, *Christian Dogmatics*, 2:134.

31. See Braaten and Jensen, *The Futurist Option*.

consummation of God's kingdom.[32] The important aspect of this position for our purposes is that election is considered as something known in time as a consequence of conversion, not conversion's eternal and efficient cause.

This corporate doctrine is a way to view predestination as beginning in salvation, asking what the doctrine implies for the church's life. In this respect it complements the phenomenology of salvation's prescription that predestination is a doctrine foremost of comfort. Communally focused, it provides a clear principal of worship. Though individuals cannot maintain their faith by a sheer act of will, a community of believers equipped with God's word embody the geography where faith can grow and individuals are assured of their predestination to eternity. This assurance will not be guaranteed, however, unless theology demonstrates how God's decrees do not threaten the gospel's temporal assurance or universal call, both of which support faith's comfort.

Perhaps the clearest implication of a corporate election model is that God's pretemporal decree (what we can confidently say about it anyway) concerns the means of providing salvation. How individuals become elect through this means is impossible to generalize and thus cannot be summarized in abstract statements (viz. that God's choice or human choice explains ultimate destinies). Instead, this study has encouraged this question to be asked on a concrete level with help from the social sciences. For those who must ask what God was thinking before the world's foundation, the answer is that he was predestinating Christ, as Karl Barth so forcibly argued, but Christ as the means of salvation and gift to the church.[33] Election is absolute/unconditional only as far as it concerns Christ as the means of salvation, and individuals are elect only on the condition that they are in him. Ephesians 1, for

---

32. Cf. Rom. 8:29-30. Kyle Pasewark's similar view of predestination shows the doctrine as a ground of comfort because it is "a condition of freedom" from sin and anxieties. Where Braaten and Jensen emphasize the eschatological dimension, Pasewark highlights predestination's existential significance. Though he ascribes to a double predestination, his interpretation of the doctrine concerns its effects beginning in conversion and the church's embrace of the doctrine in time. See Pasewark, "Predestination as a Condition of Freedom," 49-66.

33. Karl Barth emphasized that the object of God's election is not an arbitrary decree to save some individuals and condemn others. For him Christ is the truly elect one, yet also the only reprobate one. See *Church Dogmatics*, 2:2, 94.

example, emphasizes that Ephesus's church was not chosen vacuously but was chosen *"in him,"* a phrase used ten times in the first fourteen verses, directing election's focus to Christ. Again, God's decree of election as a means of salvation implies that individuals are not predestined in an absolute/unconditional sense but on the condition that they are in Christ. Election's conditional nature is precisely the hard truth for Israel in Rom 9–11, when Paul declares that only a remnant will be saved by faith in Christ rather than by lawful works. Christ's presence to the church forms the historical containment beyond which we dare not speculate or doubt, and we trust that God's gift of salvation in time cannot be compromised by thoughts that he has a deeper, contrary will than what times reveals.[34]

To emphasize election's unconditional corporate nature and conditional individual nature might, however, appear naïve. The point might be raised that if God foreknew the world and his actions in it, then he has a limited number of elect, and if this number is fixed in God's foreknowledge, then these elect are the only people that God can save. For the church, God's foreknowledge brings assurance that he foreknows his children and can unfailingly fulfill his promises to them. Even if individuals can forfeit their election by forsaking grace's source, God has provided the gifts he knew as most fitting to nourish faith. However, for those outside of the church, this assertion again highlights the seeming unfairness that some people are born closer to the divine geography than others. And to acknowledge God's omniscience is to conclude that he created the world fully aware of this unfairness. At this point theology is most vulnerable to the theologians' cross, as the history of predestination controversy demonstrates, because the Western mind,

---

34. This viewpoint can be philosophically structured by arguing that history has an ontological priority over God's foreknowledge, allowing God to foreknow and account for sin without causing it. For the phenomenology of salvation, this approach functions as a way to uplift saving phenomena as the most real reality, that is, revealing the gospel's reliably rather than leaving room to doubt that God has a hidden will behind his promises in time. At the same time, it makes God's providence a function of his foreknowledge, preserving a broad sense of God's lordship over his creation despite sin's current reign. William Craig and Alvin Plantinga both provide philosophical accounts substantiating how God's complete foreknowledge of all future events could ground his providence. See Craig, *The Only Wise God*, 127–52, and Plantinga, *The Nature of Necessity*, 164–96.

A Theology of Religious Change

at least, is ever tempted to reach a single resolution.[35] The theologian's cross is so much a part and product of our thinking that we can barely resist concluding that before time and behind the scenes of history lies an unconditional saving decree to which our notions of unconditional election correspond directly. Or, we become sickened by this thought and conclude that predestination must be the result of foreseen faith (*intuitu fidei*).[36] But theologians have failed to notice that even in opting for this conditionality creates God's absolute decree to save through human contingency. The initial emotional benefits of placing evil's origin in the human will still become crucified in the theologian's cross because the problem of foreseen faith just as with unconditional election is not, at its deepest, the paradigm's argument but the paradigm itself that creates a tendency to read Scripture through presupposed abstractions. The theologians' cross, it appears, is not an enemy from the outside that theology must flee from or fend off; it is a sickness within our very selves that is responsible for countless polarizations. The only solution I foresee is to shift election's paradigm by turning to conversion's concrete and thus self-limiting interpretation that encourages the church far less to debate than to take practical initiative to use what resources it has to communicate the gospel.

Such a paradigm shift does not, however, mean that the church has nothing to say about the tension between God's universally saving will and election's particularity. It simply recognizes that a satisfying resolution is impossible. To posit election as a historically conditioned phenomenon functions to eliminate thoughts of a decree that undercuts the gospel's temporal presence, and in focusing away from an abstract predestination concept, God's universal call can still be believed even if it cannot make election seem equitable to all people.

The issue of fairness, a "scandal of particularity," will always irritate theology. Theologians will have to settle for limited explanations of fairness. Because God has chosen to work through the church, part of salvation's inequity is a result of his choosing fallen human beings who sometimes flout their election's mission. God's response to this unfairness is embodied in the church's response, that it use what resources

---

35. See Thuesen, *Predestination: The American Career of a Contentious Doctrine*, 1–13.

36. Haug, "Predestination Controversy," 124–30.

Conversion and the Divine Choice

it has to communicate the gospel to people who do not yet believe. Even the church's frustration at God's silence and lack of monergistic action can never indicate a contrary mission or expectation than that God works to save humankind, in his own timing, through his elect. I stated earlier that part of the limitation for thinking about the theologians' cross is historical, that we hope to know more about the fullness of God's salvation in the eschaton. Though we know on the basis of God's omniscience that he must have, even factoring in the temporal contingency of human perseverance, an absolute number of elect whom he converts, we know very little else except that God's decree of predestination primarily concerns Christ and the church without cutting anyone off from salvation.

Theologians rarely reflect on how the universal hope of salvation based on God's desire to save all people is known purely by Scripture, whereas the particularity of salvation is known through Scripture and experience together. Because particularity is so obvious to experience (if we encounter people every day who reject Christ), it has more cogency than believing that God desires universal salvation. But simply because experience makes one doctrine seem truer does not entail that the doctrine, in final analysis, is actually truer. Because predestination does not have to be considered absolute but a corporate and historically conditioned doctrine, I hope that the possibility of a wider salvation will be more believable and that God's elect will be greater in number than now appears. Certain theologians have embraced the possibility that death does not end the possibility of salvation,[37] and though the possibility of a postmortem encounter with Christ cannot ground any certainty of universalism or become a normative doctrine, it might at least open to us the hope that God's ability to claim individuals for himself has broader limitations than our viewpoint from here. If we do not

---

37. See Althaus, *Die Letzten Dinge*, 188, in which he says that Jesus can reach those "beyond the limits of our history": "*Unsere Gedanken können aber auch den Weg gehen, den 1 Petr. 3:19; 4:6 und das kirchliche Bekenntnis zum descensus Christi ad infernos zunächst im Blicke auf die alttestamentliche Menscheit wiesen: Christus wird jenseits der Grenzen unsere Geschichte (wo und wann, ist uns verborgen) allen, die er in der Geschichte mit dem Evangelium nicht erreichte, noch begegnen und sie zur Entscheidung und Scheidung vor sich stellen.*" Seeberg, *Christliche Dogmatik*, 2:623–24. Schlatter, *Das Christliche Dogma*, 594–95. Lindbeck, "Unbelievers and the 'Sola Christi,'" 80; and Lindbeck, *The Nature of Doctrine*, 58–59. For a fuller bibliography see Sanders, *No Other Name*, 177–214.

embrace a predestination theology with such complexity and nuance, then the predestination of individuals might, as Haug asserts, threaten to make us incredulous toward God's universally desired salvation that is more difficult to believe than particularity (based on experience), yet crucial to election's very logic.[38]

The End and the Mid-Point

In conclusion, this question about why people believe the gospel or not has always been a difficult topic in terms of its polarizing nature, interwoven anxieties about eternal securities, and consequent hostilities over absolutely important matters. Rather than trying to solve the divine puzzle, I have tried to redirect the question toward its practical significance by arguing that the theologian's cross will always crucify us if we are lured into handling it in absolute or unconditional terms from either God's side or humanity's. The answer suggested is that this work's previous chapters make significant headway not only into conversion but actually portray God's response to the unfairness between the chosen and the outside world. By clearing out the abstract considerations of the theologian's cross and opting for a phenomenological approach that the correlational method interprets to keep saving and non-saving phenomena separate, I hope to have established an honest theological basis from where the church can trust that its faith in Christ and God's universal desire for salvation are not compromised by a secret decree or a burden to choose Christ from one's own will power.

The psychological and sociological research used to develop the phenomenology of religious change will inevitably be surpassed by more precise insights into human nature or more adequate conceptual structures adapted to an ever-changing world, but I am convinced that many of the insights discussed are classic. Though the way we talk about them might change from time to time, there will always be crises preceding religious changes, for example, and social networks providing a place of rest. The one major shortcoming of this study's scope is that it could not address the problem of cultural differences, which is a crucial factor to consider when translating the Bible or communicating

---

38. Newbigin, *Gospel in a Pluralist Society*, 80–81.

the gospel across nations. That task must be left to someone else with my hope that this study's data, which focuses almost exclusively on the western world, will still be useful to explain conversion everywhere in some (albeit incomplete) fashion.

Though we have reached the end of this book, the proposal that phenomenology is our best response to the theologian's cross is conceptually a mid-point—a location from where the reader is encouraged to go back to the beginning and view the accounts of conversion and religious change as instantiations of the divine choice. This divine choice calls the church to seek its ultimacy through Christ in time and to share this assuring message with the world outside.

Bibliography

Allison, Joel. "Recent Empirical Studies of Religious Conversion Experiences." *Pastoral Psychology* 17.166 (Sept 1966) 21–27.

———. "Religious Conversion: Regression and Progression in an Adolescent Experience." *Journal for the Scientific Study of Religion* 8 (1969) 23–38.

Alper, Matthew. *The "God" Part of the Brain: A Scientific Interpretation of Human Spirituality and God.* Naperville, IL: Sourcebooks, 2006.

Altemeyer, Bob, and Bruce Hunsberger. *Amazing Conversions: Why Some Turn to Faith and Others Abandon Religion.* New York: Prometheus, 1997.

Althaus, Paul. *Die Letzten Dinge.* Gütersloh, Germany: Gütersloher, 1964.

Austin, Roy. "Empirical Adequacy of Lofland's Conversion Model." *Review of Religious Research* 18 (1977) 282–87.

Bainbridge, William. "The Sociology of Conversion." In *Handbook of Religious Conversion*, edited by H. Newton Malony and Samuel Southard, 178–91. Birmingham, AL: Religious Education, 1992.

Balch, Robert. "Looking Behind the Scenes in a Religious Cult: Implications for the Study of Conversion." *Sociological Analysis* 41 (1980) 137–43.

Balch, Robert, and David Taylor. "Seekers and Saucers: The Role of Cultic Milieu in Joining a UFO Cult." In *Conversion Careers: In and Out of the New Religions*, edited by James Richardson, 43–64. Beverly Hills, CA: Sage, 1977.

Bankston, William et al. "Toward a General Model of the Process of Radical Conversion: An Interactionist Perspective on the Transformation of Self-Identity." *Qualitative Sociology* 4 (1981) 279–93.

Barnhart, Joe, and Mary Barnhart. *The New Birth: A Naturalistic View of Religious Conversion.* Macon, GA: Mercer, 1981.

Barth, Karl. *Church Dogmatics.* 4 vols. Edited by G. W. Bromiley and T. F. Torrance. Edinburgh: T. & T. Clark, 1936–69.

Batson, C. Daniel et al. *Religion and the Individual: A Social-Psychological Perspective.* New York: Oxford, 1993.

Beit-Hallahmi, Benjamin, and Michael Argyle. *The Psychology of Religious Behavior: Belief and Experience.* New York: Routledge, 1997.

Berger, Peter. *Invitation to Sociology.* Garden City, NY: Anchor Doubleday, 1963.

Blasi, Anthony. "The Meaning of Conversion: Redirection of Foundational Trust." In *Conversion in the Age of Pluralism*, edited by Guiseppe Giordan, 11–32. Leiden: Brill, 2009.

Bonhoeffer, Dietrich. *The Cost of Discipleship.* New York: Touchstone, 1995.

Bibliography

Braaten, Carl, and Robert Jensen, eds. *Christian Dogmatics*. Vol. 2. Philadelphia: Fortress, 1984.

———. *The Futurist Option*. New York: Newman, 1970.

Bromley, David, and Anson Shupe, Jr. "'Just a Few Years Seems Like a Lifetime': A Role Theory Approach to Participation in Religious Movements." In *Research in Social Movements, Conflict, and Change*, Vol. 2, edited by L. Krisberg, 159–86. Greenwich, CT: JAI, 1979.

Brown, Warren, and Carla Caetano. "Conversion, Cognition, and Neuropsychology." In *Handbook of Religious Conversion*, edited by H. Newton Malony and Samuel Southard, 178–91. Birmingham, AL: Religious Education, 1992.

Brueggemann, Walter. *Reverberations of Faith: A Theological Handbook of Old Testament Themes*. Louisville: Westminster John Knox, 2002.

Brunstad, Friedrich. *Theologie der Lutherischen Bekenntnisschriften*. Gütersloh, Germany: Bertelsmann, 1951.

Bultmann, Rudolf. *Kerygma and Myth*. Edited by Hans Werner Bartsch. New York: Harper Torch, 1961.

———. "Jesus Christus und die Mythologie." In *Glauben und Verstehen*, Bd. 4, 141–89. Tübingen: Mohr, 1965.

Calvin, John. *The Institutes of the Christian Religion*. Edited by John McNeill. Philadelphia: Westminster, 1960.

Carter, John. "Secular and Sacred Models of Psychology and Religion." In *Psychology of Religion: Personalities, Problems, Possibilities*, edited by H. Newton Malony, 435–49. Grand Rapids: Baker, 1991.

Christensen, Carl. "Religious Conversion." *Archives of General Psychiatry* 9 (1963) 207–16.

———. "Religious Conversion in Adolescence." *Pastoral Psychology* 16.156 (1965) 17–28.

Clark, W. H. *The Psychology of Religion*. New York: Macmillan, 1958.

Collins, Gary. "An Integration View." In *Psychology and Christianity: Four Views*, edited by Eric Johnson and Stanton Jones, 102–47. Downer's Grove, IL: InterVarsity, 2000.

Crabtree, Steve, and Brett Pelham. "Religion Provides Emotional Boost to World's Poor." *Gallup Archives*. No Pages. Online: http://www.gallup.com/poll/116449/Religion-Provides-Emotional-Boost-World-Poor.aspx (accessed March 9, 2009).

Craig, William L. *The Only Wise God: The Compatibility of Divine Foreknowledge and Human Freedom*. Eugene, OR: Wipf & Stock, 2000.

———. *Reasonable Faith: Christian Truth and Apologetics*. Wheaton, IL: Crossway, 2008.

Dawkins, Richard. *The Selfish Gene*. 2nd ed. New York: Oxford University, 1990.

Dawson, Lorne. "Self-Affirmation, Freedom, and Rationality: Theoretically Elaborating 'Active' Conversions." *Journal for the Scientific Study of Religion* 29 (1990) 141–63.

Demerath, Nicholas. *Social Class in American Protestantism*. Chicago: McNally, 1965.

Dericquebourg, Régis. "Becoming a New Ager: A Conversion, An Affiliation, A Fashion?" In *Conversion in the Age of Pluralism*, edited by Guiseppe Giordan, 131–62. Leiden: Brill, 2009.

Downton, James. "An Evolutionary Theory of Spiritual Conversion and Commitment: The Case of Divine Light Mission." *Journal for the Scientific Study of Religion* 19 (1980) 381–96.

Eberhard, Ernest. "How to Share the Gospel: A Step-by-Step Approach for You and Your Neighbors." *Ensign* (June 1974) 6–13.

Edwards, Jonathan. *The Religious Affections*. New Haven, CT: Yale University Press, 1959.

Eliade, Mircea. *The Sacred and the Profane: The Nature of Religion*. Translated by Willard Trask. New York: Harcourt, 1987.

Erikson, Erik. *Childhood and Society*. 2nd ed. New York: Norton, 1963.

———. *Identity, Youth, and Crisis*. New York: Norton, 1968.

Evans, C. Stephen. *Subjectivity and Religious Belief: An Historical, Critical Study*. Grand Rapids: Christian University, 1978.

Festinger, Leon. *A Theory of Cognitive Dissonance*. Stanford, CA: Stanford, 1957.

Forde, Gerhard. *Theology Is for Proclamation*. Minneapolis: Fortress, 1990.

Fowler, James. *Stages of Faith: The Psychology of Human Development and the Quest for Meaning*. San Francisco: Harper & Row, 1981.

Frank, Franz Hermann Reinhold. *Die Theologie der Concordienformel*. 4 vols. Erlangen: Blaesing, 1858–65.

Fredrickson, Barbara. "The Role of Positive Emotions in Positive Psychology." *American Psychologist* 56 (2001) 218–26.

Freud, Sigmund. *The Future of an Illusion*. Translated by W. D. Robinson-Scott. New York: Liveright, 1928.

———. "A Religious Experience (1928)." In *The Standard Edition of the Complete Works of Sigmund Freud*. Vol. 21 (1927–31), translated by James Strachey, et al., 167–74. London: Hogarth, 1975.

Fritz, John. *Pastoral Theology*. St. Louis: Concordia, 1932.

Gartrell, David, and Zane Shannon. "Contacts Cognitions and Conversion: A Rational Choice Approach." *Review of Religious Research* 27 (1985) 32–48.

Glock, Charles, and Rodney Stark. *Religion and Society in Tension*. Chicago: McNally, 1965.

Glock, Charles. "The Role of Deprivation in the Origin and Evolution of Religious Groups." In *Religion and Social Conflict*, edited by Robert Lee and Martin Marty, 24–36. New York: Oxford, 1964.

Gogarten, Friedrich. *The Reality of Faith: The Problem of Subjectivism in Theology*. Translated by Carl Michalson. Philadelphia: Westminster, 1959.

Granqvist, Pehr. "Attachment Theory and Religious Conversions: A Review and a Resolution of the Classic and Contemporary Paradigm Chasm." *Review of Religious Research* 45 (2003) 172–87.

———. "Religiousness and Perceived Childhood Attachment: On the Question of Compensation or Correspondence." *Journal for the Scientific Study of Religion* 37 (1998) 350–67.

Granqvist, Pehr, and Berit Hagekull. "Religiousness and Perceived Childhood Attachment: Profiling Socialized Correspondence and Emotional Compensation." *Journal for the Scientific Study of Religion* 38 (1999) 254–73.

Bibliography

Granqvist, Pehr, and Lee Kirkpatrick. "Religious Conversion and Perceived Childhood Attachment: A Meta-Analysis." *The International Journal for the Psychology of Religion* 14 (2004) 223–50.

Gutiérrez, Gustavo. *A Theology of Liberation*. Maryknoll, NY: Orbis, 1988.

Hak, Durk. "Conversion as a Rational Choice." In *Paradigms, Poetics and Politics of Conversion*, edited by Jan Bremmer et al., 13–25. Leuven: Peeters, 2006.

Halama, Peter, and Júlia Halamová. "Process of Religious Conversion in the Catholic Charismatic Movement: A Qualitative Analysis." *Archive für Religionpsychologie* 27 (2005) 69–92.

Haug, Hans. "The Predestination Controversy in the Lutheran Church in North America." PhD diss., Temple University, 1968.

Hegel, G. W. F. *The Phenomenology of Mind*. Translated by J. B. Ballie. New York: Macmillan, 1949.

Henning, Christian, and Erich Nestler, eds. *Konversion: Zur Aktualität eines Jahrhundertthemas*. Frankfurt: Lang, 2002.

Heirich, Max. "Change of Heart: A Test of Some Widely Held Theories about Religious Conversion." *The American Journal of Sociology* 83 (1977) 653–80.

James, William. *The Varieties of Religious Experience*. Reprint. New York: Touchstone, 1997.

Johnson, Paul E. *Psychology of Religion*. New York: Abingdon, 1959.

Jung, Carl. *Modern Man in Search of a Soul*. New York: Harvest, 1933.

Jung, Carl, and C. Kerényi. *Essays on a Science of Mythology*. New York: Bollingen, 1969.

Kaminsky, Joel. *Yet I Loved Jacob: Reclaiming the Biblical Concept of Election*. Nashville: Abingdon, 2007.

Kant, Immanuel. *The Critique of Pure Reason*. Translated by J. M. D. Meiklejohn. New York: Prometheus, 1990.

Kerr, Hugh, and John Mulder, eds. *Famous Conversions: The Christian Experience*. Grand Rapids: Eerdmans, 1994.

Kirkpatrick, Lee. "An Attachment-Theory Approach to the Psychology of Religion." *The International Journal for the Psychology of Religion* 2 (1992) 3–28.

Kirkpatrick, Lee, and Phillip Shaver. "Attachment Theory and Religion: Childhood Attachments, Religious Beliefs, and Conversion." *Journal of the Scientific Study of Religion* 29 (1990) 315–34.

Knoblauch, Hubert et al., eds. *Religiöse Konversion: Systematische und Fallorientierte Studien in Soziologischer Perspektive*. Konstanz, Germany: Konstanz, 1998.

Kolb, Robert. *Bound Choice, Election, and Wittenberg Theological Method: From Martin Luther to the Formula of Concord*. Grand Rapids: Eerdmans, 2005.

———. *Martin Luther: Confessor of the Faith*. New York: Oxford University, 2009.

———. Review of *Bound Choice, Election, and Wittenberg Theological Method: From Martin Luther to the Formula of Concord*. By Theodore Dieter. *Theological Studies* 68 (2007) 690–91.

Kolb, Robert, and Timothy Wengert, eds. *The Book of Concord: The Confessions of the Evangelical Lutheran Church*. Minneapolis: Fortress, 2000.

Köse, Ali. "Religious Conversion: Is It an Adolescent Phenomenon? The Case of Native British Converts to Islam." *The International Journal for the Psychology of Religion* 6 (1996) 253–62.

Bibliography

Kox, Willem et al. "Religious Conversion of Adolescents: Testing the Lofland and Stark Model of Religious Conversion." *Sociological Analysis* 52 (1991) 227–40.

Kreeft, Peter, and Ronald Tacelli, *Handbook of Christian Apologetics*. Downers Grove, IL: InterVarsity, 1994.

Lahkdar, Mounia et al. "Conversion to Islam among French Adolescents and Adults: A Systematic Inventory of Motives." *International Journal for the Psychology of Religion* 17 (2007) 1–15.

Liefeld, David. "Saved on Purpose: Luther, Lutheranism, and Election." *Logia* 15.2 (2006) 5–16.

Lifton, Robert Jay. "Protean Man." In *History and Human Survival: Essays on the Young and Old, Survivors and the Dead, Peace and War, and on Contemporary Psychohistory*, 311–31. New York: Vintage, 1961.

Lindbeck, George. *The Nature of Doctrine: Religion and Theology in a Postliberal Age*. Philadelphia: Westminster, 1984.

———. "Unbelievers and the 'Sola Christi.'" In *The Church in a Postliberal Age*, edited by James Buckley, 77–87. Grand Rapids: Eerdmans, 2003.

Lofland, John. "'Becoming a World-Saver' Revisited." *American Behavioral Scientist* 20 (1977) 805–18.

———. *Doomsday Cult: A Study of Conversion, Proselytization, and Maintenance of Faith*. Englewood Cliffs, NJ: Prentice-Hall, 1966.

Lofland, John, and Norman Skonovd. "Conversion Motifs." *Journal for the Scientific Study of Religion* 20 (1981) 373–85.

Lofland, John, and Rodney Stark. "Becoming a World Saver: Conversion to a Deviant Perspective." *American Sociological Review* 30 (1965) 862–75.

Long, Theodore, and Jeffrey Hadden. "Religious Conversion and the Concept of Socialization: Integrating the Brainwashing and Drift Models." *Journal for the Scientific Study of Religion* 22 (1983) 1–14.

Loveland, Matthew. "Religious Switching: Preference Development, Maintenance, and Change." *Journal for the Scientific Study of Religion* 42 (2003) 147–57.

Luther, Martin. *The Bondage of the Will*. Translated by J. I. Packer and O. R. Johnston. Grand Rapids: Baker, 2002.

———. *Luther's Works*. 55 vols. Edited by Jaroslav Jan Pelikan et al. Philadelphia: Fortress, 1999.

Machalek, Richard, and David Snow, "Conversion to New Religious Movements." In *The Handbook of Cults and Sects in America, vol. 3: Religion and Social Order*, edited by David Bromley and Jeffrey Hadden, 53–74. Greenwich, CT: JAI, 1993.

Marshall, I. Howard. *Kept by the Power of God: A Study of Perseverance and Falling Away*. London: Epworth, 1969.

Marx, Karl. "Critique of Hegel's *Philosophy of Right*." In *The Marx-Engels Reader*, edited by Robert Tucker, 11–23. New York: Norton, 1972.

Malony, H. Newton. *The Psychology of Religion for Ministry*. Mahwah, NJ: Paulist, 1995.

Meehl, Paul, et al. *What, Then, Is Man?*. St. Louis: Concordia, 1958.

Miller, William, and Janet C'de Baca. *Quantum Change: When Epiphanies and Sudden Insights Transform Ordinary Lives*. New York: Guilford, 2001.

Moltmann, Jürgen. *Theologie der Hoffnung: Untersuchungen zur Begründung und zu den Konsequenzen einer christlichen Eschatologie*. Munich: Kaiser, 1997.

Bibliography

Muller, Richard. *Dictionary of Latin and Greek Theological Terms: Drawn Principally from Protestant Scholastic Theology.* Grand Rapids: Baker, 1985.

Myers, David, and Malcolm Jeeves. *Psychology through the Eyes of Faith.* San Francisco: Harper Collins, 2003.

Newberg, Andrew et al. *Why God Will Not Go Away: Brain Science and the Biology of Belief.* New York: Ballantine, 2001.

Niebuhr, H. Richard. *Christ and Culture.* New York: Harper & Row, 1956.

———. *The Social Sources of Denominationalism.* Hamden, CT: Shoe String, 1954.

Oatley, Keith, and Maja Djikic. "Emotions and Transformation: Varieties of Experience of Identity." *Journal of Consciousness Studies* 9.9–10 (2002) 97–116.

Oksanen, Antti. *Religious Conversion: A Meta-Analytical Study.* Sweden: Lund, 1994.

Paloutzian, Raymond. "Religious Conversion and Spiritual Transformation: A Meaning System Analysis." In *Handbook of the Psychology of Religion and Spirituality*, edited by Raymond Paloutzian and Crystal Park, 331–47. New York: Guilford, 2005.

Paloutzian, Raymond et al. "Religious Conversion and Personality Change." *Journal of Personality* 67 (1999) 1047–79.

Pascal, Blaise. *Pensées.* Translated by Honor Levi. New York: Oxford University, 1999.

Pasewark, Kyle. "Predestination as a Condition of Freedom: Reconsidering the Reformation." In *Human and Divine Agency: Anglican, Catholic, and Lutheran Perspectives*, edited by F. Michael McLain and W. Mark Richardson, 49–66. Lanham, MD: University Press of America, 1999.

Peace, Richard. *Conversion in the New Testament: Paul and the Twelve.* Grand Rapids: Eerdmans, 1999.

Pieper, Francis. *Christian Dogmatics.* 3 vols. St. Louis: Concordia, 1950–53.

Pinnock, Clark. *A Wideness in God's Mercy: The Finality of Jesus Christ in a World of Religions.* Grand Rapids: Zondervan, 1992.

Pitt, John. "Why People Convert: A Balance Theoretical Approach." *Pastoral Psychology* 39 (1991) 171–83.

Plantinga, Alvin. *The Nature of Necessity.* Oxford: Clarendon, 1979.

———. *Warranted Christian Belief.* Oxford: Oxford University, 2000.

Rambo, Lewis. "Charisma and Conversion." *Pastoral Psychology* 31 (1982) 96–108.

Reetz, Ulrich. *Das Sakramentale in der Theologie Paul Tillichs.* Stuttgart: Calwer, 1974.

Richardson, James. "The Active vs. Passive Convert: Paradigm Conflict in Conversion/Recruitment Research." *Journal for the Scientific Study of Religion* 20 (1985) 163–79.

Richardson, James, and Brock Kilbourne. "Paradigm Conflict, Types of Conversion, and Conversion Theories." *Sociological Analysis* 50 (1988) 1–21.

Salzman, Leon. "The Psychology of Religious and Ideological Conversion." *Psychiatry* 16 (1953) 177–87.

Sanders, John. *No Other Name: An Investigation into the Destiny of the Unevangelized.* Grand Rapids: Eerdmans, 1992.

Sartre, Jean Paul. *L'Existentialisme est un humanisme.* Paris: Nagel, 1970.

Schlatter, Adolf. *Das Christliche Dogma.* Calwer, Germany: Vereins, 1911.

Schleiermacher, Friedrich. *On Religion: Speeches to its Cultured Despisers.* Edited by Richard Crouter. Cambridge: Cambridge University Press, 2004.

Seeberg, Reinhold. *Christliche Dogmatik*, Bd. 2. Erlangen, Germany: Deichertische, 1925.

Seggar, John, and Phillip Kunz. "Conversion: Evaluation of a Step-Like Process for Problem Solving." *Review of Religious Research* 13 (1972) 178–84.
Shaw, Marvin. "Paradoxical Intention in the Life and Thought of William James." *American Journal of Theology and Philosophy* 7 (1986) 5–16.
Shinn, Larry. "Conflicting Networks: Guru and Friend in ISKCON." In *Religious Movements: Genesis, Exodus, and Numbers*, edited by Rodney Stark, 95–114. New York: Paragon, 1986.
———. "Who Gets to Define Religion? The Conversion/Brainwashing Controversy." *Religious Studies Review* 19 (1993) 195–207.
Snow, David, and Richard Machalek, "The Convert as Social Type." *Sociological Theory* 1 (1983) 259–89.
———. "The Sociology of Conversion." *Annual Review of Sociology* 10 (1984) 167–90.
Spilka, Bernard et al., eds. *The Psychology of Religion: An Empirical Approach*. New York: Guilford, 2003.
Starbuck, Edwin Diller. *The Psychology of Religion*. London: Scribners, 1900.
Stark, Rodney, and Roger Finke. *Acts of Faith: Explaining the Human Side of Religion*. Berkeley: University of California, 2000.
Stark, Rodney, and William Bainbridge. *The Future of Religion: Secularization, Revival, and Cult Formation*. Berkeley: University of California, 1985.
———. "Networks of Faith: Interpersonal Bonds and Recruitment to Sects and Cults." *American Journal of Sociology* 85 (1980) 1376–95.
———. *A Theory of Religion*. New York: Lang, 1987.
———. "Toward a Theory of Religion: Religious Commitment." *Journal for the Scientific Study of Religion* 19 (1980) 114–28.
Straus, Roger. "Changing Oneself: Seekers and the Creative Transformation of Life Experience." In *Doing Social Life*, edited by John Lofland, 252–73. New York: Wiley, 1976.
———. "Religious Conversion as a Personal and Collective Accomplishment." *Sociological Analysis* 40 (1979) 158–65.
Strawson, Galen. "Free Will." In *Routledge Encyclopedia of Philosophy*, edited by Edward Craig, 743–53. London: Routledge, 1998.
Thuesen, Peter. *Predestination: The American Career of a Contentious Doctrine*. New York: Oxford, 2009.
Travisano, Richard. "Alternation and Conversion as Qualitatively Different Transformations." In *Social Psychology through Symbolic Interaction*, edited by Gregory Stone and Harvey Farberman, 594–606. Waltham, MA: Ginn-Blaisdell, 1970.
Ullman, Chana. "Cognitive and Emotional Antecedents of Religious Conversion." *Journal of Personality and Social Psychology* 43 (1982) 183–92.
———. "Psychological Well-being Among Converts in Traditional and Nontraditional Religious Groups." *Psychiatry* 51 (1988) 312–22.
———. *Transformed Self: The Psychology of Religious Conversion*. New York: Plenum, 1989.
Waller, Niels et al. "Genetic and Environmental Influences on Religious Interests, Attitudes, and Values: A Study of Twins Reared Apart and Together." *Psychological Science* 1 (1990) 138–42.
Weber, Max. *Grundriss der Sozialökonomik*. Tübingen: Mohr, 1922.

Bibliography

Wengert, Timothy. "The Formula of Concord and the Comfort of Election." *Lutheran Quarterly* 20 (2006) 44–62.

Wenz, Gunther. *Theologie der Bekenntnisschriften der Evangelisch-Lutherischen Kirche*, Bd. 2. Berlin: de Gruyter, 1997.

Wootton, Raymond, and David Allen. "Dramatic Religious Conversion and Schizophrenic Decompensation." *Journal of Religion and Health* 22 (1983) 212–19.

Zock, Hetty. "Paradigms in Psychological Conversion Research: Between Social Science and Literary Analysis." In *Paradigms, Poetics and Politics of Conversion*, edited by Jan Bremmer et al., 41–58. Leuven: Peeters, 2006.

Zurcher, Louis, and David Snow. "Collective Behavior: Social Movements." In *Social Psychology: Sociological Perspectives*, edited by Morris Rosenberg and Ralph Turner, 447–82. New York: Basic, 1981.

Index

active seekership, research on, 46–52
Allison, Joel, 75–76
alternation, 29–31, 47
Althaus, Paul, 165n37
apologetics, 45–46
Archimedes, 23, 43
Argyle, Michael, 70
attachment theory, 79–85
Augustine, Saint, 72, 76
Austin, Roy, 123
Bainbridge, William, 104–5, 113–15, 123, 127
Balch, Robert, 52, 111
baptism, 7, 161
Barth, Karl, xx, 162
Batson, C. Daniel, 21–25, 68, 153
Beit-Hallahmi, Benjamin, 70
Berger, Peter, 29, 33, 47, 50, 52
Bonhoeffer, Dietrich, 110, 154n19
Braaten, Carl, 161 n30–31
Brainerd, David, 99–100
brainwashing, 6n18, 46, 48–49, 110
Bromley, David, 111–13
Brueggemann, Walter, 160n27
Buddhism, 17, 48, 120, 124
Bultmann, Rudolf, xx, 117n2
Calvin, John, 13, 16n21
Carter, John, xvi
catechesis, role in religious development, 68–70
Christ, as conversion's center, 6
Christensen, Carl, 74–76, 79, 86
Clark, W. H., 41n3
cognitive dissonance, 43, 49, 116n61

comfort, theologically understood, xix, 5, 9, 15, 55, 57, 61–63, 81–82, 85, 95, 100n30, 146, 149, 156–57, 160–62
communication, of the gospel as a primary goal, xiii, xiv, xxi, 114–16, 152, 165
conscience, xix–xx, 55n46, 56–57, 60–61, 63, 134, 137, 139, 155, 157
conversion, defined, 6
corporate election, 161–63, 165
correlational method, outlined, xvi–xxi
Craig, William L., 144–46, 163n34
crisis, research on, 55–59
cults, 52, 110–11, 119–20, 124–25
Dawkins, Richard, xviii2
depravity, xvi, 3, 44
deprivation sociology, defined, 94
despair, 8–10, 16, 32, 63, 75, 83, 89, 134, 140, 143, 149, 154
divine geography, outlined, 151–55
Divine Light Mission, 49–50, 56, 125
doubt, challenging meaning systems, 41–44
Downton, James, 125
dynamics of change, 17–28
Eberhard, Ernest, 134
Edwards, Jonathan, 63n61
election, doctrine of, ix, xix, 64, 143n2, 144, 148n9–10, 155n21, 159–66
Eliade, Mircea, 151n14–15
epilepsy, 64
Erikson, Erik, 14–15, 24, 26, 47, 79–80, 96

Index

ethics, xiii, 3, 36, 42, 46, 54, 56, 90, 94–102, 106, 108–110, 113–16, 139, 151
evangelism, xvii, 103, 112–13, 118, 121–22, 131, 134–36, 139
Evans, C. Stephen, 90n7
existential, xvii, 8, 24, 44, 46, 49, 53, 60, 84, 90, 94, 151–52, 154, 159–60, 162
faith, defined two ways, 6n19, 9n23
faith development, x, xiv, xxii, 15, 65, 67–68, 72, 79, 82, 110, 135–35
Festinger, Leon, 43n11, 44n16, 116n61
Finke, Roger, 127–30, 138
foreknowledge, divine, 144, 163
Formula of Concord, xix, 6, 72, 134, 143n2
Fowler, James, 14–16, 42, 80
Fredrickson, Barbara, 59, 63
free will (or human freedom), xix, 3n5–6, 48–50, 53–54, 68, 144–49, 154, 156
Freud, Sigmund, 14, 72–76, 79, 81
Fritz, John, 114–15
Gartrell, David, 49–50, 52
gestalt, 21–24
Glock, Charles, 93–94, 97–100, 103–4, 106–9, 119n5
Gogarten, Friedrich, 90n4
gospel, as mark of true conversion, 1–10
grace, works despite compromising motives, 2, 10, 16, 114, 134, 140, 149
Granqvist, Pehr, 82–84
Gutiérrez, Gustavo, 104
Hadden, Jeffery, 139n50
Hagekull, Berit, 83
Haug, Hans, 159, 166
health, 4, 14–15, 25, 74, 76, 78–80, 84, 88, 98, 106–7, 116
Heaven's Gate religious group, 47n25, 52
Hegel, G. W. F., 91, 148
Heirich, Max, 31, 42–43, 121
hypocrisy, seen in positive light, 110–13
ideology, as a motive to convert, 89–92
idols, 4, 12–13, 16, 27, 36, 44–46, 61, 100–101, 114, 143, 154

Islam, 17, 51, 96, 98
James, Saint, 42, 62
James, William, 18, 20–21, 26, 49, 72, 84, 153
Jensen, Robert, 161n30-31
John, Saint, 10
joy, 42, 62, 161
Jung, Carl, 14, 16
justification, doctrine of, xx, 4–5, 57, 161
Kant, Immanuel, 150n13
kerygma, xx
Kirkpatrick, Lee, 81–82, 84
Kolb, Robert, xixn7, 33n67, 99n28, 156n22
Köse, Ali, 96, 98
Kox, Willem, 126–27
Kreeft, Peter, 144–46
Kunz, Phillip, 121–22, 131
language, role in religious change, 11, 24, 34–35, 69, 100n30, 128, 132, 138
law, divine, 8, 45, 55, 58, 63, 65, 96, 159, 161n28
Lifton, Robert Jay, 47, 50, 52, 54
Lindbeck, George, 100, 165n37
Lofland, John, 40, 51, 119–27, 129
Long, Theodore, 139n50
Lord's Supper, 7, 158
Loveland, Matthew, 29n51, 51–52, 54
Luther, Martin, xix, 3n6, 7n20, 32, 56–57, 68, 98–99
Machalek, Richard, 31, 44, 83
magic, distinguished from doctrine, 113–14, 116
Mahler, Gustav, 107
markers of religious change, 28–36
Marshall, I. Howard, 154n20
Marx, Karl, 91–93, 102–3
meaning, as key to religious changes, 41–42, 47
Moltmann, Jürgen, 93n14, 161
monergism, 5, 115, 149–50, 154, 158, 160n26
Mormonism, 121–22, 129, 131, 134
negative emotions, research on, 55–59
neuroscience, 13–14, 57–58, 140

Index

Newberg, Andrew, 13
Niebuhr, H. Richard, xviii, 92–93, 103–5
omniscience, divine, 163, 165
once saved, always saved, 150, 158
opium of the people, religion as, 91
Paloutzian, Raymond, 42–45, 47, 49, 52, 54–55, 65, 88
Pascal, Blaise, 110
pastor(s), 5, 42, 61, 85, 114–15
patience, 20, 32
Paul, Saint, 6n17, 12n3, 25, 49, 61, 125n25, 135, 137–38, 140n26, 163
Peace, Richard, 135
phenomenology of salvation, defined, 146–51
Plantinga, Alvin, 43n14, 163n34
positive emotions, research on, 59–65
postmortem encounter with Christ, 165
preaching, 32, 45
predestination, ix, xiv, xix, 144–45, 148, 153, 159–66
protean man, 47
psychology, as used in this study, xiv
Rambo, Lewis, 132n39
religious change, defined, xiii
Richardson, James, 49, 51
righteousness, 3, 9n23, 54, 59, 62–63, 96–97, 99, 113–14, 135, 161n28
role theory, 29–33, 35, 43, 97n24, 110–13, 115–16
sacramental encounter, defined, 7
salvation, as divinely inspired, 5–6
Salzman, Leon, 74–76, 83
sanctification, xviii
Sartre, Jean Paul, xviin4, 46
Schleiermacher, Friedrich, xx, 45, 58
Seggar, John, 121–22, 131
sermon(s), 20, 75, 115
Shannon, Zane, 49–50, 52
Shaver, Phillip, 81–82
Shinn, Larry, 133
Shupe, Anson, Jr., 111–13

sin, outlined, 2–4
Snow, David, 31–36, 44, 83, 124–27, 129–30
social networks, research covering, 118–33
social science, how this study uses, xiv
spark of faith, as a definition of conversion, 6, 12, 19, 39, 71, 78, 82
spirit, divine, as difficult to detect, 66–67
Starbuck, Edwin Diller, 18–21, 23–24, 26, 28, 35–36, 49, 59, 74, 96, 153
Stark, Rodney, 99n27, 103n36, 105, 108, 113–15, 118–30, 133, 138–39
Straus, Roger, 48–50, 52
subconscious, 14, 16, 18, 24, 72–73, 75, 82
suffering, 7n20, 14, 41–42, 64, 91–92, 94
switching, 29n51, 51, 54, 95n20, 129
synergism, 5
Tacelli, Ronald, 144–46
theologian, as mediator between message and audience, xiii, xv, xxi, 146
theologians' cross, 142–44, 146–48, 152–53, 160–65
Tolstoy, Leo, 94–95, 97
Travisano, Richard, 29–31, 33, 36, 42, 44, 98n26, 126–27
trust, 8–10, 14–16, 24, 26, 32, 36, 55n46, 56, 59, 62–63, 68, 70–71, 75–76, 79–80, 86, 89, 106, 124, 134, 136, 142, 147, 149, 154, 163, 166
twin studies, 70–71
Ullman, Chana, 26, 36, 62, 76–78, 82–83, 86, 120n11, 132, 138
unbelief, reasons for, 155–59
Unification Church, 111, 113, 119
Weber, Max, 92, 132n38
worldview, 2, 34, 42–43, 45, 54, 81, 89–90, 95, 101n32, 119, 131, 137–39

www.ingramcontent.com/pod-product-compliance
Lightning Source LLC
Chambersburg PA
CBHW062040220426
43662CB00010B/1590